Among the Children of the Sun

Travels In the Family Islands of the Bahamas

Marvin W. Hunt

Acknowledgements

I want to thank two good friends, David Williamson and Glenn Lewis, who were silent partners in my early Bahamian excursions. Their presence helped shape *Among the Children of the Sun*, parts of which appeared in *The Atlanta Journal-Constitution, The Washington Post, The New York Times, The North Carolina Literary Review,* and elsewhere.

I want to thank the many good Bahamians I've gotten to know through the years—my second family, really—for their kindness and hospitality; and the gifted Katie Hunt for her marvelous maps and cover.

My greatest debt, as always, is to my wife, Robin, who never said no when I planned a trip, who packed food, delivered me to the airport and always, when I came home, was (happily, I like to think) waiting for me.

Among the Children of the Sun is dedicated to the memory of three people who were dear to me: my father, the Rev. Marvin Dana Hunt; my friend Mark Taylor; and Ann Graf, Katie Hunt's mother.

For the photo gallery of my travels in the Bahamas, and engaging sidebars—ever think about birding in the Bahamas?—visit my website www.marvinhunt.com.

Contents

Prologue

OOK writing is like pregnancy, a great mysterious process that ends with a certain delivery date. The point of origin, the moment of conception, may be less certain. Looking back on it, this one was conceived the first time I visited the Bahamas, in March of 1994, when I deplaned into the engulfing wet heat of New Providence Island at the Lynden O. Pindling International Airport, a 30-dollar cab ride along Bay Street into the heart of Nassau, the nation's capital.

I followed a line of tourists up the long concourse into the International Arrivals hall of the airport. The room was spacious but a bit shabby, painted in the national colors—black, teal and yellow—and crowded with new arrivals arraying themselves into sloppy lines leading to Customs stations. Against the back wall a trio of guitar, bass and drums was playing the Soca song—it has an interesting provenance—that goes "I'm feelin' hot! hot! hot!."

It was spring break for American college students, and the lines were littered with young bucks, their caps turned around backwards, glassy-eyed, hung over. Coeds in short strapless dresses and mules who pulled at their ponytails and rolled their eyes at the wait, accompanied them. Another cadre were darkly tanned, wrinkled men and women; the men wore baggy shorts trussed up with white belts, mismatched linen shirts and well-worn deck shoes. Their wives were slim and sandaled, red-rouged, freckled, age-spotted, diamonded.

The line crept forward, the college kids kicking their rucksacks and backpacks a few feet ahead at each shifting of the line. The rich older people, carrying only one bag each, had their papers out and in order.

1

They'd done this many times before. Customs was hardly a rite of passage. For them entering the Bahamas was an easy, familiar ritual. Ahead, after they cleared the airport, half an hour into Nassau, fine yachts or well-appointed cottages with freshly made beds across the harbor on Paradise Island awaited them.

The kids were on the lam from college, with two related imperatives: to get drunk and laid. They would be cabbed along the narrow winding road from the airport east on West Bay Street and deposited at overpriced, aging hotels at Cable Beach, or resorts farther along West Bay, past Fort Charlotte, the massive late 18th century fortress that guards the harbor, into the narrow, labyrinthine heart of Old Nassau. Some would board cruise ships anchored in the harbor.

By nightfall, the older, affluent crowd would be knocking back umbrella drinks and looking forward to tasty dinners. Later, I imagined, while the college crowd was getting into trouble, the wealthy couples would be hugging each other and falling asleep in familiar tropical boudoirs.

It's a safe bet that no tourist that day would be venturing farther along East Bay Street past Fort Montague into the east end of Nassau, to Fox Hill, where windows were shuttered and businesses dimly lit behind iron bars, where life was dangerous, where guns and knives too often ruled the night. I certainly wouldn't. Nassau was only a layover for me. I was on my way to Eleuthera, one of the Family Islands, a short flight and a world away from Nassau.

But even if I had been traveling on to Fox Hill that afternoon, I would have been much safer then than now. The capital of the Bahamas (700 lovely islands and cays strewn over a stretch of ocean ranging south from a parallel with Ft. Lauderdale to within forty-five miles of Hispaniola), Nassau is enduring a hideous reign of violence fueled not only by international drug smuggling, which there's still plenty of, but by more pedestrian conflicts—local drug turf wars, gang violence, angry neighbors settling scores, common thuggery and robberies gone bad. What all of this killing has in common is increasingly lethal weaponry, which is proliferating in the crowded neighborhoods of Nassau with horrific consequences. Packing everything from handguns to assault rifles, Bahamians are now killing each other at a ghastly rate. Last year the Bahamas, whose population hovers around 300,000, recorded ninety murders; all but a handful of those occurred in crowded Nassau, where perhaps seventy percent of the nation's population is concentrated. And 2011 was even bloodier. In April, *The Nassau Guardian*—a pillar of the Commonwealth's robust press—announced that one person was being killed in the Bahamas every sixty-eight hours, or 2.67 days. In July, the paper reported that the 2011 murder rate was forty percent above that of 2010. On the last day of 2011, the nation recorded its 127th murder. And with its economy, which depends almost entirely on tourism, still stagnant, things will likely only get worse in the future.

Though no less tragic for it, Bahamians are killing each other, not tourists. Holed up in a resort at Cable Beach or on Paradise Island, you're not likely to be assaulted or killed. If you wander beyond the central dock and adjoining markets of Bay Street, however, you're courting real danger. At the very least, you might come upon hysterical family members wailing over a bullet-riddled corpse. So my advice to you is to stay on the reservation. And that's sad to say because Nassau has such an incredibly rich history, one that distantly mirrors its turbulent present. Everywhere on New Providence are vestiges of this nation's luridly colorful and notoriously lawless beginnings, when one of the most extraordinary chapters in human history was written. That history I'll survey, if you'll indulge me, before beginning my travels among the children of the sun.

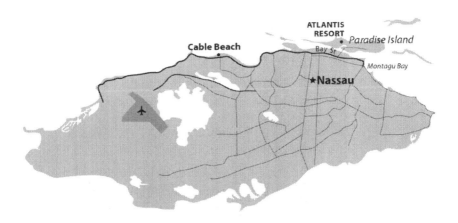

NEW PROVIDENCE

Chapter 1
A Long, Piratical Beginning

FOR more than twenty years, from 1696 to 1718, Nassau was, off and on, the capital of what is called the Pirate Republic. It was a period when a society of disgruntled, defiant, courageous and often brilliant seaman—freebooters, privateers, buccaneers—ruled the island of New Providence and many other islands in the Bahamian archipelago. In the later years of the pirate republic, 1716-18, the streets were crowded with merchants who thrived on the pirate booty, with harlots and ruffians plying their trades in ramshackle huts and carousing in open-air saloons. Jamaica's Port Royal, which was sunk into the ocean in an earthquake of biblical vengeance in 1692, is its only analogy.

The pirate haven of Nassau was framed by a pair of English governors. On April Fools Day, 1696, newly appointed Nicholas Trott became the first (hardly the last) governor to grant sanctuary to notorious criminals. That day the infamous pirate Henry Avery, on the run from the English navy, steered his sloop around Hog Island, as Paradise Island was then known, into the harbor and came ashore at Fort Nassau, where the British Colonial Hilton now stands, and requested a meeting with the governor. In a private conference, Trott granted sanctuary to Avery, who had assumed the identity of a simple merchant, in return for a bribe amounting to £860—more than three years' the governor's salary—with Avery's magnificent ship, the *Fancy*, laden nearly to the gunwales with chests of gold coins, pieces of eight, jewels, muskets and gunpowder, as well as huge quantities of ivory plundered from Africa, thrown in for good measure. Facing inevitable capture by the British navy, and certain death at the end of a rope, if not death at sea, Avery was eager to unload his booty.

Trott, facing his own exigencies, was more than willing to accept the offer. Trott's decision to grant Avery and his men sanctuary would greatly increase his firepower and more than double his seventy-man garrison at Fort Nassau, with its twenty-eight guns, the island's only defense. Chronically undermanned and underfunded, Trott feared that the French would any day sack the village and overwhelm its crumbling citadel, taking this strategically important Bahamian island under foreign rule.

The beginning of the end of New Providence's pirate republic came twenty-two years later, on July 27, 1718, with the arrival of the newly appointed governor, the extraordinary Commodore Woodes Rogers, who would wrest control of the island from the outlaws in short order and bring the Golden Age of Piracy to a close.

The son of a prosperous merchant captain, Rogers was born in 1679 in Poole, England, with salt water in his veins. His family soon moved to Bristol where the young man was apprenticed at sea. He wived wealthily, marrying the daughter of an admiral, and set out on his seafaring career as a slave trader, at which (unfortunately) he did very well. With the outbreak of the War of Spanish Succession (1702-12), however, Rogers's career took a radical and unforeseen turn. Intent on exploiting Spain's troubles, Queen Anne's government licensed sea captains as privateers, granting them "letters of marque" that authorized them to chase and plunder the enormous Spanish treasure fleet that sailed the Pacific from the Philippine islands around South America, from the Spanish Main through the Caribbean and the Bahamas to the Azores and home to Spain. For the English, it was a win-win deal. The privateers roamed the oceans like lone wolves, indulging the Age's unbridled wanderlust, with the very real prospect of coming back fabulously wealthy, or not ever coming back. The Queen and Crown, comfortably ensconced at Windsor, would claim the lion's share of the booty.

Spain ferried much of the world's treasures in the hulls of its enormous galleons. The greatest of these colossal ships were fearsome fighting vessels that dominated the Atlantic and Pacific Oceans, hauling Spanish troops to the New World and beyond, across the Pacific to

Eastern Asia, returning mind-boggling treasures from these destinations back to Spain. For good reasons, Spanish galleons were the quarry of choice for English privateers. The plunder from a single Spanish ship could bring an English commander literally a king's ransom.

Rogers, through his family's connections, got his letter of marque in 1708 and became commodore of a fleet of two ships, the *Duke* (350 tons, 36 guns), which he commanded, and the *Duchess* (260 tons, 26 guns) under the command of Stephen Courtney. Also serving under Rogers was the legendary privateer, explorer, self-taught naturalist, inept captain and all around son-of-a-bitch, William Dampier, who had already circumnavigated the globe three times and recounted his breathtaking adventures and discoveries in best-selling books.

On September 1, 1708 the *Duke* and *Duchess* set sail from port of Kinsale and made their way southwest across the Atlantic toward the Drake Passage. Within a month, the usual ravages of life at sea set in, with scurvy taking the first sailor's life; soon fifty men were down with the illness. The crew reduced to dire straits, the fleet passed the Falklands on Christmas day and rounded the tip of South America into the Pacific in early January.

Some weeks later, the *Duke* and *Duchess* approached the island of Juan Fernandez, 600 miles west of Chile. Here, four years earlier, the Scotsman Alexander Selkirk, a crew member aboard one of a fleet of English ships hunting Spanish booty, the *Cinque Ports* (Dampier himself was captain of another ship in the fleet, the *St. George*), had decided to remain on the island rather than venture farther on the worm-eaten *Cinque Ports*. He elected to maroon himself rather than take his chances on the voyage home.

On February 1, 1709, Rogers's crew spotted a fire on the beach and, coming ashore on the craggy, mountainous and verdant Juan Fernandez, saw a lone man draped in goatskin waving a white cloth tied to a stick. It was Selkirk, for all appearances a wild man: His matted hair draped over his shoulders and his beard grown to his chest, his bare feet thickened with calluses as tough as horses hooves. He had lived alone on Juan Fernandez for four years and four months. Having forgotten his native tongue, at first Selkirk could only utter the word "maroon" to describe his circumstance. Over the coming days, as he rediscovered speech, Selkirk related the incredible story of his survival, showing his rescuers the cave in which he lived for some time, the mountain streams from which he drank, the trails he had carved up across mountain passes down into a verdant valley where he built his living quarters—a hut in which he slept and a separate kitchen building.

Selkirk had not only survived on this remote island, he had thrived. He ate seals, fish, turtle eggs and lobsters, drank the milk and dined on the flesh of goats he ambushed and cudgeled. He became a virtual Pan, nimbly chasing down and tackling the animals on bushy crags. He stole and corralled their kids which he raised, milking them and making cheese. When he could no longer resist his natural urges, he fucked them. He feasted on seasonal bounty—bird eggs, wild radishes and cabbages, turnips, oats and plums. At night he enjoyed the company and protection of the island's feral cats which he tamed to keep at bay the rats that threatened to feast on Selkirk while he slept.

Night and day he tended his precious fire, which was extinguished only twice in the fifty-two months, the 38,000 hours he lived on Juan Fernandez. The first time he lost the flame after chasing a goat off the edge of a precipice hidden by brush. Man and beast tumbled in a free fall to the ground, Selkirk landing on the goat, killing it, and seriously injuring himself. Somehow, he managed to drag himself back to his hut were he suffered in extremity from his wounds and exposure. Managing to relight his life-sustaining flame, Selkirk spent months recuperating. The other time a Spanish raiding party landed on the island and Selkirk fled inland. The Spaniards sacked his camp, looted his meager possessions and left.

When the English arrived on the island, they found Selkirk hale and hearty but reluctant to leave. He feared that the captain of the *Cinque Ports*, whom he loathed and feared, might be among his rescuers. Soon his anxieties were allayed, however, and he joined the crew of the *Duke* on its hunt for Spanish galleons. A month later, on March 26, they captured a Spanish prize, the 50-ton *Santa Josepha*, which they converted to a hospital ship and appointed Selkirk master of. The fleet sailed up and down the west coast of the Americas, taking two more small Spanish ships and then the larger, more valuable French-built *Havre de Grace*, on April 15. But the prize was costly: during the battle, Rogers's brother John was shot through the head and killed. His body was committed to the sea. Rogers called his brother's death an "unspeakable sorrow."

Later that month the privateers sacked and burnt the Ecuadorian port town of Guayaquil, but not before the citizens had hauled most of their treasures into the jungle. Sickened by tropical fevers, the English nevertheless desperately sought a greater prize. In late December 1709,

Rogers's watch sighted a possible quarry on the horizon. This was the lumbering 450-ton *Nuestra Señora de la Incarnaciŏn Disenganio*, worth, in William Dampier's estimation, one million pounds sterling. The English privateers pulled along side the *Nuestra* and opened fire. The ensuing three-hour battle ended with the *Nuestra* striking her colors and surrendering to the English. But Commodore Rogers was left the worse for it. Shortly into the action, a musket ball ripped through his upper left jaw, scattering his teeth across the deck, and lodged in the roof of his mouth. Despite his ghastly wound, Rogers managed the battle by writing his orders on a scrap of paper. That night he nearly choked to death on a bone fragment that lodged in his throat.

A week later, with Rogers's face grotesquely swollen, the English ships spotted an even larger prize, the *Nuestra Señora de Begoña*, a nine-hundred ton behemoth armed with forty cannon *en route* on its maiden voyage from Manila to the Spanish transshipment outpost of Acapulco. Rogers watched from the deck of his flagship as five hundred cannonballs fired from the English ships bounced harmlessly like marbles off the hull of the massive galleon. Soon, his own fleet was shot through and through and Rogers was forced to break off the attack, leaving the Manila galleon to make its way undaunted. But not before Rogers was wounded again, this time by wood shrapnel that tore through his boot, carved the flesh from his heel down to the bone and took off part of his ankle.

The wounds received in these encounters would torment Rogers for the rest of his life. He would require a cane to walk and had to endure the psychological as well as physical pain of a terribly disfigured face.

The English fleet continued west to Batavia (present-day Jakarta) where a surgeon cut the musket ball from Rogers's mouth and he recuperated from his wounds. In the meantime, he sold the *Havre de Grace*, and his crews cleaned and repaired their vessels. But there was little peace in paradise. Rogers's crew became restless and threatened mutiny, accusing the Commodore of abusive treatment and of secreting treasure that rightly belonged to them. Even greater trouble—lawsuits—came when the East India Trading Company, which had exclusive rights to the English interests in Batavia, accused Rogers of encroaching on the Company's charter.

Four months after arriving in Batavia, the fleet weighed anchor for home, sailing west around the Cape of Good Hope, where Rogers's ships joined a convoy sailing north along the west coast of Africa. The convoy arrived at the mouth of the Thames in early October 1711. Selkirk was now master of the captured *Incarnacion*, rechristened the *Bachelor*, as it was towed to dock in London.

Seventy members of the company had died during the three-year voyage around the world. The total plunder amounted to about £148,000, far less than was expected. Immediately Rogers and the Bristol owners who had financed the expedition were beset by their creditors, and the East India Company laid claim to much of the venture's profits. When the dust settled, when all the debts and penalties and bribes had been paid, Rogers and his backers were left with a paltry sum, not enough for Rogers even to cover the debts his family had incurred in his absence. To escape his creditors, the commodore declared bankruptcy. Still, Rogers fared better than many of his crew, who got little or nothing for the labor, the dangers and hardships they had endured for three years.

Selkirk, however, did quite well for himself. His two and a half shares netted more than £800, a princely sum for a man of his humble station. He soon found himself the talk of the nation, his ordeal recounted in two books and an influential essay. People sought him out. Rogers, for his part, exploited the story of the marooned sailor in his own account of the voyage, as did Captain Edward Cooke in his narrative of the same expedition. The popular and influential essayist and playwright Richard Steele extolled Selkirk's virtues in an essay that made Selkirk out to be a model of Christian stoicism and courage in the face of daunting circumstances. But Selkirk's story really caught fire with the 1719 publication of Daniel Defoe's *Robinson Crusoe*, often cited as the first English novel. Neither Crusoe nor his island bears any resemblance to Selkirk or Juan Fernandez Island, of course —Juan Fernandez was mountainous and temperate and sometimes snowy. But Defoe's tale of the marooned goat man, the merest shadow of the historical Selkirk, was destined to become a permanent fixture, an archetype really, of the western imagination, fueling the dreams of countless young men drawn to the fantasy of living alone on a deserted, tropical island.

Unlike the pious moralist Crusoe, Alexander Selkirk returned home a troubled man. Cribbed by domesticity, he drank heavily and brawled, once beating a man nearly to death. He married one woman and then, it seems, without dissolving that marriage, wed another. Typically, when cornered by his troubles, Selkirk took to sea. He met his end aboard the *Weymouth* in the mouth of the Gambia River on the

West coast of Africa, on December 13, 1721, where he died at forty one of a fever, leaving behind his two wives to wrangle in the courts over his estate.

The *Weymouth*'s log records that Selkirk, like scores of his shipmates who succumbed to the same contagion, suffered fever and chills, headaches, muscle pains and bloody diarrhea, then bleeding from his nose and mouth as he died. Their symptoms suggest a final irony: these may be tell-tale signs of hemorrhagic fever, something like the Marburg or Ebola filovirus, which are indigenous only to Africa. These horrible diseases are zoonotic, animal-borne. That is, there are no intermediary hosts such as mosquitoes for the virus; it's transmitted through direct contact with bodily fluids, typically blood, of an infected animal—monkeys or chimps, for example—or infected persons. Precisely how these diseases were first transmitted to humans is unknown; the contagion may have been spread in a number of ways —eating "bush meat," for example—but some scientists have posited intimate contact between man and beast as the origins of hemorrhagic fever. The etiological thread of these contagions may go back to sexual contact with an infected animal: the revenge of the animal kingdom against Selkirk, who had abused goats on Juan Fernandez Island.

Back in England, Woodes Rogers emerged from his legal tangles penurious but renowned, celebrated as a brilliant captain and a war hero. Even though he was only a sheet of paper, his letter of marque, away from being a pirate himself, he became obsessed with destroying piracy worldwide. His initial foray against the buccaneers (from the French *boucanier*, a person who smokes meat in a barbecue frame called a *boucan*) was undertaken in 1713 when he persuaded his Bristol backers to finance the purchase of a 460-ton merchantman *Delicia*, fitted out with thirty-six guns, a vessel that would be Rogers's sea-faring home for the next eight years. He sailed to Madagascar, a haven for pirates, there to buy slaves which he would sell in Batavia and, if successful, return a handsome profit to his investors. His clandestine plan was to infiltrate the pirates of Madagascar and learn their ways and means. What he found upon arriving were tribesmen from whom he bought slaves, and a markedly underwhelming pirate state. The ragtag band of Madagascar outlaws lacked a vessel sufficiently large to threaten shipping and, after some tense weeks of negotiations, he managed to convince a number of them to return with him to England and beg

Queen Anne for pardons. After disposing of his human cargo in Batavia, Rogers sailed for home in 1714, the *Delicia* laden with money and treasure.

Next, he set his eye on the Bahamas, the other, much better organized and menacing republic of pirates. For some years the Bahamas had had no government at all, nothing to challenge the pirates who raided the rich shipping lanes into the Caribbean with impunity. In 1717, he and a wealthy merchant, Samuel Buck, formed The Copartners for Carrying on a Trade & Settling the Bahamian Islands. With the backing of 163 prominent traders, Rogers and Buck convinced the Lord Proprietors who had legal control of the islands —and had lost £2,700 to piracy—to cede their authority to the Crown which, for a token, they then leased the Bahamas to Rogers and his associates for twenty-one years. In return Rogers agreed to undertake the mission without a salary. On January 6, 1718 Woodes Rogers was appointed Captain General and Governor in Chief of the Bahamas.

When Rogers set sail for New Providence Island in early summer 1718, he wielded a mean stick and a tasty carrot. The carrot was a King's Pardon, a guarantee of amnesty for any rogue who would renounce piracy and pledge allegiance to the new government. This amnesty would prove an indispensable tool in wresting authority from the buccaneers. The stick was a formidable fleet of Royal Navy warships: the thirty gun fifth-rate frigate HMS *Milford*; the 273-ton, twenty gun sixth-rate HMS *Rose*; and the 113-ton, ten gun sloop-of-war *Shark*. These ships carried a manifest of 550 soldiers and sailors, and 130 English, German, and Huguenot settlers. They escorted Rogers's personal fleet—his flagship, the *Delicia*, the 135-ton, six-cannon *Samuel*, and the 75-ton, six-cannon *Buck*—to the Bahamas. Never before had such a force been mounted against the Pirate Republic.

Word of Rogers's mission reached New Providence well in advance of his arrival on July 24, by which time all but one of the most powerful pirate captains had accepted the pardon or scattered. The principal holdout was the Jacobite sympathizer Charles Vane, a vicious, wily and peripatetic captain who had taken dozens of prizes throughout the Caribbean and the American Colonies, often savagely beating, marooning, even hanging some of his victims. Even as Rogers approached the island, a death-head flag fluttered over Fort Nassau —Vane's assertion that this was still pirate country.

But Vane was about to be ambushed. Rogers's armada approached from the west, surprising the pirate captain and his fleet in the Harbor, its flanking beaches now littered with the wrecks of vessels looted and burned, the tropical air fouled with the stench of animal carcasses rotting on the beach. Vane's escape route to the west was blocked by Rogers's advancing fleet, and his largest prize, a 250-ton, twenty-gun French ship which Vane had taken as his flagship, couldn't pass over the shallow sandbar known today as Potters Cay to the east. Vane was trapped. He sent a message to Rogers accepting the King's pardon—he had played this hand before—but this was merely a ruse to buy time to devise a plan. In the middle of the night Rogers was awakened and called to the deck where he beheld an incredible sight. Vane's men had offloaded his flagship's booty, soaked its decks with tar, and set it aflame. The fireship was now riding a trailing wind toward the Royal Navy's *Rose* and *Shark*. In the frantic minutes that followed the Navy crews scrambled to weigh their anchors and swing their sterns to the east. With the wind at their backs, the English captains raced for the open sea as the flaming pirate ship neared them, its skeleton crew firing cannons at the Royal Navy convoy. The English vessels successfully outdistanced the fireship, but Vane's ploy had been successful. It bought him and his men time to gather their bounty and board a shallow-draft Bermuda sloop, the *Katherine*, and make their way out of the harbor to the east just after sunrise. The English gave chase in the *Buck* but this heavier vessel, now sailing on the high tide, was unable to catch the swift sloop as it rounded the east end of the island and caught the wind. In a final gesture of defiance, Vane had the *Katherine* fire on the *Buck* before Vane and his crew escaped into the safe immensity of the open seas.

When Rogers came ashore the next day to much pomp and circumstance, he was greeted by, among others, the magnificent and fearsome Benjamin Hornigold, a notorious pirate, founder of the Nassau pirate republic, who had accepted the pardon and would prove an invaluable aid to the survival of the new government. Rogers inherited a Nassau in shambles, its fort, looted of all but one cannon, tottering near collapse. Rogers set about consolidating control of the island, marshalling its inhabitants to work with his hundred-man construction company to rehabilitate Fort Nassau. Despite great difficulties—a sickness that swept the colony killing eighty-six of Rogers's company, the early and unexpected departure of the Royal Navy ships, and the indolence of the natives—Rogers, with the assistance of Hornigold and other reformed freebooters, was, improbably, able to secure the island. In a matter of six months' time, order was restored and peace descended like manna on New Providence, though there was always the fear and very real danger that Vane or the Spanish would attempt to retake the island. The end of the Golden Age of Piracy was effectively at hand, an end punctuated by the hanging on December 12, 1718, of eight pirates on the beach near what is today Woodes Rogers Walk.

In the twenty-two years framed by the gubernatorial bookends of Nicholas Trott and Woodes Rogers, New Providence Island was home and refuge, at one time or another, to the most dangerous and notorious pirates of the Caribbean. And for two years, 1716-1718, it was a genuine pirate republic, a commonwealth of rogues. Now the stuff of romantic legend, fossils encased in beautiful amber, the reality of pirate lives was much different. Most were violent, drunken scoundrels, ruthless and bloodthirsty, though brave and capable sailors nevertheless. Their real virtues were seamanship and the fact that their society was perhaps the first modern democracy. What follows is a brief account of some of the most notorious Bahama pirates, beginning with Vane himself. These brief lives are based upon the 1725 edition of *A General History of the Robberies and Murders of the Most Notorious Pyrates* (the Rosetta Stone of pirate history) and Colin Woodard's *The Republic of Pirates* (2007), the most recent and informed history of the period.

Nothing is known of Vane's birth or upbringing, though he was likely a Londoner, born perhaps in Wapping, which was the epicenter of London's seafaring community, home to sailors and chandlers —shipwrights, sail makers, carpenters, sutlers, purveyors of ship stores, provisioners of everything needed for seafaring. Wapping was also the site of Execution Dock, where the young Vane may have witnessed numerous hangings of pirates, including five of Henry Avery's men dispatched in the fall of 1696, their bodies were staved in the mud at low tide and not removed until their bloated corpses had been submerged under three high tides.

Vane first appears in the records a world away from London, in Port Royal, Jamaica, where his pirate career was already underway. He was in Nassau early in 1718, at the height of the Bahamian pirate republic. At that time Vane, then the informal leader of the outlaws, had humiliated Captain Vincent Pearse who, arriving in Nassau on February 23, had carried the King's Pardon to the pirates. Vane accepted clemency and then under cover of night escaped across the Potter's Cay bar to the east. Over the next several days he prowled the waters east of Nassau, eventually taking a trading sloop from Jamaica. In an act of brilliant audacity, Vane sailed his prize back into Nassau Harbor where, behind the cover of the shoal which Pearse's vessel couldn't cross, he defiantly looted it. It was, as Colin Woodard writes, "political theater par excellence." Vane's insolence emboldened the 209 pirates occupying Nassau, many of whom reverted to their old ways, and by the end of March, Pearse's position as the King's authority had become untenable and he was obliged to weigh anchor and abandon Nassau once again to Vane and the pirates.

After fleeing Nassau under the greater pressure of Rogers in the summer of 1718, Vane sailed south and then north again along the coast of North Carolina where he saluted his old friend and Nassau pirate Edward Teach (or Thatch), aka Blackbeard, near his hideout of Ocracoke Island, then turned south again for Charleston, which he blockaded and took eight ships carrying ninety slaves in the span of a day and a half. From Charleston he sailed back to the Bahamas where he sacked the island of Eleuthera, robbing its settlers of their livestock. Now flush with food and liquor, Vane and his crew went on an extended binge, a lost month that ended when their stores were consumed, and the viciously hung-over pirates were obliged to set sail for new quarry.

Vane's career began to unravel in November when his watch spotted a French frigate passing nearby. The pirates hoisted the black flag and approached their prey but as they neared it, the French ship rolled out cannons and fired on Vane's two-ship convoy. Surprised, Vane broke off his attack. The crew was divided about what next to do. Vane argued that they were outgunned and should give quarter while most of his crew insisted that they attack. Though he was in the minority, Vane asserted his prerogative as captain and the pirates turned tail. Judging that their captain had humiliated them, the crew branded Vane of all things a coward and by a majority vote, as was the rule among pirates, ousted him as captain, electing John "Calico Jack" Rackham to take command of the fleet. Vane and fifteen of his supporters were put aboard one of their smaller prizes and cast off.

Deprived of his ability to threaten His Majesty's colonies, Vane sailed southwest to the Bay of Honduras where he refitted his vessel with guns and took a half dozen prizes, retreating after each foray into the cover of the Bay. But soon a terrible hurricane wrecked Vane on an uninhabited island; most of their supplies and provisions were lost to the sea. Throughout the winter and into the spring of 1719 Vane and his men suffered in "great straits for want of necessaries," according to the author of *The General History of the Pyrates* (1725). At long last a Jamaican ship anchored off the island and Vane discovered that the captain was an old compatriot who had taken the pardon, one Holford. Holford refused the pirates safe passage, fearing that Vane would "knock me on the head and run away with my ship a'pyrating." Vane and his crew were set ashore. Soon another ship anchored nearby and Vane was presented with another chance at escape. He convinced the captain to take him and his men on as crew members but by the unlikeliest of coincidences, before the ship got underway, it was visited by Holford who was returning to the area to fetch a cargo of lumber. Dining with the captain, Holford happened to spot Vane in the galley. He informed his host that this was the notorious buccaneer Charles Vane, who was promptly shackled and transported to Jamaica where Vane was tried, convicted and hanged on March 29, 1721.

The flamboyant "Calico Jack" Rackham, so called for colorful Indian calico he wore, was Vane's quartermaster until he led the challenge that deposed Vane and was elected commander of the pirate fleet. Having been elevated to his first command, he never looked back. Rackham's was a pirate career of singular audacity, if also recklessness. He courted danger in the waters of Jamaica under the nose of the island's authorities, taking small prizes before sailing back to Nassau in May 1719 where he successfully petitioned Rogers for amnesty, a move that allowed him and his crew to keep their plunder, which they set about cashing in. Rackham and his band caroused for weeks until their stocks were depleted and, once again profoundly hung-over (a familiar Bahamian malady today as it was then), they had to take to the sea again.

At some time in this hiatus, Rackham met and fell in love with the notorious cross-dressing female pirate Anne Bonny, a "notorious harlot" then married to a middling pirate who had been pardoned and was now acting as one of Rogers's informers. Making no attempt to conceal their affair, the outrageously dressed Rackham and the violent and transgressive Bonny were soon the talk of the town. Indeed, their audacity was shocking. They approached Bonny's husband and demanded an annulment, to which Bonny agreed in return for a cash settlement. But when the couple set about to find a respectable witness to attest to this arrangement, the news reached the puritanical Rogers who threatened that if Anne Bonny carried through with her plan he would throw her into prison and "force Rackham to whip her." Bonny relented and promised to return to her husband. Of course, she had no intention of keeping this promise, and soon afterwards, Captain Rackham and his seething, passionate consort took to sea as pirates.

At this point, the other notorious cross-dressing woman pirate, Mary Read, enters the story. The author of *The General History of the Pyrates* offers a report that fairly drips prurient excitement. He tells us that Read and Bonny met aboard Rackham's ship, when, both dressed as men, neither aware of the other's gender, they were immediately attracted to each other. Both drawn to someone they took to be a fair young man, in secret one then the other revealed her true identity. What a surprise! But the story isn't accurate. They indeed may have gotten to know each other in something like this manner, since both regularly dressed as men, but they met back in Nassau, not at sea. Still, some genuine and powerful attraction drew these two women together. Sensing this, Rackham was fiercely jealous of Mary Read. Stronger evidence is to be found in the bond of passion and courage these women exhibited on the subsequent cruise. They famously threw themselves together into battle with utter abandon, "running gunpowder for the men, fighting in battles, and terrorizing their captives."

Rackham's preference for hunting in Jamaican waters proved foolhardy. Raiding small vessels and then retreating into coves, "Calico Jack" was a conspicuous menace to Jamaican shipping. Soon the pirate hunter, Captain Jonathan Barnet had had enough. Barnet captained a well armed, swift sloop; he knew these waters better than perhaps anyone; and he had the focus, determination and confidence of an Eliot Ness. He set out to bring Rackham to justice. Barnet sighted the Calico gang near one of their hideouts and gave chase. After several hours during which—unthinkably—Rackham's crew seems to have gotten drunk, Barnet finally cornered Rackham and opened fire, destroying the main mast and sails of Rackham's sloop. The drunken pirate crew fled below decks, leaving Bonny and Read, inseparable to the end, to face the enemy alone. The story goes that when Read demanded the men come up and fight, they refused and she fired into the hold, killing one of the cowering crew.

The fight ended with Barnet taking Rackham, Bonny, Read and the remainder of the crew prisoners. Rackham and his male accomplices were tried, convicted and sentenced to hang. Calico Jack was held in the same prison at the same time as his old rival Charles Vane, both men waiting a noose. It's not known whether they encountered one another. On the day he was hanged—November 18, 1720—Rackham received a visit from his lover, Anne Bonny. She offered little sympathy and a sharp censure. "I'm sorry to see you here," she told him, "but if you had fought like a man, you need not have hanged like a dog."

As for Bonny and Read, they were both found guilty and sentenced to die. But they "pled the belly." Claiming they were pregnant meant that, upon proof, they couldn't be executed before giving birth. It was found that indeed they both were with child. How they got themselves pregnant in such short order isn't known, but there must have been a line of lustful men waiting to make sure they did. In any case, neither woman was hanged. Mary Read died of a fever in prison, while Anne Bonny may have been rescued by her father, a wealthy South Carolina planter who wielded considerable influence in Jamaica. No record of her fate survives.

His personality and disposition belie the comic potential of Benjamin Hornigold's name. Decidedly unfunny, he was a man of remarkable integrity and superior skill as a ship's captain. A privateer during the War of Spanish Succession, with the signing of the Treaty of Utrecht in April 1713, he, like others in the same situation, found himself short of work. Forced to scale back his operations, he recruited a small force on the island of Eleuthera and began to raid Spanish shipping along the coast of Florida and Cuba, operating now as pirate rather than privateer. This venture proved successful and sustainable—he operated this way for nearly two years—in part because Hornigold was able to sell his bounty to traders in the thriving colony of Harbour Island just off the northeastern tip of Eleuthera. In time his crew grew to 100 men, and Hornigold, sailing swift and well armed sloops, took a score of ships over the next two years. By the late winter of 1714, Hornigold and his men had amassed a fortune of £60,000. In time, Hornigold joined other buccaneers working in the area—Samuel "Black Sam" Bellamy and the French pirate, Olivier la Buse—to form a loose consortium of outlaw ships that operated with near impunity in the waters of the Bahamas south to Cuba and west to the Florida coast, sailing sometimes alone and at other times as a united fleet.

It isn't accurate, in the opinion of Colin Woodard, to call Hornigold an English patriot, though many have. Like his men, to be sure, he was fighting against a system of entrenched abuse carried out by the standing navies and merchant fleets of his time. And yet his sympathy with the wartime allies England and Holland showed itself in his refusal to attack ships from these nations, unless his necessity was extreme. In fact, the international nature of this consortium would weigh against Hornigold's prejudices. According to the pirate articles, 50 percent of the profits from captured bounty went to the captain, the remainder being divided among his crew according to rank. For common seamen, who had been abused and cheated by the Royal Navy and merchant captains, this was a far more lucrative arrangement than they had enjoyed as privateers. And as pirates, moreover, they had much greater control over their destinies than they had ever known as legitimate sailors. In battles the captain had absolute command of the fleet, but at other times the crew had the right, as we have seen, to impeach a captain. This arrangement put a tremendous pressure on pirate captains to seize ever richer prizes, regardless of the nationality of their prey.

But Hornigold would take English and Dutch prizes only as a last resort. Notably to la Buse, but also to many others in the pirate fleet, Hornigold's policy was senseless and costly. In July 1716, policy tensions came to a head when Bellamy and la Buse proposed attacking an English ship off the coast of Hispaniola. Hornigold ruled against them and a tense and heated debate ensued. It concluded with a majority rule against Hornigold who was stripped of his position as head of the consortium. Many of his crew defected to Bellamy and la Buse, and Hornigold was cast out in his flagship, the *Adventure*, with twenty-six loyal men. He was warned not to return to these rich hunting grounds.

While Bellamy and la Buse remained in the Caribbean regularly taking prizes, the disgraced but undaunted Hornigold retreated to Nassau and began consolidating a new center of power that would become the Republic of Pirates. The geography of Nassau's harbor—a geography that Vane would later exploit brilliantly—was ideal for Hornigold's designs. It was an excellent anchorage, guarded by the length of Hog Island to the north, with a quick egress to open water to the west, and a protected haven for smaller boats behind the sandbar at Potter's Cay to the east.

Having been sacked four times by the French and Spanish during the war, Nassau was a shambled ghost town when Hornigold arrived in the summer of 1716, manned by only a few stragglers who lived in huts and survived by fishing. Hornigold and his men set about attacking Spanish and French shipping in the Straits of Florida, fencing their loot through unscrupulous traders on Harbour Island, sixty miles east of New Providence. With his profits, he fortified the ruined Fort Nassau with cannons, and stationed a captured Spanish ship—armed with thirty-six guns—at the western entrance to the harbor to guard his flank.

The fledgling pirate republic under the command of Benjamin Hornigold was now firmly entrenched. Over the coming months the population of Nassau exploded as disgruntled sailors and unscrupulous traders, freed slaves and mulattos, rum merchants and whores filled the streets. From time to time, Hornigold's old rival captains—Bellamy and la Buse and William Jennings—took refuge there, as did a host of other notorious figures such as the periwigged Palsgrave Williams, son of the attorney general of Rhode Island, who abandoned a life of wealth and ease to take up piracy to avenge what he saw as the English authorities' abuse of Williams's stepfather's Scottish family.

With Rogers's arrival in Nassau in July, 1718, as we have seen, everything changed. Most outlaws who rejected the pardon—Vane and his allies stayed behind to challenge authority—fled to Jamaica or Hispaniola or another safe haven. Those who didn't run or resist took the pardon, none more eagerly or sincerely than Hornigold himself. When war again broke out with Spain, Rogers generously rewarded his convert with a letter of marque, allowing him to hunt trophies in the Spanish Main. His tortuous career had taken him from privateer to pirate and now back to privateer. The Spanish caught him somewhere near Cuba where he died, either in prison or by some other means in early 1719. No one knows for certain what fate brought Benjamin Hornigold to his end. Sailing out of Nassau Harbor in 1719, the father of the pirate commonwealth disappears from history.

The Rogues Gallery of Nassau pirates also included the wealthy (and hapless) Barbados planter, Major Stede Bonnet. Bonnet was a land man, the son of a prosperous family of sugar cane growers; born and raised on a plantation, he had no deep ties to the sea. But after the death of his son, Bonnet fell into a deep depression that led to a nervous breakdown, from which he emerged with an improbable fascination with pirates, given the fact that pirates had wreaked havoc on planter interests in Barbados and the rest of the Caribbean basin for years. In 1716, he commissioned the building of a fine sloop which he christened the *Revenge*, and in the middle of the night deserted his plantation, leaving his wife behind to raise their infant daughter and two young sons. His family would never see him again.

Bonnet soon proved himself completely inept, once foolishly attacking a Spanish man-of-war during which he was severely wounded and the *Revenge* nearly lost. Later, Blackbeard, having watched the bungling Bonnet mishandle the *Revenge*, took command from him, obliging Bonnet to settle in with a good book in his captain's quarters. Nevertheless, he gained the respect of Nassau pirates by virtue of his aristocratic bearing and his audacity, but principally for his splendid new ship. Double-crossed and abandoned by Blackbeard in Beaufort Inlet, North Carolina, Bonnet took back command, at least nominally, of his own vessel, the *Revenge*, and sailed up the Pamlico River to Bath, then the capital of North Carolina, and secured a pardon from Governor Charles Eden who, as we shall see, often colluded with pirates. Bonnet and his crew soon reverted to their old ways, however, and for the last few months of his life, the Major fared much better as a pirate, though this success was due mainly to his capable quartermaster Robert Tucker. The *Revenge*, renamed the *Royal James* to create the illusion of Crown loyalty, took perhaps a dozen or more ships from the Cape of Delaware down the Virginia coast. But the bounty ended abruptly. The South Carolina pirate hunter, William Rhett, in command of a far superior force, surprised the pirate vessel at anchor in the mouth of the Cape Fear River, near the village of Southport. In the ensuing engagement, the combatants' vessels ran aground on the serpentine shoals of the Cape. They fought a pitched battle that lasted five hours until the rising tide lifted Rhett's boats while the *Royal James* remained stuck. The pirate crew had no choice but to surrender. Today, on the eastern side of the small town of Southport is a marker at Bonnet Creek, site of a small residential development, commemorating the battle and describing Bonnet as "small and round."

Bonnet was taken prisoner and conveyed in shackles to Charleston where he was tried, convicted and sentenced to die. He briefly escaped prison but was quickly captured and returned to jail. Terrified by the prospect of what he was facing, Bonnet lived his remaining months in a sustained panic. He broke down again, and in a most un-aristocratic manner, begged and groveled for pardon, writing pathetic letters to the authorities. So sorry was the figure Bonnet cut that Rhett, who captured him, is said to have raised money so that Bonnet could sail to London to plead his case before the king. But there would be no mercy for the Major. Charleston's merchants, who had lost so much to the piracy, demanded his execution, and South Carolina Governor Robert Johnson ceded to their will. Bonnet and twenty-nine of his crew were hanged at what is now the Battery in Charleston on December 10, 1718.

Through much of his peripatetic career, Benjamin Hornigold had one prize student, one loyal lieutenant who stayed by his master's side through thick and thin. This was Blackbeard himself, who in time would become the most notorious of the Nassau pirates. Edward Teach (or Thatch) was born sometime around 1680 in Bristol, according to the author of *A General History of the Pyrates*, though he cites no evidence to corroborate the claim and there are no Teaches or Thatches, Woodard reports, listed in the city's tax records for 1696, the only year for which records survive. If he was, he may well have known Woodes Rogers who was also a Bristolian of roughly the same age. Very recently, a competing claim has emerged that Teach was a native of North Carolina. There is no concrete evidence of this, but this origin might support Woodard's suggestion that Blackbeard was a mulatto, a suggestion based on his unusual appearance—tall and lanky and dreadlocked. This is countered by his ability to read and write—he kept a detailed journal that fell into the possession of the Royal Navy but was subsequently lost—indicating that he was properly educated. Blackbeard like other pirates cultivated an outrageous appearance, but his particular guise seems to have been meant to terrify his victims and awe his crew. The *General History* tells us that his beard was thick and black, "which he suffered to grow of an extravagant length; as to breadth it came up to his eyes." He tied off braided strands of beard and hair with ribbons and twisted fuses into the ends, which he sometimes lit, enveloping his head in a wreath of fearsome smoke. In battle, he wore a sash across his chest in which he carried three pistols sheathed in holsters like a bandolier. But this wasn't his most fearsome aspect. What struck fear and dread in observers were his eyes which were "fierce and wild," creating the heart-stopping impression of "such a figure, that imagination cannot form an idea of a fury, from hell, to look more frightful."

The *General History* also suggests that he might have turned to piracy because he lacked preferment in the navy, reporting that "he was never raised to any command, till he went a-pirating." While this may allude to the period of his service as a privateer, it may suggest a deeper source of Blackbeard's hostility. If his ambitions as a legitimate seaman were unfairly thwarted, and if this created a seething hatred of naval authority, he was certainly not alone. Many pirates had been frustrated or abused in lawful naval service.

Teach first enters the record as a member of a Jamaica-based privateering crew that hunted Spanish prizes during the War of Spanish Succession, perhaps already honing his craft under Hornigold's tutelage, learning the art of sailing, acquiring the skills of seamanship, and charting the waters of the Caribbean. With the end of the war, Hornigold and Teach found themselves without a livelihood and so turned to piracy. For the next three years, Teach served with Hornigold, rising through the ranks to become quartermaster. In 1716, around the time Teach started calling himself Blackbeard, Hornigold granted him his first command, a twenty- or thirty-ton sloop taken near Harbour Island. By the following year he had risen to become the fourth most powerful Nassau pirate, commanding a crew of seventy from the quarterdeck of his six-canon vessel.

When Major Stede Bonnet's fine ship, the *Revenge*, sailed into Nassau Harbor bearing the scars of Bonnet's near disastrous attack on the Spanish warship, with the foolhardy and seriously wounded captain nursing his injuries, it didn't take long for the "Flying Gang" to realize that Major Bonnet was not fit to command a ship. In return for granting Bonnet shelter, he agreed to give over command of the *Revenge* to Blackbeard. Bonnet could keep his cabin, but Blackbeard would rule the roost. Soon, Blackbeard was cruising the Gulf Stream north past the Carolinas and Virginia on his way to the Delaware Bay, in his first independent command of a ship. As a quartermaster he was the consummate loyal student. As commander, he would prove ruthless and savage, though he did not, as one might suppose, wantonly murder his victims.

With the bedridden Bonnet entirely useless, Blackbeard set about on a reign of terror in the waters off the mid-Atlantic coast that lasted more than a year. His first prize was the *Betty* ferrying wine from Madeira to Virginia. Blackbeard looted its cargo, took its crew aboard the *Revenge* and set the ship on fire, sending it to the bottom. His next victim was a British merchant ship carrying 150 passengers from

Dublin to Philadelphia. Blackbeard's hatred of the English was fierce, in part, presumably, because of his own mistreatment, but also because members of Sam Bellamy's gang had been captured and were awaiting hanging in Boston. Bellamy was already dead and Teach took the condemnation of his crew personally, considering Massachusetts as an outpost of the British Empire. He would wreak havoc upon the city that was about to host the hangings of members of his fraternity. He bullied everyone aboard the English ship, took what he wanted or could use and, contrary to Hornigold's practice, dumped the remaining goods in the ocean. Over the coming weeks, he plied the waters from the Delaware Cape to New York and east to Bermuda, taking prizes throughout the triangle—at least 15 ships in all.

Shaken and humiliated captains spread word throughout the Colonies and England of Blackbeard's barbarous attacks, of watching as their crews and passengers were terrorized and their cargoes dumped overboard. Blackbeard was already approaching legendary status, so that he was credited with a number of attacks he couldn't have performed, being hundreds of miles away. A rumor circulated that Blackbeard intended to sack Philadelphia itself.

Likely merely another rumor, in any case this threat never materialized. Instead, Blackbeard sailed south into the Caribbean where he rendezvoused with Hornigold, Blackbeard now commanding two ships, the *Revenge* fitted with twelve guns and 120 men, and a forty-ton Bermuda sloop mounted with guns and manned by thirty pirates. He had by now surpassed his teacher in reputation if not in skill. In November, near the island of St. Vincent, Blackbeard captured the greatest prize of his career, a crowded 250-ton slaver, *La Concorde*, whose crew, depleted by sickness, couldn't manage its cargo of nearly 500 slaves and repel an attack from the fiercest pirate at sea at the same time. After a brief engagement *La Concorde*'s captain struck his colors.

Large and yet nimble, this craft was perfectly suited for conversion to a pirate flagship. Blackbeard deposited the slaves ashore, impressed the craft's quartermaster and surgeon, and set about converting it to a warship. The refitted Guineaman, now bristling with twenty two guns, he rechristened *Queen Anne's Revenge*, to signal Blackbeard's Jacobite loyalties. Over the coming months she would bring dread and terror to the busy shipping lanes of the South Atlantic and Caribbean. Pirate ships now cruised these waters virtually unchallenged, with *Queen Anne's Revenge* the reigning black queen of the seas.

With Bonnet in nominal command of the *Revenge* and Blackbeard sailing *Queen Anne's Revenge*, the pirates cruised the Leeward Islands taking a large merchant ship, the *Great Allen* from Boston. Blackbeard unleashed his fury on the crew. He shackled and beat the ship's captain, Christopher Taylor, while the pirate crew ransacked the ship for valuables, taking an exquisitely wrought silver chalice that became a legendary trophy. Finding little else of value, Blackbeard marooned Taylor and his men on a remote shore of Martinique. They watched from the beach as Blackbeard burned the *Great Allen* to the waterline.

In November, 1717, Blackbeard and Company launched an audacious siege of the island of Guadeloupe, burning its town and taking a French ship laden with sugar. They continued raiding in the French West Indies, looting and burning ships near the island of St. Christopher. Their take included the *Margaret* which carried valuable livestock. By this time, Blackbeard's reputation was such that crews abandoned their ships rather than stay to fight, taking to rowboats at the sight of the black flag hoisted atop Blackbeard's flagship. All the while, he was increasing the firepower of *Queen Anne's Revenge*. By the end of the year, she carried thirty six guns.

At about this time, Blackbeard learned of the King's Pardon, which had been issued that September, and a strange and profound change, subtle at first, began to overtake him. He virtually disappeared from sight for several months in Spanish-controlled waters, beyond the reach of English eyes and ears. Now known as "The Great Devil," intelligence reports place him in the vicinity of Vera Cruz in command of a four-ship armada—one of which, probably *Queen Anne's Revenge*, carried 42 guns—their ships loaded with "much treasure." In March of 1718, Bonnet, now again apparently commanding the *Revenge*, spotted a massive Boston merchantman, the *Protestant Caesar* of four hundred tons. Foolishly, Bonnet attacked. The ensuing three-hour sea battle ended, typically, with Bonnet running away in the darkness. Bonnet's men had had enough of their master's incompetence. When they met Blackbeard's ships at Turneffe, they pleaded with him to replace the captain which Blackbeard promptly did, placing Bonnet under what Woodard calls "house arrest."

Meanwhile, whatever elation the victorious captain and crew of the *Protestant Caesar* felt was short lived. A few weeks later, Blackbeard spotted the Boston ship—whose name must have piqued his wrath—at anchor in the Bay of Honduras, laden with fresh-cut logs. His fleet ran up their black flags and death's heads in a daunting display of power and vicious intent. In what must have been a keenly embarrassing time for Bonnet, the *Protestant Caesar* surrendered to Blackbeard without firing a shot. As was his usual practice, Blackbeard stranded the captain and crew, then looted and burned their great vessel.

From the Spanish Main the pirate armada sailed north for the next month, arriving off the coast of South Carolina in May. Here Blackbeard pulled off his greatest coup, the blockade of Charleston. He positioned his four ships in the mouth of Charleston Harbor so he could intercept traffic coming and going. To the dismay of the city— women and children, it was reported, "ran about the street like mad things"—Blackbeard captured five prizes in just a few days. The most important of these was the London-bound *Crowley* which carried a number of prominent Charlestonians. At this time, many of Blackbeard's crew, perhaps the captain himself, were suffering from serious illness, probably venereal disease. Blackbeard needed medicine, and he now had a precious cargo of citizens he could use to blackmail the city. He sent one of these unfortunate souls in the company of two pirates across the harbor into town where after a series of serio-comic delays the authorities capitulated and a chest of medicines was delivered to *Queen Anne's Revenge.* Leaving behind looted ships the pirates sailed out of the harbor with the medicine, 4,000 pieces of eight worth £1,000 and the clothes belonging to their captives whom, in a final humiliating gesture, they stripped. He had paralyzed the most important Colonial city south of Philadelphia for nearly a week.

From Charleston, Blackbeard sailed north, capturing two more South Carolina-bound ships, but taking only slaves. But something had changed. Since hearing of the King's pardon Blackbeard had begun to shift his priorities. Most likely, he realized that the heyday of piracy was nearing its end, and that if he was to survive he would soon need to find a secure haven and drastically reduce his visibility. This would mean jettisoning his prizes and much of his crew, stripping down to a leaner operation and restricting his movements. This seems to be why he made his way up the coast toward North Carolina where he probably suspected, rightly as it turned out, that he might find protection, indeed even a patron, in Governor Eden. But first he needed to break up his company. He did so in what is now Beaufort Inlet, a day's sail north of Cape Fear. The two sloops in his flotilla, the *Adventure* and the *Revenge,* along with the Spanish prize he had taken in Charleston, passed over the bar at the mouth of the channel flanked by two deserted banks, Shackleford and Bogue, then safely negotiated the shallow labyrinthine inside passage to Beaufort harbor. Following these, Blackbeard sailed *Queen Anne's Revenge* across the outer bar and then deliberately, it appears, ran her aground on a shoal. He sent word up the channel to his other ships asking that they return. They did, and attempted to free her from the bar but to no avail. *Queen Anne's Revenge* was now listing and it was soon clear that Blackbeard's great flagship, perhaps the most infamous and feared vessel in the western hemisphere, was lost.

Next, in a surprise move, Blackbeard returned command of the *Adventure* to Bonnet and transferred his sailors to the other vessels which made their way back to Beaufort. Almost immediately Bonnet sailed back past the wreck, probably skirting around Cape Lookout at the southern end of what is now Core Banks, putting in at the Pamlico Sound and the wide river feeding it, and sailing up the Pamlico to Bath where he secured his pardon from Eden.

Meanwhile, Blackbeard with a hundred or so co-conspirators had turned on the rest of his crew, marooning sixteen of them on Bogue Banks, where I vacation summer and fall. Another two hundred men he stranded in Beaufort. Finally, his crew reduced to "forty white men and sixty negroes," Blackbeard set a course for Bath in their Spanish prize, taking with him the £2,500 in treasure the gang had amassed.

Bonnet heading south with his pardon and Blackbeard heading north to get his, probably passed each other sometime over the coming days but didn't rendezvous. The two men would never see each other again. Bonnet was on his own. As fate would have it, neither had long to live.

Having broken up his fleet and shed the bulk of his crew, Blackbeard sailed up the Pamlico to Bath. He asked Eden for a pardon, which the Governor readily granted, giving him to boot the rights to the Spanish ship; then Blackbeard, legally free and unindictable, took up residence in the village. It's said that he married the sixteen-year-old daughter of a local planter—his fourteenth wife—in a ceremony presided over by Eden himself. If this is true, Blackbeard was hardly ready to settle into a quiet life. He drank heavily and caroused for days on end. In one of the most sensational accounts of Blackbeard's career, as doubtful as it is lurid, the author of the *General History* reports that he savagely abused his young bride, forcing her to prostitute herself to "five or six of his brutal companions . . . one after another, before his face."

In any case Eden granted Blackbeard the customs right to sail for St. Thomas, perhaps wishing to rid himself if only temporarily of this dangerous and unstable townsman. Instead, the pirate sailed north to Philadelphia where he seems to have come ashore and walked the streets fearlessly, stopping in shops to buy goods—in effect taunting the Pennsylvania authorities. He left Philadelphia the second week in August and set sail for Bermuda, taking two French ships on August 22 after a fierce fight in which Blackbeard's vessel was damaged and some of his men wounded. The pirates transferred the cargoes of sugar and cocoa to one of the French prizes which they kept and, uncharacteristically, sent the other empty vessel on its way. They returned to North Carolina, anchoring behind uninhabited Ocracoke Island where they stripped the French ship of its riggings and spars and transferred much of the cargo they had looted to a boat which they took to Bath. Blackbeard presented Governor Eden's accommodating neighbor, Tobias Knight, with sweetmeats, sugar and cocoa. *En route* back to his ships anchored at Ocracoke, he boarded a piragua captained by a local trader who apparently didn't recognize the pirate and resisted. Blackbeard took pistols, clay pipes, brandy, a silver cup and £66, threw the piragua's oars overboard, and beat the owner with his sword until it broke. Two days later he sailed the *Adventure* back to Bath and reported to Eden that he had found a French ship loaded with cargo abandoned at sea. Now plainly colluding with the pirate— not even the most naïve landlubber would have believed Blackbeard's story—Eden granted him the ship under the right of salvage, and permitted him to burn it as a threat to navigation, allowing him to legally destroy the evidence.

Informed of what was happening in North Carolina through the summer and fall of 1718, Virginia's Governor Alexander Spottswood, no paragon of virtue himself, grew increasingly dismayed. A notorious pirate operating under the protection of legal authority was not only in a position to paralyze shipping along the Carolina coast. With nothing to oppose him Blackbeard, from his base in the Pamlico region, only a day's sail south, obviously posed a threat to Virginia. Woodard is no doubt correct in claiming that Spottswood had an ulterior motive. He was in trouble with his own assemblymen who had evidence that he was diverting land to his ownership and money to his coffers. As much to divert attention from his own nefarious activities, Spottswood hatched a bold—but manifestly illegal—plan to bring an end Blackbeard.

Informants had kept the Governor apprised of Blackbeard's activities through the late summer and autumn of 1718. He knew that the pirate operated in the Pamlico River and Sound between Bath and Ocracoke, and so devised a two-pronged plan of attack. He commissioned and fitted out two sloops, the *Jane* and the *Ranger*, under command of Lieutenant Robert Maynard, which would sail down the Outer Banks to Ocracoke Island on the chance that they might surprise Blackbeard at anchor. Simultaneously, he sent a small force on an arduous overland route through the Great Dismal Swamp via Edenton to Bath in the event that the pirate might be surprised and taken in the village.

Maynard's fleet rounded the south end of Ocracoke in the late afternoon of November 20th and sighted Blackbeard's *Adventure* anchored in deep water on the island's southeastern side known today as Teach's Hole. Alongside the *Adventure* was a merchant vessel belonging to one Samuel Odell whom the pirate was hosting in an all-night drinking bout. Maynard laid off in the distance through the night, waiting until morning to attack. At nine AM on the 21st, the *Jane* and *Ranger* weighed anchor and sailed for the *Adventure* and its merchant companion. Almost immediately the attacking vessels ran aground on a sand bar, losing whatever element of surprise Maynard might otherwise have gotten. The crews of both sloops began noisily heaving ballast and water barrels overboard. Hung over, the pirate crew coming up on deck saw the unfamiliar vessels buzzing with activity and must have realized immediately they were about to be attacked. As the *Adventure* raised its sails, the *Ranger* came free of the bar, its crew rowing furiously through the still air toward the pirate flagship. As the *Ranger* neared, Blackbeard's men fired off a volley of musket shot followed by a furious broadside from its cannons, cutting down the *Ranger*'s rigging and killing its commander, Midshipman Edward Hyde, outright. But as the *Adventure* swept past, a volley of musket fire from the crippled *Ranger* struck the halyard supporting the pirate ship's mainsail, which slowed the *Adventure*. This was a crucial bit of good luck for Maynard because at about the same time, he managed to free the *Jane* from the sand and its crew began desperately rowing for the pirate ship. Had the *Adventure*'s mainsail been fully functioning, Blackbeard would surely have escaped the ambush.

When the *Jane* came within earshot of the *Adventure*, the two captains famously exchanged words. "Damn you villains, who are you and from whence came you?" Blackbeard shouted, drink in hand. "You can see we are no pirates," Maynard replied. At the official inquest into the battle, Maynard testified that Blackbeard, turning up his cup, "drank damnation to me and my men, whom he styled Cowardly Puppies, saying he would neither give nor take Quarter."

With the ships now at close range Blackbeard fired a broadside—his cannons loaded with grape and partridge shot, creating a shotgun effect—at the *Jane*. At the same time, the fierce veteran pirates began lobbing makeshift grenades—bottles stuffed with gunpowder, musket balls and iron fragments—onto the *Jane*'s deck. The resulting carnage was horrific. Twenty-one of Maynard's crew were killed or wounded and the ship's deck was awash in blood. When Blackbeard boarded the Navy sloop, he had every reason to think that he had won. But Maynard had an ace up his sleeve, having kept the remainder of his men safely below decks. With the smoke clearing, Maynard ordered his men on deck and Blackbeard, like a bear cornered by a pack of dogs, found himself surrounded by a dozen sailors intent on killing him. As pirates boarding the *Jane* engaged the Navy crew in hand-to-hand combat, the two captains, swords drawn, squared off in what must have been a chaotic fight punctuated by ritualized, duel-like moments. Maynard made the first thrust, striking Blackbeard's cartridge belt, and bending his sword back toward the hilt. Blackbeard hacked at Maynard, striking the lieutenant's sword and slicing his fingers. Maynard discarded his blade, drew his pistol and fired point blank at Blackbeard, gravely wounding him. Leaping to the aid of his captain, Abraham Demelt, the *Jane*'s helmsman, slashed Blackbeard across the face. Others fired pistol shots into the reeling pirate captain who continued slashing at all around him.

The coup de grâce came, it was reported, from a Scotsman who struck Blackbeard with a single blow to the neck, nearly decapitating him, leaving his head attached to his shoulders by a flap of skin. This may be true; it may not be. The author of the *General History*, a writer very fond of graphic detail, doesn't mention this grisly finale, saying only that Blackbeard died while "cocking another pistol." Neither did Maynard include this climax in his official account of the battle, saying rather that Blackbeard collapsed "with five shot in him, and 20 dismal cuts in several parts of his body."

One way or another, Blackbeard was decapitated and his ghastly death's head hung from the *Jane*'s bowsprit. The headless corpse was thrown overboard into the Pamlico Sound where, legend has it, it swam three times around the ship before sinking.

The swimming corpse has haunted me for decades. I knew little about the other Nassau pirates, but I knew the legends of Blackbeard since I was a boy. I grew up, one might say, with the mythic pirate —the devil incarnate, with his flaming dreadlocks, his wild eyes flashing, draped with pistols, slung with swords, harboring untold treasure—as a summer companion. For nearly twenty Julys, my parents took a house on the south bank of the Pamlico River, two miles across the flat water from Bath. On many a still sultry afternoon, with the river flashing distant mirages in the relentless sun and thick air, when we tired of water skiing or the fish weren't biting, my brother and I slowly cruised the banks of the Pamlico north and south, scanning the shore for a freshly fallen tree that might have heaved up a chest of loot, a treasure beyond our wildest dreams. Blackbeard's undiscovered hoard must, we wanted to believe, lay waiting to be found. We sometimes camped on a small Huck-sized island two miles downriver, nobody but us, combing the beaches for treasure. We found nothing and Marc will figure later in my travels, sadly.

November and December 1718 were very bad months for pirates of the Caribbean. Blackbeard and his crew died on November 21. His pathetic pleas having failed, Bonnet and twenty-nine of his crew swung on the 10th of December, and Rogers hanged eight more pirates in Nassau two days later.

Rogers's meting out of the December justice ensured that pirates would never again rule the Bahamas. But his troubles were far from over. His administration ran out of money in 1719, and he was obliged to carry the colony's debt on his own, running up a tab of £20,000 by year's end. Still, he managed to complete the restoration Fort Nassau, fitting it out with fifty-four cannons, and established a ten-gun battery at the eastern end of the island. He had the *Delicia*, 100 soldiers and 500 militiamen to fend off enemies of the realm. He had sufficiently fortified and armed Nassau so that when war broke out with Spain again, despite the fact that Nassau was of immediate interest to England's archenemy, the Spanish made only a half-hearted attempt to invade New Providence, an assault the colony easily repulsed.

Crippled, physically ill and mentally exhausted, deep in debt, he resigned his post in late February 1722 and sailed for England.

Rogers fully expected His Majesty's government to cover the debts he incurred while governing the Bahamas, but he was disappointed. His petitions were ignored and he fell deeper and deeper into depression, obscurity and desperation. Unable to satisfy his creditors, he was soon languishing in debtors' prison—this extraordinary man, this rare creature, this national hero brought so low.

But Rogers wasn't to be down for long. Another reversal of fortune awaited him, this Phoenix rising again, when a writer working on a history of pirates approached him for assistance with the project. This was the author of *A General History of the Roberies and Murders of the Most Notorious Pyrates*, published in 1724. Captain Charles Johnson is a *nom de plume*. No plausible candidate by that name was writing at the time. For much of the twentieth century, the book was attributed to the great Daniel Defoe, who immortalized Selkirk as Crusoe. This attribution is deeply satisfying not only because Defoe clearly sought out pirates, but also because Defoe published so much that he "defies bibliography." He's said to have died of dropsy, pen in hand. Why not give him the *General History*?

It would have been great indeed to have added the Rosetta Stone of eighteenth-century piracy to Defoe's bibliography, but that attribution unraveled in 1988 when inconsistencies between this book and other pirate pamphlets by Defoe were pointed out. A more likely candidate, the seaman and journalist Nathaniel Mist, has recently taken Defoe's place as the book's likely author. Still, it must be said that the identity of Captain Charles Johnson has never been certainly determined.

Whoever he was, the author of the *General History* was a gifted and experienced writer who solicited first-hand information about the Nassau pirates from Rogers, information that he alone could have known. The *General History* was a smash hit, selling out its first print run within a matter of months. A second edition followed and then an expanded third edition the next year, and a fourth in 1726. The popularity of the *General History* brought Rogers back to the public's attention. He was rescued from obscurity and oblivion by Johnson's success. The nation acknowledged Woodes Rogers for the true patriot and naval hero that he was. The King granted Rogers a pension retroactive to 1721, and reappointed him Governor of the Bahamas. Now acclaimed as a great man, Rogers, aged fifty, sat for a splendid portrait of the Commodore and his family in almost regal fashion, by none other than William Hogarth. The Rogers portrait hangs today in the London Maritime Museum.

When Rogers and his son arrived back in Nassau on August 25, 1729, he found an island in shambles, having been raked by a vicious hurricane. Though pirates no longer threatened the outpost, he faced daunting administrative hurdles and the continuing deterioration of his health. He survived these but sickened and died on July 15, 1731. Woodes Rogers was buried on the island, New Providence, which he had done so much to rescue and preserve. The site of his grave is unknown. It's haunting to think that somewhere beneath the stately whitewashed buildings of Old Nassau, beneath its traffic-choked thoroughfares, beneath the footfalls of wandering tourists, the dust of the great Woodes Rogers, the most important figure in Bahamian history, is mingled with the sand of New Providence.

His legacy endures in the Bahamian national motto: *Expulsis Piratus, Comercia Restitua*—"Pirates Expelled, Commerce Restored."

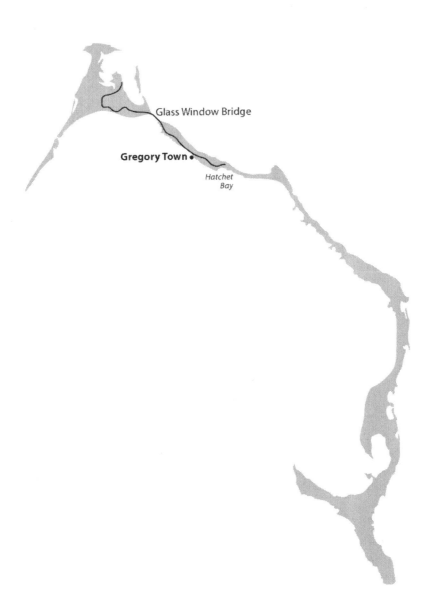

Glass Window Bridge

Gregory Town •

*Hatchet
Bay*

N

ELEUTHERA

Chapter 2
Eleuthera: At Play in Fields of Stone

The Eleutheran Adventurers "were forced (for diverse months) to lie in the open air, and to feed upon such fruits and wild creatures as the island afforded."
~ *Massachusetts Governor* **John Winthrop**, *1649*

THAT day back in 1994 when I first arrived in Nassau, the first of what would become many trips to this airport and capital city, I didn't fit with either the seniors or the juniors. For me Nassau was only a stopover. I wouldn't leave the airport. I would spend four hours waiting for a flight to Eleuthera, hunting ground of the old pirates, and one of the twenty-eight "Out" or "Family Islands." Virtually every Bahamian traces his or her roots to the Family Islands, the preferred term for the islands and cays (pronounced "keys"), since nearly everyone in Nassau and Freeport was born in the Family Islands, or came from people born in these islands.

We cleared Customs and turned right into the lobby; the tourists headed out the doors to waiting taxis—late 80s Detroit land barges, Electras and El Dorados, with shiny leather upholstery, broken door handles and air fresheners dangling from rear view mirrors. Nothing about these drivers hinted at their historical importance. Yet they were as monumental and crucial to the future of this island nation as pirates or modern politicians. Some of them were old enough to remember 1958 when Nassau's cabbies had prepared the way for independence from Great Britain by going on strike, and so crippling the nation's economy which then, as now, was almost entirely dependent upon the travel industry. In 1697, as in 1958 and today, travel is the engine that drives this nation.

That year, 1958, the National Assembly, dominated by a group of white businessmen known as "The Bay Street Boys," after Nassau's main street, granted exclusive rights to a syndicate of white taxi drivers to serve the then new International airport, half-an hour from the heart of Nassau. Immediately, black cabbies went on strike, blockading the road to the airport with their cars. Tourism choked out, like a motor suddenly starved of fuel or air, when tourists couldn't get into town. Suddenly everything stopped.

As word of the strike spread into Nassau, other workers joined the stoppage. Hotel and construction workers walked out, and the Bahamas came under a general strike that would last nineteen days and effectively shut down the Royal Crown Colony of the Bahamas. By crippling its economy, cab drivers had taken collective action that spelled the doom of the apartheid political structure that had ruled the Bahamas for three hundred years.

The strike was resolved and black cabbies returned to the queues at the airport, but inexorable processes had begun that would lead inevitably to independent governance under black majority rule. In July of 1965, Lynden O. Pindling, a representative of the new black-nationalist Progressive Liberal Party (PLP), stood before the National Assembly to protest another desperate piece of legislation passed by the white-dominated Assembly aimed at thwarting majority rule. In a brilliantly theatrical gesture, Pindling grabbed the signatory mace—a gift from the Loyalist South Carolinians in the eighteenth century—and pitched it out of the window where it burst into shards in front of agitated demonstrators gathered on the street below.

Pindling turned his attention to the Assembly. "Authority belongs to the people," he shouted before the stunned legislators, "and the people are outside." As leader of the PLP, Pindling oversaw the transition to internal governance and would become the nation's first Prime Minister when the Bahamas achieved independence from Britain in 1973, bringing to completion a political revolution from minority to majority rule, from white to black, no less impressive than South Africa's, only without the bloodshed.

36

I got my bag and walked to the other side of the airport, the domestic wing. Here life was very different. The metal door of the men's bathroom was permanently jarred open, the molded plastic seats in the waiting room were cracked and duct-taped and full; the floor scraped and stained. I was surrounded now almost entirely by black people. Crisp shirts and bright flower-print dresses, broken sandals and grimy T-shirts. There were women scolding and cajoling youngsters; some cradled sleeping, others bawling, babies. Young men wearing basketball jerseys, floppy hats and gold chains ambled about. Older men lugged family burdens—cardboard boxes duct-taped shut and suitcases held together with twine—across the floor. One man wheeled a rusted window air conditioning unit along on a dolly. An old woman gently rubbed the back of a child who was bent over, his hands clasped over his ears. The air was ripe with smells I'd never known.

I queued up in the noisy line of people checking in and read the departures board; the names were strange and evocative—Eleuthera, San Salvador, Exuma, Great Inagua and Mayaguana, Cat Island, Andros and Great Abaco, Crooked Island and Grand Bahama. I knew nothing about these islands, but their names, their syllables, seemed carved of some mysterious beauty.

Moving forward step by small step, it occurred to me that at some point in my walk through the airport that day I had stepped over an invisible line, a demarcation between two worlds of the Bahamas, one of leisure and privilege, the other of work and whim and exigency and surprise which had little to do with tourism, where men and women went about living ordinary lives that from an outsider's point of view seemed extraordinary. I had the feeling of being alone on a strange planet—which is the deepest pleasure of traveling. Though I knew nothing of life in the Bahamas, I was comfortable moving up in line, trusting that beneath the apparent chaos of the cacophonous room there were rhythms I could only glimpse, energies and synergies I didn't recognize, forces, motivations that moved the crowds along in some order I was just now encountering. I was happy, trusting and now very hot.

I stepped up to the Bahamsair agent, an attractive woman dark as mahogany who wore her hair pulled back in a tight bun. Her neatly tailored teal uniform fit her well. Her nametag said Brenda.

"And where are you flying this afternoon, sir?" Her smile was sweet and her teeth bone white.

"Eleuthera."

Her outrageously long fingernails were decorated with stars.

"That's a pretty place," she said. "My cousins live on Eleuthera, in Tarpum Bay." She smiled again, coyly I thought, and looked down while writing on my ticket. I stared as she wrote, tracing the pretty curve of her hip down her leg, straining inconspicuously to see what shoes she was wearing.

"I hear it's a beautiful island," I said. "Think I'll like it?"

"Yes, for sure you will like it a lot. Very friendly people in Eleuthera."

"Behave yourself," she said, handing me back my ticket.

"Do I get a window seat?"

"You can have whatever seat you want, Mr. Hunt."

She liked me, I thought. I was growing happier by the moment.

"The plane today is not full. Just find a seat."

"And behave myself?" I asked.

"Yes, please. Behave yourself."

I had been invited to the Bahamas as a tag-along on a geologic expedition mapping sea-level changes on Eleuthera. Conrad Neumann, a geologic oceanographer, was a friend of mine, a drinking buddy. And his colleague Paul Hearty taught at the College of the Bahamas. Conrad and Paul were doing important work, potentially revealing master clues to the recent history of global climate change.

Geologists can map the rise and fall of the ocean by the nature of the rocks that make up Bahamian islands. The farther inland the rocks register inundation signals the extent of these rises and falls, these global sea changes, over geologic time. The evidence suggested a dynamic that the principal investigator, Conrad Neumann of The University of North Carolina at Chapel Hill, called "The Madhouse Effect"—rapid fluctuations, in geologic terms, in the sea level, some occurring in the brief period of 5,000 years.

I had a promise from a newspaper editor to consider a story about the trip, if I came back with one.

Eleuthera is a sprung fish hook 110 miles long and only a mile or so wide at its widest. Its eastern shore is wildly beautiful, the northern sector a line of dramatic cliffs against which the blue Atlantic crashes incessantly, the waves traveling uninterrupted along the Tropic of Cancer from West Africa. Eleuthera's western, lagoon coast is a line of low ledges and sandy coves, and settlements with great names—

Tarpum Bay, Rock Sound and beyond, to places I would visit many years later. South of Governor's Harbour, Eleuthera is a lower, curvaceous stretch of island along which major resorts are open now, and others are under construction. North Eleuthera has long been a tourist destination. Now Southern Eleuthera is fast gaining on the north.

At the North Eleuthera airport, a short flight from Nassau, I met my compadres for the week to come—Conrad and Paul J. Hearty of the College of the Bahamas. We ate conch fritters and had a drink in the steamy lounge while waiting for our rental car to show up. One drink became several, as the car didn't show up when it was supposed to. Finally, just as I was getting grinny, it arrived and we loaded ourselves into a 1987 Buick Grand Marquis. Conrad got behind the wheel and, feeling very good, we launched out on a ride from the airport south through The Bluff, Upper and Lower Bogue twenty miles south from the airport toward Gregory Town and Cambridge Villas, where we'd be staying for the week.

At the narrowest point on the island, the isthmus called Glass Window, we crossed the bridge dividing the Atlantic, which crashed deep blue and white on the left side, and on the right, the balmy, electric green Bight of Eleuthera. Thirty feet below on the lee side, a pickup truck lay upside down just beneath the clear shimmering water of the Bight, its chassis looking like the underside of an enormous sea turtle.

Gregory Town in the north central sector of Eleuthera was a settlement of pastel-colored houses scattered on a hillside overlooking the turquoise Bahama Banks. Flanked by a restaurant and bar, Cambridge Villas was a yellow concrete building of two stories at the bottom of the hill, toward the harbor. Out back was a pool surrounded by oleander, bougainvillea and, in the distance, hibiscus and Poinciana trees—all in bloom. After more rum and a delicious meal of cracked conch, mashed potatoes, sliced tomatoes, and fruit, I asked our proprietor, Harcourt Cambridge, about the Glass Window crossing.

"That truck go over in a rage," he said. "Sometimes when clear blue sky be here in Gregory Town there will be a storm out at sea. That storm will drive up big waves that break over Glass Window. No warning at all, just that mean wave we call the rage come breaking over the road. Carry your vehicle into the water. I know the man who owned that truck you saw," he continued. "He's lucky to be alive to tell about it. You must be careful, you see, at Glass Window, even on clear days." Mr. Cambridge sat up straight and shook his head in warning. "When I was a boy, my mother told us, 'when you crossing Glass Window and you see the rage break over, you wait and count seven waves, then run like hell.' "

I turned in for the night, stupidly drunk and tired, wondering how that pickup driver survived being hurled over the bridge thirty feet to the rocks and shallow green water below. Around sunrise, I had a dream about water, but not a drowning dream. I was standing on the bridge rail at Glass Window, looking out over The Bight of Eleuthera and thought I could fly; I spread my arms and leaned out. The next instant I was underwater, looking up through shimmering frames of vision at a world turned upside down. I listened to myself breathing comfortably underwater.

The first European settlement in the Bahamas, Eleuthera was reached in 1648 by religious dissenters from Bermuda who named it with a Greek neologism for "freedom." Another group of zealots arrived from Bermuda the following year. Expelled by Bermudian loyalists after the execution of Charles I in January 1649, these stubborn republicans and dissenters, sixty of whom, including three Independent ministers, set sail in a borrowed pinnace. Captained by William Sayle, a trader who had twice served as colonial governor of Bermuda, the voyagers included an old preacher named Patrick Copeland.

Their fifty-ton ship foundered on a reef on the lee side of the island near the present settlement of Governor's Harbour. One person drowned and the vessel was lost, including all provisions, dry goods, tools, seed corn and stock animals. The marooned colonists "were forced (for diverse months) to lie in the open air, and to feed upon such fruits and wild creatures as the island afforded." Bowed but not broken, the Eleutheran Adventurers, as they came to be called, lived for a time on the beach and later migrated to the northern tip of the island, gathering in a cave still known as Preacher's Cave on the north face of the island to worship and pray for delivery.

In New England, meanwhile, word of the difficulties the Adventurers were enduring prompted Governor Winthrop to petition Boston churches to come to their aid. Money was raised to provision the Eleutheran colony, and a ship laden with life-saving food and seed, cattle and tools reached the island the following year. In gratitude for the crucial help from New Englanders, the Eleutheran Adventurers sent back ten tons of brazilwood that raised £124 for the charter endowment of Harvard College. Some of the old college library was built of this wood.

The gift of brazilwood to Harvard seems starkly ironic today, since there are few ancient forests left in the Bahamas. In 1492 Columbus describes San Salvador, 200 miles southeast of here—the most likely site of his first landfall in the New World—as a densely forested island with thick groves and immense stands of hardwoods. In typical fashion, the early European settlers of the Bahamian islands began razing the subtropical forests, then rich in mahogany, tamarind, brazilwood, Spanish cedar, yellow pine and lignum vitae, to make plantations. It was a tragedy in the making, this deforesting, a tragedy caused by the unusual geology of these islands. The Bahamian archipelago is a limestone platform covered by a thin layer of topsoil. Crops flourished for a couple of years, with no hint of trouble to come. But cotton and sisal were avaricious, leaching the thin stratum of topsoil of nutrients. In only a few years the plantations failed, leaving only one alternative to abandoning their holdings: clearing more forest to plant new fields. These failed in succession, and more and more forest was cleared to make fields for crops. In short order, wind and rain eroded the barren fields. Desiccation spread like a blight from island to island, the plantations inevitably failing as fast as settlers could clear fields, exposing more and more denuded land to erosion. By 1725, the cultivation of these islands had dramatically lowered the forest canopy, and hardwoods were giving way to gnarly bush land.

With the ominous failure of their crops and the establishment of the Commonwealth in England, many of the original Eleutheran Adventurers—setting a pattern that would be repeated in the next century with Loyalists fleeing the American Revolution—abandoned their "Freedom" island and returned to Bermuda. Others emigrated to Massachusetts and Jamaica. Even William Sayle returned to Bermuda in the mid-1650s where he was appointed governor for a third time. But some colonists remained on Eleuthera, settling on offshore cays, Spanish Wells and Harbour Island, still predominantly white communities, prosperous and heavily touristed. These offshore settlements left the mainland of Eleuthera open for occupation by Africans who survived slave ships that wrecked here in passage to the

American South and who, in the words of Michael Craton and Gail Saunders in their definitive social history of the Bahamas, "could not easily be assimilated into the founding households."

The unchecked destruction of aboriginal woodlands resulted in what you see today on every Bahamian island: vast stretches of low windswept, impenetrable bush ringed by coconut palm (*Cocos nucifera*) and Australian pine (*Casuarina litorea*)—two imported species impossible to eradicate—along the beach. Imported in the 19th century to control erosion, the Casuarina has proven a particularly ruinous irony for the Bahamas. This species has proliferated so virulently that it now dominates the Bahamian shoreline, shedding a blanket of acidic needles near the beach that kills native runners and leaves behind fields of sand blown away by storms, exposing more and more of the limestone platform. Open to the sun, the edge of the limestone dried and broke into blocks, roughly rectilinear. Another rise in sea level—only a foot or so over eons—resubmerged these blocks from the beach out to about 20 feet in depth. Hucksters and entrepreneurs claim these structures are manmade—the sunken city of Atlantis on Bimini is the prime example. This is nonsense. Beach rock, which sometimes does look like a collapsed wall or an ancient street, is an entirely natural eruption of Bahamian geology.

This points to another stark irony: the beautiful waters of the enormous Bahamian archipelago are beautiful precisely because they are barren. Crowded with spectacular fish, the gorgeous Bahamian reefs of which, thankfully, there are uncharted miles, are oases in a vast underwater desert. You could see that upside down truck in the Bight at Glass Window as clearly as through a tear drop precisely because there's no life down there muddying the water.

With Cambridge Villas as base camp, and me tagging along, Conrad Neumann and Paul Hearty set about their ongoing work of piecing together a geologic history of the Bahamian islands. In geologic measurements, what Stephen J. Gould called "deep time," the evidence gathered by Neumann and Hearty indicates sudden dramatic fluctuations of the sea level during the last interglacial cycle. This is what Neumann calls the "Madhouse Effect"—rapid fluctuations of world climate before the Holocene Epoch (the last 11,000 or so years) when geologic change seems to have slowed. In fact, for all our fear of global climate change, some scientists make the case that the human presence on earth, as we have propagated and cooked, emitting fumes into the sky, as we industrialized and began to spew a host of gasses into the atmosphere, seems not to have accelerated but retarded climate change, stabilizing the planet at an optimal level suited to human life.

We spent out first full day in the field in the northern interior, mapping ridges that Hearty described as chevrons, ancient concretized sand deposits accreted by storms when the sea level was much higher than it is today. Wind-swept water coursed over the beaches and drove up inland ridges. The water retreated over time, leaving these thicketed hills. At places roads had been cut through these ridges, revealing strata of rock that contained the record of thousands of years of geologic activity—a bonanza for geologists.

This work took us into rough country, over rocky tractor paths beside orange and banana orchards lined with guava and mango trees, up hills and down ravines. Driving through a banana orchard we came upon a lone man moving stones from the base of trees. Paul said hello and asked if the boss man was around. The man looked down and mumbled something haltingly in English. It sounded like Creole.

"Haitian," Paul said pulling away, "Despised in the Bahamas. Probably here illegally." Haitians, who have fled to the Bahamas for decades, are a source of social unrest in the nation. Haitian shanty towns dot the Bahamas; the largest number of Haitians squat in New Providence, but the two settlements—The Mud and Pigeon Pea—on Great Abaco are the largest in the nation. Recently, the government warned that large-scale violence between Haitians and Bahamians might break out on these islands. In the far south, on Great Inagua, Haitians sometimes wash up on its beaches, drowned or nearly drowned when their overcrowded, ungainly boats founder. The survivors are taken to Nassau to recuperate and then repatriated. This happens a dozen times or more every year.

At midday we stopped on a remote paved road cut into the summit of a high hill. The breeze was strong and steady, slightly cooler at this altitude. Beside the road engineers had left standing a stone tower 15 feet high as a pedestal for a utility pole. For geologists, such ridges provide a mother lode of information, telescoping rock features exposed over many thousands of years. They were like children at Christmas; I was more interested in the smashed carcass of a Bahamian boa constrictor by the roadside.

Neumann and Hearty sampled rock strata that contained microscopic fenestrations indicating that this chevron-shaped hill, this far inland, had been formed by wet sand along the wave break of an ancient shoreline. When the moisture evaporated the sand became, over the eons, a porous, bleached limestone composed of fenestra—fossilized vessels—and oolite—egg-shaped mineral grains precipitated out of the ancient ocean. Appearing in the interior of the island, these compositions tell the story of successive storms pushing these sand ridges up while the ocean gradually receded, more than 100,000 years ago.

Conrad and Paul were so absorbed in their work at this rock tower they didn't notice the brown and white van that pulled to a stop behind Bahama Mama. A half-dozen men and women, trailed by a shy necktied boy, got out.

"We are witnessing," said a handsome man in his Sunday suit.

"Oh, yes? That's interesting," said Conrad, turning away from the rock toward them. "We are too. Looking at the rocks. At tiny bubbles in the rocks." The rocks, not God, mattered to Conrad. He was blinded by science.

"Yes. Yes. That's interesting." The Bahamian nodded thoughtfully. The women in their fine print dresses nodded and smiled.

"We are visiting our lost brethren in the area," he continued.

"Ah, well, then," Conrad ventured, "We're not lost. I've been here before. We're geologists. Well . . . not him," he said pointing to me.

Here on this obscure road in the Eleutheran bush Faith met Inquiry at high noon under a blazing sun, with embarrassingly few souls in sight. Believer and scientist alike read sermons in stone, but very different ones.

Conrad launched a brief account of essential geology, heavy on the concept of deep time—certain not to inspire serenity in The Believers.

Chief Witness wasn't fazed. "We have no problem with rocks being three billion years old," he said. "Genesis 1 tells us only how the earth was created for man's habitation. No, I do not wish to deny the record," he said. "What matters is that God created every creature." He swept his arm toward the bush. "And asked Adam to name them."

"Even some Christians miss the point of Genesis 1 which tells us that the continents rose up out of the seas at God's command." He turned to his flock. "At one time the whole world was underwater. Is that not right, Mr. Geologist?"

"Yes," Conrad said, equivocating, "knowing how all this was formed, what it is, only increases the mystery, doesn't it?"

"Praise the Lord," said one of the women. The others nodded and smiled.

For the next few minutes Chief Witness addressed us perfunctorily on matters of doctrine. Conrad, Paul and I nodded and smiled. Simple politeness on both sides allowed two master ideologies, science and religion, to engage and disengage without insult or violence.

The Believers wished us farewell, got back into their van and drove off, leaving behind *Watch Tower* pamphlets titled "Will This World Survive" and "Why You Can Trust the Bible."

Two years after Hurricane Andrew had ravaged Eleuthera, destruction was apparent everywhere. Driving these inland roads, many of them rubble, we passed walls, sheds, roofs and cars that were strewn about like so much trash. Eighty percent of buildings in the northern sector of the island had been damaged or destroyed; most were abandoned. We passed an empty A-Frame house whose doors and windows had been blown out. A half-submerged Chevy was visible in the little bay at the back of the house. In the front yard fledgling burrowing owls stirring in the afternoon took no notice of us.

Later in the day we drove back toward Glass Window and turned back north along Whale Point Road. Here another ridge had been cut through to make a roadbed. While Conrad and Paul chipped away at rocks, I climbed the bank and made my way through sea grape and palmetto bushes, around enormous termite mounds, toward the Atlantic. The sun was well past meridian, and it was baking hot under a cobalt sky. Where the vegetation ended, an expanse of unbroken limestone weathered to a bleached slate color and carved into peaks and wedges began.

It would be a difficult walk but I could see the ocean, darker blue than the sky, stretching to the horizon from 200 feet away and hear it thunder at the base of the cliff. Soon I was standing at the top peering down at the ocean seventy feet below. The Atlantic was hammering the rocks, throwing a brilliant white spray half-way up the wall. The breeze was so stiff that terns flittered at eye-level against a sky whose blue had deepened even more richly in the last few minutes.

The scene was vividly colored—gray rock sprouting tufts of green vegetation, white birds, the porcelain sky and dark ocean—and stretched to infinity. I chose the smoothest rock cradle I could find and sat down rapt in wonder, engulfed by the overwhelming spectacle. Alone for a change, I thought I might be the only white person who had ever been to this spot. I remembered earlier that day, at the base of the bridge at Glass Window, reading a cryptic message written in a stanchion when the cement was wet: "Columbus he be standing up / all the way round." I fancied myself a latter-day Columbus, exploring a New World.

After a while I stood up and trekked back toward the car, following the cliffs north and then turning west inland across the field of unbroken rock. Ahead rose a ragged stone wall that seemed to have been carved out by waves. But how could waves reach this height? Up close, the wall was a maze of what seemed to be concretized tree roots.

Carrying on, I met Conrad and Paul who had come looking for me.

"Hey, you should see this stone wall I found. It looks like its got roots running through it." They looked at each other.

"Where?"

"Back there."

"Let's go."

When we reached the wall they started hooting. Then they unholstered cameras and began shooting. Between shots, they peered at the rock through magnifying glasses.

"Rhizomorphs!" Paul shouted.

"Better than what you see in texts," Conrad added, busily scribbling in his notebook.

I had stumbled upon a structure formed eons ago when sand surrounding fossil roots had concretized. The roots had decayed, and over time waves had eaten away at the shelf, leaving tangles of tubular molds exposed in astonishing detail.

Conrad and Paul were excited and I was proud to have become a part of their work. I thought of Columbus again and didn't hesitate to exploit the moment. "This place shall henceforth and forever more be called Marvin Gardens," I shouted.

For me the name still stands, though in all likelihood no geologist has seen Marvin Gardens since that afternoon in 1994.

On the way back to Cambridge Villas, Paul slowed our Bahama Mama to a crawl beside a white man and woman riding bicycles. He waved as we passed and they exchanged "see-you-tonights."

"Steve and Sarah," he said. "I met them last night at Elvina's."

Tired from the day's travel, I had turned in early the night before while Conrad and Paul had gone bar hopping in the village.

"Sarah's a doll. They'll be at Cush's tonight."

Gregory Town was lively after dark. The bar at Cambridge Villas was home to a friendly group of locals and a few tourists who drank until late at night. And there were at least three other watering holes in Gregory Town where we could mingle with Eleutherans. Cush's was a disco a couple of miles south of town on the Queen's Highway. When we arrived around 10 o'clock on Saturday night, a crowd of islanders was dancing to soca, reggae and salsa tunes played by the Eleuthera Express, a four-man band set up against the wall of a dance hall no larger than a rich man's living room. When we arrived the place was rocking. Well lubricated already, we fell into the party without a glitch. Not even when a pretty Bahamian woman turned her back to me and ground her hips into my crotch did I feel anxious; her boyfriend at the bar, talking intently to the tender, seemed miles away.

The party at Cush's grew in fascinating ways. We were soon joined at our table by a well-preserved heiress to a chocolate fortune, two German teenagers, and Steve and Sarah we had passed earlier in the day. They'd come to Eleuthera from their home in Massachusetts, shortly after filing for divorce. I didn't ask why. Perhaps they'd had second thoughts and hoped to patch things up in Paradise. In any case, Steve was a surfer and Eleuthera offered good surfing on the cheap. The stretch of the Atlantic just south of Gregory Town, the only real surfing spot in the nation, offers some of the best and least crowded runs in this part of the Atlantic.

Steve was reticent, dark-skinned, thick-browed, and wore a most unsurferlike corporate haircut. I heard he was quite good on his board.

His estranged wife Sarah was a petite, attractive, sun-worshipping legal assistant who had tired of surfers. Later, I saw Sarah and Paul talking familiarly at a corner table, cupping their ears to hear each other over the blasting chords of Eleuthera Express. Sarah was, I thought, all too ready to be rescued from her husband.

The next morning Steve went surfing, and Sarah came with us to the cliffs. We parked Bahama Mama on the road to Whale Point, shimmied up the bank and made our way through the dense bush out across the moonrock. Soon we were at the top of the cliff, staring down into the surf exploding in the face of the wall. Paul and Conrad roamed north and south, hammering off chunks of rock and peering at them though their miniature magnifying glasses. I wandered off to photograph the curious bonsai trees that clung to life on the rocky hill behind the wall. In cup-shaped recesses in the limestone I found thin sheets of red dust covering white sand.

Here was another astonishing discovery. This was sand from the Sahara Desert, hauled aloft by winds, carried on the Trades across the Atlantic, and deposited here in this remote cliff top on Eleuthera, an ocean away. This deposit, like my camera and my sandals, came from places I'd never been. I scooped some samples into a plastic bag. I still have that red powdery sand somewhere in the attic.

Nearer the cliff edge, I could hear the surf pounding. The sky was crystal clear, blurring only near the horizon. The sun was deadly. I started to feel anxious. Danger lurked everywhere. At any minute, walking toward the edge, I might spook a scorpion, or trip and impale myself on the blades and pikes that time and weather had sculpted in the limestone underfoot. I could have a heat stroke here, for Christ's sake, or tumble from the cliff-top and die in the angry maw of the ocean.

I looked around to find the others. Paul and Sarah were nearby but I couldn't see Conrad. They shouted that they hadn't seen him. Maybe he'd taken a tumble, I thought. I set off in the direction I'd last seen him, climbing up and down one ridge and to the top of the next. My heart was pounding when I reached the crest and looked down into the ravine.

There below me, Conrad, The Father of Bahamian Geology, was floating naked in a natural pool twenty yards wide. It had been formed in the ravine where the cliff dipped to a mere 10 feet above the ocean; the pool's lip was the cliff's edge, an infinity pool. Over centuries, the action of waves breaching the cliff and flooding the pool had caused large stones to mill out a dozen chest-deep chambers within it.

Conrad, wearing only his floppy white hat and red bandana tied rakishly around his neck, was grinning at me from one of these chambers, his own private bath.

"Do I remind you of something?" he shouted. "The beluga of the Bahamas?"

Just then a breaker rose over the wall and struck Conrad from behind. Above the foam I saw his white butt roll over and disappear. He came up laughing and sputtering as his hat surfed toward the head of the pool.

The scene was at once comic and idyllic. I stripped to my underwear and sandals, folded my clothes on a rock out of the water's way, and walked gingerly into the pool.

"So, you ever been naked before?" Conrad asked incredulously. "You do that like a man who's never taken his clothes off."

"Isn't this illegal?"

Conrad guffawed, "Yeah, you wait for de cops. Deh be comin,' mon," he said in Bahamianese.

Soon, I was relaxing naked in my own natural Jacuzzi, watching small sergeant-majors striped in yellow and black darting about. Reclining at eye-level with the surface of the pool, I gazed out on the strange perspective created by the rolling ocean beyond the pool and the small drama at my legs where the small fish were flashing. In a few minutes Sarah and Paul appeared on the ridge above the pool. Paul was naked; Sarah was in a bathing suit.

Her modesty melted and soon she was lounging naked in her own chamber, a taut brown cat with a spectacular body. We were free voyeurs in paradise. For the next hour we floated unashamed and unembarrassed in the pool, and sunbathed on the flat ledges verging it. Many thousands of years old, this rough-hewn Eden had perhaps never been seen by anyone.

We named it Neumann's Pool at Marvin Gardens.

The next day we drove south along the Queen's Highway through Hatchet Bay and James Cistern toward Governor's Harbour. The beauty of the drive—at points we could see the blue Atlantic and green Caribbean in the same vista—was tarnished by the enormous amount of trash that littered the highway. Washing machines, engine blocks and entire cars rusted in the bush and along beautiful beaches.

Much of this heavy refuse was strewn by Hurricane Andrew, but much of it had been dumped by Eleutherans. Though signs in every village urged people to "Join the Cleanup," it was not easy to be tidy on Eleuthera, or on any Bahamian island, for that matter. In this nation of islands, you can't move material by long hauling trucks or trains or cars. Everything must be shipped or flown island to island. This adds an enormous onus to the Bahamian economy, slowing down the delivery of everything that's imported—which is nearly everything—and making everything vastly more expensive, and vulnerable.

The same is true of virtually every Caribbean nation, to one extent or another, but nowhere is the vulnerability of an island nation more evident than the Bahamian problem of water. "Water, water everywhere" Coleridge wrote, "but not a drop to drink." He might as well have been describing the Bahamas. The larger, more northern islands have all the fresh water. The southern islands less, in some cases—Great Inagua, which we'll visit later—no fresh water at all.

Andros in the northern tier is the largest Bahamian island and the richest in fresh water. Every day seven million gallons are barged from North Andros to Nassau on New Providence, which long ago outstripped its ability to satisfy the water needs of its citizens and throngs of tourists. This rate and volume clearly can't be sustained without inevitable interruptions. How deep the Andros reserves are can only be estimated.

Imagine the chaos and human suffering that would ensue within days if a tanker sank *en route* to or from New Providence. In November 2008, the nation faced a near crisis when one of its water tankers—the *Titus*, which hauls nearly three million gallons of water into Nassau daily—was delayed returning to the fleet after being dry docked for repairs. Water levels in Nassau were "tremendously depleted," according to *The Nassau Guardian*; residents as well as hotels and resorts were urged to take measures to conserve water.

Water is not the only stark vulnerability this island nation faces. It manufactures very little, and its ability to produce large crops—owing to the rocky, hardscrabble geology—is limited. Neither can it efficiently transport goods. These islands, despite their proximity to what might still be the wealthiest nation on Earth, are fundamentally trapped in a tourist economy—constantly concerned about electricity and water, generators, and trash.

"Bahamians like their garbage so much they line the roads with it," Paul said.

But there was another, more artful, not to say spiritual, dimension to this trash. We passed a crude cairn of kitchen utensils seemingly piled to have some religious meaning and, frequently, tin cans stuck onto the ends of tree branches—location markers or merely decorations. This was, as we shall see, more than it seemed.

North of Governor's Harbour we turned east toward the Atlantic on a winding road that took us to another rocky hilltop. Where the road had been cut through the ridge we parked next to fifteen vertical feet of rock strata. We sat and ate; they talked, I listened as they ate and looked at this wall: another rhizomorph. This one a collage of fossilized crab claw, palm fronds and remains of fallen trees embedded in the rock. For the geologists, here was more evidence of ancient catastrophic geological events, the gnarly remains of past times, ancient, undiscovered until this lunch break. Conrad and Paul talked about how far this facet might push the record back. This half hour, I thought, was what science was all about. Sitting here, looking at a very old slice of geologic life. Down the hill the Atlantic spread out toward Africa. I had a true souvenir of what was across this vast expanse of the Atlantic.

At the bottom of the hill was a grove of coconut palms and the blue ocean beyond. We finished eating and drove down to the pure white beach and pale green water. The palm grove belonged to an elderly American woman whose estate backed up to a lovely cove protected by a small cay and an offshore reef. Near the shore the water was clear and pale green and the beach pure white. The woman's gardener was there, cutting branches, but no one was at home. The place looked abandoned in a paradise of palms and shrubs and wind and beauty.

We parked on a path down to the beach. Paul and Sarah walked north to spend the afternoon at an isolated cove. I walked with Conrad south along the beach, thinking he had been hurt by Paul and Sarah going off together, by themselves. Half a mile farther south we came to the northern reach of (the since closed) Club Med, set on an arching mile of spectacular pink-white sand and emerald water. I had never snorkeled, never had a mask on my face. Conrad tooled out to the reef line while I sat on the beach. Back on shore it was clear that, despite the great beauty of the swim, something was wrong.

"The entire reef is dead." Conrad said. "Covered with fleshy algae?"

What had killed it?

"Not sure," he said breathlessly. "So many factors conspire to destroy reefs. Nitrogen runoff from sewage, higher summer temperatures. Who knows? The pressure on a reef is enormous. Change the ecological balance even slightly and algae take over. Reefs either keep up, catch up or give up, and this one's given up. The last time I was here, it was thriving."

I wondered how many patrons of the Eleuthera Club Med, which took more than its share of the island's resources and created more than its share of waste, knew that their beautiful beach was guarded by a dead reef.

Later that day we took the car south along a wagon path to Casuarina Bay. On the beach I found a plastic bottle labeled:

Fresh Washing

Yuhwa

Lemon Liquid

For Shining Dishes

And Softer Hands

On the reverse side was Chinese script and at the bottom "Made in Shanghai."

Later, we picked up Paul and Sarah and drove the couple of miles into Governor's Harbour, a settlement large enough to have a convenience shop, police station, and a stoplight. It was Whit Monday, and the town was celebrating with a festival in the market square by the wharf. Crowds milled about. Kids played stickball on a roughed-out diamond. A band played calypso songs in the gazebo. Methodists from churches across the island were grilling chickens at one end of the square.

On Cupid's Cay near the mouth of the harbor we stopped for drinks at Ronnie's Hi-D-Way Satellite and Disco Lounge, a seedy but friendly place, dark and air-conditioned; it advertised island oddities such as pizza and steak sandwiches. Oprah was on the TV. Behind the bar was a price list in bold caps: "Cigars $2.75, Lighters $1.00, Alka Seltzer $.75, Condoms $1.00." Lanocaine laced "Stud 100s" went for $10.00 each.

The place seemed to be floated by the traffic of yachts and small cruise ships that put in at Governor's Harbour.

An hour later, seriously buzzed, I reeled out of the darkness of Ronnie's into the still withering heat. We stumbled into the car—Paul driving—and wound our way back through town. The holiday had spawned a wonderful street festival, delicious food being grilled, rich aromas wafting the air, music blaring, dancing, and drink. We stopped by the Methodist stall and bought take-out dinners of chicken, conch salad and macaroni, then cruised north toward Gregory Town.

Breezing up the Queen's Highway, it was cool and our mood was friendly and comfortable. We seemed to have gotten to know each other all at once. Sarah said her sun-burnt lips were falling off. Conrad said, "In Dublin I picked up a loose woman and her legs fell off."

Conrad sang sea shanties as we drove north toward Gregory Town, and was all around brilliant. He could spin great yarns. He told a morbid story of a boat-builder who dug graves on the side and swore that if a man died suddenly, you had to bury him quickly. If he died slowly, he'd rot slowly. You could take your time planting him. I told the story the Grave Digger tells Hamlet in 5.1 about how long a body will keep in the grave before rotting. If the body wasn't rotting before it died—if it didn't have the plague—it would last eight years. If it were the body of a tanner (Shakespeare's father worked in the leather trade), it would last nine. Conrad told a story he'd heard in Maine about a nurse who'd been ship-wrecked with her two children. She'd kept them all alive by using a length of rubber tubing to administer salt-water enemas. The intestines had drawn out the salt.

Near Hatchet Bay we ate our boxed dinners—blood-pink chicken but delicious conch salad—under Casuarinas on a low ledge overhanging the Caribbean. Afterward we went snorkeling. There was an extra mask and snorkel for me but no fins. This wasn't a beach but a dicey walk down to a ledge and then a plunge into water fifteen feet deep. I had never been in water this deep before, had never worn a snorkel and mask. I was terrified for about ten seconds. After that initial wave of fear, it was brilliant, instantly euphoric. The water was tepid and buoyant and clear through to the bottom.

There were purple sea fans, fire coral the color of mustard, blue tangs, wrasses and sergeant majors and a thousand darting creatures. A mottled tiger grouper lurked under a ledge, rolling its bug eyes and gulping water. I came from this baptism a new man. This was the beginning of a grip of underwater, which will soak this book as it develops.

That night in the restaurant at Cambridge Villas, I met Ted Goldsmith whose company supplied goods to mom-and-pop stores on the island. Goldsmith was a Jew from Miami who spoke in a gentle raspy voice, wore a sharply defined beard and a silky blue running suit. He talked about the lingering effect of Hurricane Andrew, dressing up his conversation like someone talking into a tape recorder.

"You know, it's really sad," he said, "these poor people being blown away like that. They had it hard enough before the storm." He shook his head. "They just didn't deserve what happened to them. It was cruel. Many of them lost everything."

"Since then it's been almost impossible to collect on accounts. Still, we get along. I admire the way they can lose so much and rebuild and stay happy. They just can't pay their bills."

I asked Goldsmith if he ate the food he supplied to Eleutherans.

"No, I carry my food with me. But I have no problem with these people."

He pointed in the direction of two pilots at the bar, who flew props into North Eleuthera from Ft. Lauderdale and seemed to stay at Cambridge Villas often. One was an overly friendly drunk who claimed to have graduated from Oxford with an English Lit degree, called me "Professor," and spat when he spoke. He quoted Shakespeare and Keats imperfectly, and thought they'd been contemporaries and claimed to write children's stories, make movies and didn't, needless to say, inspire confidence as a pilot.

Goldsmith continued: "But in Spanish Wells, I have real problems. Big ones."

Spanish Wells, a cay just off the northeast coast of Eleuthera, is white and Protestant. Spanish Wells is so named because it was the final watering hole on the return trip to Spain—a continuous and magnificent parade of cargo and warships, galleons included—sailing through the Straits of Florida, up from the lower Caribbean. The island was unpopulated at the time, of course, merely an outpost, but if we had lived in Spanish Wells in the eighteenth century, sitting down by the harbor in the afternoon, we would surely have witnessed great merchant and military vessels commanded by the richest nation on earth, loading casks of water in Spanish Wells. This was the launching point for the great contrary sail from the New World back across the Atlantic to the homeland, to fabulous riches, to fame and devotion.

Goldsmith was talking to me three-hundred years after Spanish ships put in at Spanish Well, but its separatist character remains. "Because I'm a Jew, I can't sell anything in Spanish Wells. They're very, very closed up there. Just won't let me in." Mainland Eleuthera was different: "Here, I'm comfortable."

Goldsmith ordered another Kalik, "The Beer of the Bahamas."

Then as now, personal and property crimes seemed virtually unknown in Gregory Town. I saw only one policeman in town that week in 1994, a thin man leaning against a building next to Cambridge Villas. An hour later a US Coast Guard helicopter like one I'd seen landing at Governor's Harbour the day before buzzed Gregory Town. That night, drinking rum at Pineapple Cove Resort (now the Cove), the then owner, a foul mouthed ex-pat from New Jersey, told me that a big drug shipment had arrived the day before. A plane had landed at Governor's Harbour, off-loaded its cargo, refueled and taken off again, all under the watchful eye of Bahamian police. Today, the cops were making a show for the American authorities who'd heard of the delivery a day late.

"The only way to get hurt around here," he said, "is to assault a cop. That you don't want to do. A couple of years ago some hood from Nassau, a stranger, showed up at Elvina's. He sat there for most of the day drinking beer and waiting for his drugs to arrive. He'd parked his car halfway in the road, so somebody walked in and asked him to move it. So the hood walks outside, shoots the tires out of the man's car and then guns him down in the street."

"When the cops got to Elvina's he took a shot at one of them"— George made a pistol of his clasped hands and said "bang"—and disappeared into the bush.

"The bozo missed. And he was shit out of luck. It's all right to kill a local merchant, but don't shoot at a cop. Well, you know, nobody on this island was going to hide him. He stayed in the bush for a day or two before he came out at Hatchet Bay, half-starved and eaten up. Four cops with Uzis and a body bag were waiting for him. Bang, bang. End of story."

George wiped his Pilate's hands in the air and laughed.

"Stupid son of a bitch."

The next day Hearty made the most important discovery of the week. Investigating the cliff behind an abandoned quarry he had named for Sarah, he stumbled upon a fossilized beach 70 feet above sea level. This was evidence of a sea-level marker at the stage-nine period on the island, a glacial meltdown some 400,000 years ago (if my notes are correct) when the sea level rose rapidly and radically. Even I could tell that this was a beach.

"I'm finished," Hearty shouted triumphantly. "Enough, already! I've seen all I could hope to see."

We went home early to Cambridge Villas. By the pool the drunken pilots from Ft. Lauderdale shot a promotional film featuring Paul and Sarah, Conrad edited a scientific paper in the main room of our apartment and I was rereading V. S. Naipaul's *Miguel Street*, a brilliant collection of sweet, funny and poignant stories set in Trinidad, Naipaul's boyhood home.

The screen door banged open and in came Dominic, 12, and his younger cousins Elvado and Mario. From their names I couldn't decide whether they were native Bahamians, Haitians, or perhaps Cuban. They were drumming up money for St. Gregory's Church a couple of blocks away. Elvado plopped down on the sofa beside me and pressed his finger into my sun-burnt shoulder. "Is you a China man?" he asked. "Say some Chinese."

"No, I'm an American."

"You know Michael Jordan?" asked Dominic.

"No, but we went to the same college."

"What college that?"

Elvado, still fingering my shoulder, broke in. "Why you need sun block?"

"Because I'm a white man."

"White like Larry Bird," Dominic said, laughing shyly. "He richer than Michael Jordan?"

"I don't know."

"Michael Jackson the richest man in the whole world," said Elvado matter-of-factly.

"Michael Jordan's father got murdered," said Dominic, who knew his sports and was proud of one-upping his cousin.

"He was killed," said Conrad, "in our state."

"California," Dominic added confidently.

"North Carolina." Conrad corrected.

"My uncle live in Nassau," Elvado said, apropos of nothing.

Meanwhile 8-year-old Mario had been going through our things. Now he was tying Paul's bandanna around his head and playing with the binoculars. Dominic snatched the glasses from Mario's hand and made for the porch.

He peered through the wrong end. "You is far away, Mario."

We sent the boys packing with some dried soup, a bag of rice and money for the church.

That evening, after Sarah left to meet her husband, we sat on the porch and talked as the sun sank behind Cambridge Villas. A Magnificent Frigate bird soared overhead, its ruby throat distended and lit up by the sun. We were thrilled by this strange creature, the pterodactyl of the modern age. Conrad said it got its name from sailors who released them at sea. If a Frigatebird didn't return to the ship, land was near. If it did return the crew said, "frig it!"

In the middle of the night we awoke to a violent electrical storm. Thunder literally shook the building. Lightning flashed like a strobe, lighting up our apartment so that we could walk about without flashlights. Out back, rain blew diagonally in sheets across the pool. The oleander and bougainvillea writhed frantically. At one point the landscape was lit up like a halogen light for several seconds, revealing green stripes on towels that blew wildly on a clothes line.

The next morning we said our good-byes to Mr. Cambridge and drove north through light debris, over the bridge at Glass Window, to the airport. Soon our Bahamasair flight to Nassau was banking over the island. I strained to get another look at Gregory Town but couldn't see it. I remembered that Frigate bird and promised one day to touch down on Eleuthera again.

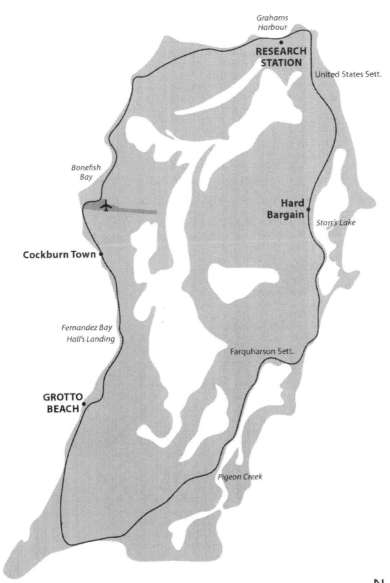

Grahams
Harbour

**RESEARCH
STATION**

United States Sett.

Bonefish
Bay

**Hard
Bargain**

Storr's Lake

Cockburn Town

Fernandez Bay
Hall's Landing

Farquharson Sett.

**GROTTO
BEACH**

Pigeon Creek

SAN SALVADOR

N

Chapter 3
Columbus, Iguanas and Mother Wit on San Salvador

"I, in order that they might feel great amity towards us, because I knew they were a people to be delivered and converted to our holy faith rather by love than by force, gave to some among them red caps and some glass beads, which they hung round their necks, and many other things, of little value."

~Christopher Columbus

A S my Bahamasair flight from Nassau descended east over San Salvador, I could see that the Queen's Highway ringing the island cut right across the end of the runway. Touching down, our Dash-8 turboprop rushed past an oversized stop sign where two cars were waiting to cross. I knew San Salvador was small but this was crazy.

If he could speak from the dead, Christopher Columbus, who made first landfall in the Americas probably on this island at 2 AM on 12 October 1492, might testify to fatal meetings on San Salvador. If not he, then certainly the Lucayan Arawak Indians who met Columbus on the beach that morning. Unfortunately, there are no Lucayans left to recount the atrocities committed against their ancestors. That task fell, ironically, to Europeans, first to Peter Martyr (fl. 1510), chronicler of Columbus's American voyages, and then to Bartolome de las Casas

(1474-1566), Bishop of Chiapas, who became the scourge and minister of his nation's policies in the Caribbean. A native of Seville, las Casas enjoyed a privileged position in the early stages of the Spanish occupation of the New World. His father and uncle had sailed with Columbus on the second voyage to the Americas, and las Casas himself arrived in Hispaniola as an *encomendero* in 1502. In 1510 he participated in the conquest of Cuba and was granted a sizable estate. But las Casas was about to experience a Pauline conversion. That year, at the beginning of what promised to be a very lucrative career as a landed slave holder, las Casas heard newly-arrived Dominican monks preach against the evils of slavery. What he heard transformed las Casas from a conquistador to a bitter and relentless enemy of Spanish policies. He took holy orders in 1510, renounced his *encomienda* in 1514 and preached his first sermon against slavery that year. For the rest of his life las Casas was a dagger in Spain's imperialist hide, ceaselessly decrying his nation's inhumanity before papal and imperial authorities, documenting in impassioned and graphic language the ruthless exploitation and wholesale extermination of the indigenous people of the region under the yoke of slavery. This was, as las Casas and others reported, a Spanish humanitarian crime, a virtual genocide. The Black Legend of Spain.

From the start, the European ventures in the Caribbean were torn by contradictory impulses. On the one hand, Spain was driven by a desire to exploit the resources of the New World, to discover El Dorado and mine its gold. Her intelligencia, raised on the utopian visions of Genesis and Plato and Ovid, however, were looking for something else, the hoped-for discovery of a better race of man, living not so long after the Fall. Arthur Golding's 1567 translation of Ovid's *Metamorphoses* rendered a passage familiar to learned men throughout Europe, in elegant fourteeners—fourteen syllable lines meant to imitate Latin prosody:

> *The lofty pine tree was not hewn from mountains where it stood*
> *In seeking strange and foreign lands, to rove upon the flood.*
> *Men knew no other countries yet than where themselves did keep;*
> *There was no town enclosed yet, with walls and ditches deep.*

The fallen nature of European culture was evident in the very existence of ships unknown in the Golden Age, whose masts were hewn from "The lofty pine tree."

The people of the Indies were "simple souls," among whom, according to Richard Eden's 1555 translation of Peter Martyr's *De Orbe Novo* (1511), "a few clothes serve the naked. Weights and measures are not needful to such as can not skill of craft or deceit, and have not the use of pestiferous money . . . . They seem to live in that golden world of which the old writers speak so much, wherein men lived simply and innocently without enforcement of laws, without quarreling, judges and libels, content only to satisfy nature, without further vexation for knowledge of things to come."

The horrible irony was that harvesting the Americas required the destruction of the very New World Edenites the more thoughtful explorers hoped they had discovered, and whose natural virtues learned and thoughtful Europeans like Martyr and las Casas wished to preserve. In practical terms, they wanted to "save" the Lucayans, to convert them to the true religion, of course, but this conversion came with the threat of brutal suppression and reprisals. Landing on a new island, the Spanish would routinely gather the natives and read aloud "The Proclamation," a document that made legal the seizure of land, under royal and sacred authority, from the native inhabitants and required them to subjugate themselves and convert to Christianity upon pain of death. On beaches throughout the Caribbean, this document was read to Amerindians in Spanish.

Unable to resolve the contradictory drives of the Spanish incursion into the Caribbean, unable to serve two masters at once, las Casas sided with the Indians early on. His *History of the Indies* (1527-36) is, according to one of its editors, "both an indictment and a prophesy: the price of Spain's moral aberration will be nothing less than the nation's political, economic and moral suicide." In the *History*, he describes Amerindians in terms that recall in detail the myth of prelapsarian Eden as well as the Golden Age, at the expense, understandably, of exact characterization. The Indians were people "so blessed. . . in gentleness, simplicity, humility and other natural virtues, it seems Adam's sin left them untouched." The Lucayans, he continues, "know not how to kill or fornicate, have no prostitutes, adulterers, thieves or homicides and adore no idols."

The first Spanish "harvesters of Lucayo Indians," las Casas reports, had only to exploit the possibility that the overwhelmed Indians might believe the white men coming to them in ships were divinely sent. The conquistadores "were received as they always are before our deeds prove the contrary," he wrote ruefully, "that is, as angels from Heaven."

He explains the ploy the Spaniards used to dupe the natives into abandoning their islands for Hispaniola, the Spanish base of operations in the region. The Spanish "said they came from Hispaniola, where the souls of their beloved ones were resting in joy, and that their ships would take them there if they wanted to see them . . ." On Hispaniola the dispossessed and enslaved Lucayans "found neither father, mother nor loved ones but iron tools and instruments and gold mines instead, where they perished in no time; some, from despair at seeing themselves deceived, took poison; others died of starvation and hard labor." When the Indians proved too delicate for mining, "the enemy of human nature" set them to work as pearl divers. But even this bit of efficient resource management—the Lucayans were excellent swimmers and divers—was callously not to say wastefully applied. Las Casas writes that the Spanish "used to stuff shiploads with hundreds of Indians of both sexes and all ages, pack them in like sardines and close all the hatchways to prevent escape, thus shutting off air and light. And, since ships carried food and water only for the Spanish crew, the Indians died and were thrown into the sea, and the floating corpses were so numerous that a ship could find its course by them alone, without need of a compass, charts, or the arts of navigation."

In his last days las Casas, vindicated and elevated to the Bishop of Chiapas, issued a chilling prediction.

"Should God decide to destroy Spain," he wrote, "[it will be] clear that Spain deserved the punishment for the destruction we have brought to the Indies."

Peter Martyr d'Anghiera (1457-1526) was also outraged. Martyr tells how some Amerindians, having escaped to the mountaintops of Hispaniola, adored the breezes that "wafted from their native country; with extended arms and open mouths they seemed to drink in their native air, and when misery reduced them to exhaustion, they dropped dead upon the ground." Unable to escape the Spanish, others fell down and "willed themselves to die."

For the bronze-skinned Lucayans of San Salvador, the meeting of Europe and America that October morning in 1492 spelled disaster. Within five years of Columbus's arrival the Lucayans had been decimated. Forty years of disease—typhoid, malaria, smallpox, dysentery, pneumonia—and the policies of the "Black Legend" of Spain completely exterminated them, leaving not a single Lucayan alive in the entire Bahamian archipelago.

Called Guanahani by the Lucayans and Watling's Island by Europeans from the time of the early settlements to 1926 when it was rechristened with its Columbian name, San Salvador is a bean-shaped island stranded in the Atlantic 200 miles southeast of Nassau. Thirty miles around, fewer than a thousand people live on the island today —about the same number of Lucayans who lived there in 1492—all in settlements strung along the main road. Talk about beachfront property. Most of the small, brightly colored houses on the Queen's Highway looked out through palm trees on to flat, stunning-white beaches and sweeping expanses of emerald green water and dark blue beyond. Inland, there seemed nothing to San Salvador but bush, shallow brine lakes, and an impressive lighthouse.

Paul Hearty and Conrad Neumann were waiting for me at the Bahamian Field Station at Graham's Harbour on the northern shore of the island, a three-acre compound converted for research purposes in geology, archeology, and marine sciences in the 1970's when the Navy abandoned its rocket tracking station here. Using the Field Station as their base, Paul and Conrad, along with the advanced undergraduate and graduate students in Conrad's class, would continue their work on the formation, composition and natural evolution of the Bahamas.

As a research facility the Field Station on San Salvador was modest but adequate: a library, lecture halls, laboratories, a dive shop and a dark room. Digs were at least comfortable: a sink, chest of drawers, twin beds, a lamp and a ceiling fan in each room. Shared bathrooms. Our half-hour meals were austere and inflexible—breakfast at 7:30, lunch at noon, dinner at 5:30. Since the nearest restaurant was 15 miles away in the main settlement of Cockburn Town (pronounced "Coburn Town"), unless you happened to have a rental car handy, you didn't dare be late for a meal.

After finding my room and unpacking, I walked a mile east from the Field Station along the Queen's Highway to North Point, a gently curving half-mile spit that protected Graham's Harbour from the thundering Atlantic. Above North Point, walking along a narrow trail 30 feet above the water, I gazed out at a scene that reminded me of Glass Window: on one side the clear, placid, shallow water of the harbor shimmered a pale green in the still intense sunlight; on the other side the deep, deep-blue Atlantic heaved and crashed against a cliff face, sounding, when I closed my eyes, like the heavy, desperate breathing of a sea-monster in the throes of death.

At the top of a ridge I rummaged through a stumpy concrete observation tower left behind by the Navy. Lit a bright orange by the slanting afternoon sun, the rusting hulk of a small tanker that had come to grief on the rocks and broken in half came into view. She shuddered as swells rolling past Man Head Cay reached and rose over her, washing through her hold, throwing a pure white spray up near the top of her stack, the only part of her that retained its paint—a bright yellow. It was a reminder of the economic history of the Bahamas, recalling a time when wrecking—along with sponging, turtling and harvesting ambergris—was a major source of income for Family Islanders.

Soon I was standing at the top of a sheer drop thirty feet above the water, a cut fifty yards wide where the current ran swiftly from the harbor back to the ocean in a slackening tide. Thrilled and chilled, I watched the lethal black shadows of two sharks cruising in ambush at the end of the run.

Back at the highway I followed the road east around the bend, past the school at the edge of the settlement of United Estates where brown children in striped brown uniforms, their book bags slung over their shoulders, were loitering at the end of the school day. Farther along I came upon a sprawling turquoise shack surrounded by nautical bric-a-brac under an ancient almond tree. The sign out front said "Club Ed—Ed's First and Last Bar." This was a delicious sneer at Club Med, whose fenced-in compound I had passed on the cab ride in from the airport at Cockburn Town. I walked in, hoping for a cold beer, but the place was empty. I walked on through the village, promising to stop by Club Ed on the way back. A few hundred yards farther, I struck out east from the road along a path through the bush toward the Atlantic. Nearby was a rock face that rose straight up from the beach. Paul had described just this kind of formation, suspecting that this was evidence of substage 5a on the island, rock dating from a period 100,000 years ago when the sea level abruptly returned to current levels following an interglacial meltdown called substage 5e 20,000 years earlier. At 5e the ocean had risen precipitously and inundated the Bahamian archipelago. 5a rock would further substantiate the theory that sea levels have risen and fallen rapidly—catastrophically—in recent geologic history.

I hacked through a wilderness of love vine and poisonwood, around a rusting car and bicycles, toward the beach. At the top of the ridge, I came to a clearing between two fig trees and a ruined "leaf house"—a square, one-story, stone-and-mortar building with a pyramid roof that had once been thatched. Leaf houses are among the oldest architectural structures in the Bahamas, one stage later than the slave house. When you see these "leaf houses" you should stop and imagine the extraordinary lives that occupied them for generations.

I walked gingerly through the doorway into the main room, treading warily over broken floor boards where the bush grew up into the room. I found a good spot to photograph the ocean through a window, a shot of blue water and white breakers nicely framed by the desiccated gray of the wooden sash. Darkness on the edges.

A woman walked into the clearing ten feet away from me. She was older, heavy set, wearing a faded green dress, her head wrapped in a yellow cloth. I was suddenly embarrassed and thought for an instant how I might explain my trespass. She might be afraid that this white man appearing out of nowhere in a ruined house might be a threat. But she wasn't afraid, nor did she care about my explanation. She said "all right," the way Bahamians of a certain age do when greeting a stranger.

"My grandfather built this here old leaf house," she said. "I was born and raised in it."

From where we stood, I could see the verge of a white sand beach running south out to a point, and the ocean. A reef line retarded the swelling ocean to form a beautiful little cove virtually at this woman's childhood doorstep. The breeze up here was steady, warm and sweetly scented.

"So this was your land when you were little?" She laughed.

"Well, this was my father's land. Now it's mine."

I said it must have been wonderful to grow up on this ridge, with fig trees to climb, and the beach just down the ridge.

"Yes, it was very nice here when I was growing up. My father strung a hammock between them trees, and after supper we would lay up in that hammock and watch the ships come by out there. Such nice breezes those nights. Pretty lights from the ships."

I asked what she was going to do with the land now that it was hers.

"Build me a house here and move back. Plant a garden. I been working in Nassau for 35 years. Long time there, child, long time. I'm tired and I'm coming home. 'Course, all them that I was raised with is long gone from here." Silent as a shadow, sadness moved across her face and was gone, leaving her features placid and serene again. "All things in the fullness of time," she said.

"My nephew is somewhere around here marking off the land. You'll see him if you go down through this growed-up bush."

"Well, I better go on down and see what he's doing," she said, "he's a hard worker, tough to keep up with." And she continued on her way toward the beach.

I walked back to Club Ed and entered the cool darkness at the bar. American college students studying at the Field Station had carved their names and schools into tables and chairs, and drawn caricatures with felt-tip pens on the walls. It didn't take long to find evidence of Conrad Neumann. His name was written on one wall, and on the opposing wall was a faded Xerox copy of a Neumann mass Christmas mailing, with captions depicting significant events of a year in the life of the Neumann family. Conrad drew one of these every Christmas and sent photocopies to friends.

Ed, a lanky, hard-boned man of 60 with teeth like rows of a ruined fence and rheumy eyes, came out of hiding. He looked terrible. I ordered a beer. We talked. His wife had been taken to the hospital in Nassau, and Ed, animated and plainly drunk, was making the most of her absence. I said I wanted to go to Man Head Cay, home to the last of San Salvador's iguanas, just off the northern tip of the island. Could I hire a boat, I asked, to take me out to that humpy, white-cliffed shingle a half-mile off North Point?

"What you want to go to Man Head Cay for?" Ed asked. I told him I wanted to photograph the iguanas and couldn't risk snorkeling out over the cut with my camera in a plastic bag. I needed a boat.

"I gotta boat, nice one too. I take you dare tomorrow in my boat," he said, grinning proudly. "You see plenty iguanas. You catch me one. Better dan chicken, good Lord." Ed bellowed out another drunken laugh.

Would twenty dollars be enough to run me out and fetch me a couple of hours later?

"Yeah, dat's good money. And you see dem iguanas dare too. I guarantee it, Marvin." I was surprised that in his condition Ed remembered my name.

I went to pay for my beer and realized I had only twenty dollar bills in my wallet. I took one out, knowing full well that Ed couldn't make change for it.

"No, no, I can't do nothin wid dat," Ed said, shaking his head from side to side. I didn't want to drink on credit, though Ed would probably have floated me a beer. Besides, I was tired and eager to seal our deal for the boat.

"Take this," I said, handing the crisp bill to Ed, "and have that boat ready tomorrow at noon."

"Gimme another and your boat is paid for." I gave him another twenty.

Ed beamed and laughed loudly. "Marvin, you a righteous man. Yessir, dat you is." He squeezed my hand and clapped me on the shoulder. "You gonna see some iguanas tomorrow, yessir."

I left Ed's knowing I'd made a mistake. Giving money to a drunk man, however affable, is foolish. That night at the Field Station I fell in with a group of students who were planning to walk to Ed's for a drink. When Ed had gotten my beer that afternoon I'd noticed that only a few Becks were left in the refrigerator; I guessed he'd drunk most of his stock. Ed being whiffled and low on beer, I advised them against walking to Club Ed. But one young man struck out alone on the darkened road.

After breakfast the next morning Conrad assembled his students around a flatbed truck in the parking lot for a briefing on the day's work along the island's west coast—first at Fernandez Bay where we would snorkel out to a patch reef, then back to Cockburn Town to investigate an ancient fossilized reef exposed by the falling sea level, and finally 15 miles south to Grotto Beach to see "the meeting of modern and ancient beaches in a dynamic environment."

Just before we left, Conrad pointed to the sweeping bay that fronted the Field Station. To the east an arc of cays and reefs, marked by a white line of breakers, trailed off the end of North Point which I had explored the day before.

"I can imagine that Columbus," Conrad said, "sailing up the Atlantic coast of the island in 1492, saw that reef and anchored in the Trades on the outside. It would have been difficult to get his ships inside North Point, so he must have taken smaller boats over the reef and rowed into this bay."

Evidence from his log indicates, in fact, that Columbus sailed around the northwest corner of the island and landed here at Graham's Harbour, assuming he's talking about San Salvador and not the other major contender for first-landing, Cat Island to the north. I could almost see three ships bobbing inside that line of breakers at North Point, and the launches sloshing up on the beach 100 yards from us, Columbus standing erect, grim-faced and expectant as he made landfall. Later he would sail west and then south to Fernandez Bay where he met the Lucayans.

By nine o'clock Conrad and his students were rumbling west in the truck on the main road through tiny settlements at Rocky Point, Sue Point, Bonefish Bay and then south through Cockburn Town. I followed in a rattletrap Chevy van I'd rented at the Field Station. At Fernandez Bay, we snorkeled a hundred yards offshore to an expanse of reef. It was probably twenty-five feet to the bottom, the coral heads splendidly beautiful, harboring the profuse marine life that's common in these waters: parrotfish, triggerfish, groupers, barracudas. Purple sea fans swayed in a setting rich in coral varieties—Elkhorn, brain and mustard. The reef might have looked healthy to a casual diver. But even I could see that large swaths of brown algae covered much of the area. These lovely fields of coral were slowly but surely dying. That was the lesson Conrad meant to convey.

Back in Cockburn Town we ate box lunches in the town square where women sold straw hats, coral rings and wood carvings across the street from Spanish-styled buildings, the only evidence of Iberian influence I saw on San Salvador. After lunch it was back to work. The sun was roiling in a cloudless, frying sky when we struck out on foot north along the gray fossil reef. Conrad and his students collected specimens of ancient club and brain coral exposed in the face of the concretized reef when the sea level began to fall 125,000 years ago.

An hour later we were back on the main road, hugging the coast south toward Grotto Beach near the tip of the island. South of Fernandez Bay we passed a marker on the beach commemorating

Columbus's landing and on the other side of the road a reconstructed Lucayan village of grass huts arranged in a rough circle. It was the only evidence—and that specious—of the Lucayans I had seen on San Salvador. A few miles farther along, the hard surface abruptly ended. From here it was a lurching, teeth-rattling rumble 10 miles over the rocky roadbed to the south flank of a small bay.

This was Grotto Beach, breezy, deserted and stunningly beautiful. At the top of a small dune overlooking the steeply pitched beach, I sat in the shade of an airy cabana, looking out at the bay through wisps of sea oats. On the far side a low brown rock wall rose above heaving water the color of liquefied emeralds. To my left, a reef line guarded the bay where swells rolling in from deep blue water broke in brilliant white flashes. Opposite the reef line, the bay closed to a narrow head where the ocean pounded at a line of shallow caves beneath a rock ledge.

This structure, which gave Grotto Beach its name, was what Conrad and his students had come to see. We climbed onto the ledge and Conrad explained this meeting of ancient and modern beaches, but I was too busy taking pictures to listen carefully. Soon I seemed to fall into a trance, mesmerized by exhaustion, the soft rasp of the breakers and the astonishing scenery. While others worked the rock ledge, I drifted down the beach, settled for a while on the sand, and then went for a swim as the sun sank toward the Exuma Sound.

Afterwards, I sat alone for half an hour gazing at the scene, completely engulfed in the abandoned feel of Grotto Beach. I could hardly believe my eyes when there appeared, like a maritime apparition such as the mermaid, a lone surfer paddling in on his board from the breakers.

The next morning I read *Hard Times* in my room while Conrad and Paul, students in tow, traveled south along the Atlantic coast to Storrs Lake, one of the half-dozen hypersaline lakes on San Salvador. Here Conrad and his students would wade in mucky water three times saltier than the ocean, searching the bottom with their hands and feet for lumps of precipitated lime called stromatolites. These lithified heads, which look like stacks of giant mushrooms flattened on top of one another, are fossils of the greatest antiquity, so old and rare that until recently they were thought not to be extant in the modern world. Providing the earliest fossil evidence of life on earth, stromatolites reveal organic processes in the ancient past that gave rise to the first life in marine waters.

I had lingered at the Field Station because I wanted some time alone in the van to explore San Salvador's Atlantic coast and meet the islanders. Dan Suchy, director of the Field Station, had provided the names of several old people who had spent most or all of their lives on the island and were good storytellers. I had directions and the van all to myself. I planned to take my time driving down to Storrs Lake and, if the geologists weren't there, to drive on to Almgreen Cay and then farther to The Bluff and Pigeon Creek at the southeast corner of the island.

San Salvador's Atlantic coast was 20 miles of pristine drama, reachable in most places only by hacking your way through thickets of sea grape, palmetto, and waist-high bush. The Queen's Highway on this side of the island was rougher than along the western side. Below the settlement at United Estates, the ocean disappeared behind a sand ridge topped with scrub brush and stumpy trees. At Hard Bargain the road narrowed and deteriorated further as it turned inland along Storrs Lake. Here the vegetation darkened and thickened so that it scraped both sides of the van. There was no sign of the geologists at Storrs Lake so I lurched on in the van, its brakes squealing every time I touched the pedal, through dry billabongs and rubble past Almgreen Cay toward a rocky point called The Bluff.

Just past Fortune's Hill, on a slope rising above the road, I came upon the overgrown ruins of the Farquharson Estate. For thirty years in the early nineteenth century Charles Farquharson (1760-1835), a Scot, operated a plantation on this site. Widowed or abandoned by his wife in the Carolinas, Farquharson was a loyalist who obtained one of the two original land grants on San Salvador, a 200-acre tract of land near Pigeon Creek. Defeated and despised by the American rebels, he like other loyalists left the Carolinas for *terra incognita* at Pigeon Creek where he built a house and began to acquire slaves to work his land. His journal of 1832-33 provides an invaluable account of plantation life in the last years before the 1834 emancipation of slaves in the Bahamas.

Alone and isolated he took as his common-law wife a black woman called Kitty Dixon, by whom he had several children. Islanders politely referred to Kitty as Mrs. Farquharson; Farquharson in his will called her simply "my faithful companion." Worked by as many as 60 African and mulatto slaves, the Farquharson plantation raised cattle, cotton and vegetables. Compared to plantation owners in the more fertile northern Bahamian islands, however, Farquharson remained a poor man during his three decades on San Salvador, even though his plantation was virtually self-sufficient, producing its own timber, food, rope, salt, building materials and most of its equipment. The inventory for 1831-32 lists a mere 12 bales of cotton shipped to Nassau. In this hardscrabble land only his cattle brought Farquharson a steady, if small, income.

By no means an abolitionist, Farquharson seems to have been an enlightened man for his times. Nowhere in his journal does he refer to his workers as slaves but rather as "the people" or "the hands." He was evidently a fair master who looked after the health and welfare of his workers, if only out of enlightened self interest. The scarcity of resources and the uncertainties of life at Pigeon Creek threatened everybody alike, drawing white and colored people together. Michael Craton and Gail Saunders believe that Farquharson "recognized the delicate balance between his own dependence on his slaves and their dependence upon him." As a result of such interdependence, some historians believe that here as elsewhere in the Bahamas slaves didn't experience to the same degree the horrible indignities and suffering of slaves on plantations in the lower Caribbean and American south.

This isn't to say that there aren't racial problems now or weren't then. Farquharson's journal provides one of several contemporary accounts of a slave uprising in the Bahamas. The trouble occurred in 1832 when in Farquharson's absence his highhanded son James, himself of mixed blood, struck a highly respected African slave called Alick with a crop. The next morning the slaves appeared at the big house armed with clubs and staves, and for the next several days a state of open revolt existed at the plantation. When Farquharson returned, he confined the leaders of the uprising and later shipped them to Nassau for trial in the slave court. As further evidence of the historical tolerance of Bahamian culture, Governor James Carmichael Smyth, an abolitionist at heart, recommended lenient treatment of most of the offenders, finding just cause for their actions.

Otherwise, turmoil was rare on the Farquharson plantation. The dominant experiences for most were labor and rest punctuated by fear when someone was sick or injured or when a hurricane struck, and excitement when a ship approached the coast. Only three ships regularly visited San Salvador during the years Farquharson kept his journal, when San Salvador was known as Watling's Island, though hundreds passed within sight of his plantation on their way to Cuba and the lower Caribbean. Farquharson himself left the island only rarely, traveling to Nassau perhaps twice a year.

Their isolation was such that ships became a fetish among the settlers of Pigeon Creek. Archaeologists working at the Farquharson plantation in the 1970s found images of schooners, warships, sloops and barques carved in the plaster walls of the main house and some of the outbuildings. These drawings, write Craton and Saunders, were "symbols and signs of a desperate loneliness and of the tenuous links between such distant outposts and the larger world of European commerce, culture and civilization."

Up here in the ruins of the plantation, it was easy to imagine the ecstasy of seeing a wooden ship rocking in the wind above the green top of the bush line, making its way to anchor at Snow Bay.

On the return trip to the Field Station I stopped at a little house painted bright orange on a hill above United Estates belonging to 70-year old Mabel Williams. Born and raised on the island, she had three sons and a daughter before leaving San Salvador for Nassau where she worked as a domestic for nearly three decades. She returned to the island of her birth in 1990. Her children and grandchildren remain in Nassau. She sees them twice a year, once when they come to San Salvador and again when she visits them in Nassau. Photographs lining the walls of her modest home are her only daily reminders of her distant family.

Mabel Williams greeted me wearing a faded print skirt and a red bandanna wrapped tightly around her head. She laughed in modest disbelief when I said I wanted to talk to her about her life on the island.

"Did they send you over here from the Field Station, honey?" she asked. "They always sending somebody over here to talk to this old woman. I has to tell so many stories, honey, so many stories." She laughed again, settled in a fine print chair, and began to tell the story of a woman's life on San Salvador.

"I was born in that little leaf house just behind here, up on the hill. When I grew up here they weren't no vehicles at all. Only the priest in Cockburn Town, he had a vehicle. The rest they get around by foot or on horseback, you see. And this here road"—she pointed behind me out the window to the pot-holed, rubble-strewn Queen's Highway— "this road here weren't nothing but a dirt track, man. I've seen my mama with a half sack full of flour on her head, walk from Cockburn Town way round and come round and come round till she get here.

"And then they had the ferry boat leave from the bottom of the lighthouse. The road go down from the lighthouse to the lake where the boat come in. And so if the ferry boat is full, then all them that can't get on, they got to walk around, man."

Cockburn Town was on the other side of the island, probably 20 miles away by the Queen's Highway. The ferry that ran from the lighthouse at Dixon Hill to Cockburn Town long ago stopped plying the Great Lake in San Salvador's interior.

"It was real rough, now, real rough. There was no electricity till four, five years ago, honey. It was dark, I mean dark. When you walk from church at night it was so dark you can't see your hand in front of you. If there ain't no moonlight, then your foot go down in this puddle hole, something like that. Man, it was rough. But we come through it, we come through it."

"Now the children of today, they was born in luxury, like it was always that way. But every time I have to lecture them, I have to go back to my childhood days, how it was then." There was a faint weariness in her voice, as if the act of remembering was exhausting and painful. "But I have to let them know how it was when I was a child. They say, 'but Mabel, how can you remember all that? You ain't got no note pad, no book. How you remember all that?' they asks me." She put a finger to her forehead. "But it's all right in here."

"When I was a child, the houses here was all rock-wall houses with thatch roof. We called them leaf houses. That was my mother's house right out there, where I was born." She pointed through the north wall of her house toward a building I couldn't see. "In those days there was no money, no jobs. You don't have no doctors. I have to tell the young people what it was like when you had babies.

"You had midwives take care of the birth. And, you know, they had not so many problems then with having babies. They had the mother's wit, you know. And the midwives, they train from the older set. And the midwives, before they die, they pass that know-how on; they train you, you see. You would work along with them. And you know every settlement have their own midwives then."

I asked about her father. Something in her eyes said that I had asked an inappropriate, obtrusive question.

"You know, my mother was a single girl and when you are single and you have children, the fathers don't check with the children. They don't take care of them, they don't give them anything, something like that, you know."

Mothers without husbands were easy prey for men with something, anything, to offer. "It's just like, okay, you may have one, two children, okay, and you don't have anything to give that child. You know your child is hungry, you know they need clothes, and you don't have it. And somebody say, 'I can give you so and so. Come to me such and such a time and I can give you so and so.' And you go. All you're thinking about is, Lord, I'll have something to give my child in the morning. That's all you're thinking. Your mind is on the child."

"Many times when I was a child I remember being hungry, many times. So much times my mother say, 'anyhow child I don't know how you going to school this morning.' But if she have some grits, she cook that grits. And you have to wait until she put the water on the fire—the wood fire, now. You have three"—she pronounced "three" as "tree"—"rocks and a couple wood sticks. And you have to wait till that water boil. Then you put your grits in the Dutch oven and you feed your children with dat, nothing else, now, nothing on top of dat grits. I mean you eat dat grits, and you feel good too!"

Mabel Williams learned bush medicine the way women learned midwifery and other survival skills, from her mother. "I got to know a lot about bush medicine from my mother, and she get it from her mother. And that's how I got to know about the bush medicine." With the nearest major medical center more than 200 miles away in Nassau, San Salvadorians have access to basic health care only: a single clinic in Cockburn Town served the island's entire population. In such conditions, bush medicine still plays an important role in controlling chronic medical conditions such as high blood pressure and diabetes, and in treating common ailments and injuries.

"The bush medicine is for different complaints. When I was a child I say, 'Oh mama, my stomach hurts, oh mama, my belly hurts. It hurt me.' And she 'Okay. come wid me.' And we go to the spoonwood tree. Spoonwood, it's very bitter, bitter. You pick off 'bout tree leaves off the tree, and you chew them leaves, and you swallow the juice from that. And fifteen, twenty minutes, you feel the pain dying away, just dying away. Or suppose you have gripes in your stomach, keep breaking around your stomach, you get the spoonwood and you get the guava bud. And you mix that guava bud with the spoonwood, and you boil that, and that cut all the pain."

"Just like the medicine today, some of the bush medicine is stronger than some. Some work fast, and some work in two, tree weeks. So much medicine is for different complaints. Take, for instance, if you have the jaundice. We on San Salvador have no doctor for jaundice, so mama go there to the broom bush. And you get the thistle too. And you put them two together and you boil that and that clear up everything. You won't have no more fever, no more headache."

Mabel Williams led me out into the yard to show me some of these curatives: shepherd needle for high blood pressure—("I took this shepherd needle this morning," she said)—hurricane weed for stones, pepper grass for indigestion, pound cake bush for diabetes and period pain, jumbay to settle nerves, and Gum Elemi to staunch bleeding and heal wounds.

Before leaving I walked with her up the hill to the ruins of her mother's leaf house. I took her photograph standing in front of the window out of which she was blown, eight months pregnant, by a hurricane that swept San Salvador in November 1941. "That was a terrible, terrible day," she said, "The sun never dawn."

Mabel Williams was a treasury of "mother's wit" from a time and culture fast fading. It would of course be a disservice to her, and thousands of other people like her, to sentimentalize a life of unrelenting difficulties that Mabel Williams would not wish to relive. But those struggles in the beautiful but implacable landscape of San Salvador and later in the hustling world of Nassau had produced in her a remarkable strength, faith and dignity that shown through clearly in our conversation, virtues that perhaps only great struggles can produce in people. It's unlikely that her children or grandchildren, whose lives have been irrevocably shaped by their experiences in Nassau, will ever learn midwifery or the secrets of bush medicine from their matriarch. Perhaps only a few will note her passing.

A mile from the Field Station I stopped by Club Ed for a drink. But nobody was minding the store, so I drove on back to the station. At breakfast the next morning a student who'd gone for a drink at Ed's the night before had pounded the door but no one came. He peeped in Ed's window and saw a tall, thin man twirling circles in the middle of the empty bar, singing to himself. This didn't bode well, I knew, for my boat ride to Man Head Cay the next day.

I got to Ed's at 10:30 in the morning and knocked on the door. When nobody answered I called his name several times and walked around the building trying every door I came to. I waited on his verandah in the shade of the almond tree with several of Ed's scrawny, sleeping dogs for company. I chafed at the possibility of having paid forty dollars for a beer, but the breeze was blowing gently from the ocean and the almond tree cast an umbrella of shade over the chaise lounge I was lying in. The only sounds were the occasional whirring of hummingbirds feeding at the bougainvillea blossoms and Ed's dogs scratching. It was fresh and cool and bug-less under the almond tree. Soon I nodded off.

I awoke at the sound of footsteps and opened my eyes to see a face looking down at me.

"You livin' the life, mon," he said, obviously pleased to see me waiting for the bar to open. It was one of the Johnnies I'd met yesterday.

I told Johnny about our boat deal. He was surprised. "Ed don't got no boat. He got a engine but he sunk his boat."

Ed had snookered me. Ed who had clapped me on the back and asked about my hometown and my job, Ed who'd assured me that I would spend this afternoon photographing iguanas on Man Head Cay. I thought of that forty dollars, but what I really hated losing was the chance to see the iguanas. Having given up the rental van the day before, I now faced the prospect of spending the rest of my time on San Salvador with no wheels. I walked back to the Field Station in the heat of the late morning, ate lunch alone in the cafeteria, and thought how to salvage the rest of the day.

Despite signs warning "Don't snorkel alone" posted everywhere, I collected my mask and fins and snuck out of the compound, jumped the cinderblock wall near the entrance to the Field Station, dashed across the road and disappeared into the bush, emerging out of sight on the other side at the beach. The sky was a washed-out blue, the tide high and the water, except for gentle swells, flat and smooth as the facet of a gemstone. There were no boats in the harbor or on the beach; the shore arcing out toward North Point was as flawless and precisely curved as a suture needle.

Alone and undetected, I fought back the urge to strip and go naked into the water. I couldn't risk coming out bare-butt in paradise and meeting some inquiring stranger to whom I should have to explain my transgression of right law, naked. I teetered out across the submerged beach rock at the water's edge and slipped quietly into a warm bath. I propelled myself over the shallow reach into 15 feet of water. Below me were the jutting edge of the outermost rock and the sandy bottom the color of finely crushed skulls. There were very few fish here—only a couple of small damselfish nibbling at the hair-like algae that grew from the lip of the rock, and a large skate buried on the bottom. Sea fans swayed as gentle swells began lifting and lowering me at the surface. I dove underneath the rock ledge and peered into the shadows but didn't see anything, then corkscrewed up toward the surface and cruised on my back just beneath the ceiling of water. Nothing threatened the serenity of a weightless moment. I felt no apprehension, no presentiment of danger. Suspended here I could hear my heart beat steady and slow as I gazed up through the surface at buff balls of cloud riding high in the sky. Turning over, I paddled along to the thin whistle of air passing through the snorkel tube next to my ear, listening to the mesmerizing sound of my own respiration. I moved effortlessly toward North Point in a dream state only briefly suppressed when I dove to peer into a crevice or pull myself underneath a ledge. Atavistic glimpses of earliest childhood, inarticulate felt-memories of a life I once lived, somewhere, swept through me. I had slipped out of time; space seemed infinite yet somehow tractable; distances immaterial.

In *Water and Light*, his account of a diving trip in the Turks and Caicos Islands at the southern extreme of the Bahamian archipelago, Stephen Harrigan writes from "beneath the ocean" :

> I am searching for a sort of maternal oblivion. I want to dissolve away, not to die but to recede into the sleepy, safe, nonthinking being I used to be, before I was expelled from the womb and supplanted by my conscious self. Water is the human mind's most powerful mother symbol—a reminder of the benevolent, nurturing void from which we all emerged. Pregnant women, in their dreams, see floods and gentle waves and ocean tides, see their children borne seaward on moving sheets of water or slowly bobbing to the surface, reaching out their tiny hands for rescue. At the baptismal font—designed, it is said, to suggest the womb of Mary—the sacrament of rebirth is conducted by touching the forehead with flowing water or by immersing the entire body so that the candidate can surface newborn, blinking and shining with grace. When the Vedas speak of water, the

word is *matritamah*—"the most maternal." Even the letter M, the universal "Mother letter," is an ideogram meant to depict the movement of waves across the surface of water.

This is a wonderful rendering of what it means to dive, what going underwater for extended periods of time feels like, this return to the womb.

I took a shallow trajectory that carried me swiftly along toward the eastern shore of the harbor. A few minutes later I glided over another structure that seemed manmade. Beneath me, stretching out as far as the eye could see, was an avenue of flat limestone slabs laid out three abreast along a gentle slope declining into deep water. The precise rectilinear jointing of these slabs gave the astonishing impression of an ancient ruined thoroughfare, like the main street of Pompeii. The Egyptian priest Solon, whose story Plato relates in the *Timaeus*, claims that the submerged island of Atlantis, having achieved utopian perfection in the 10th millennium BCE after subduing to its rule every Mediterranean nation but Athens, was located in the Western Ocean somewhere beyond the Pillars of Hercules. An underwater "road" similar to this one off the Bimini coast, which I would dive on years later, has supported a persistent theory that Atlantis was a Bahamian island.

This is, of course, fantastic nonsense. These submerged carbonate streets, common throughout the Bahamas, are entirely natural phenomena created when beaches are exposed at lower sea levels and weathered flat. In time they dry and crack into rectangular blocks like paving stones. Though the deeper blocks are ancient, these structures form with remarkable speed at the present shoreline where you sometimes find bottles and cans embedded in them. Bahamians quarry them to build patios and garden walls.

At the moment, however, demystifying what was to the naked eye a dramatic archaeological find did nothing to cloud my imagination. I could almost see a trail of fallen plinths and columns and capitols and broken wheels littering the way along this underwater road into the dark of the ancient past. Buried somewhere in the sand, I could believe, were baubles and bracelets, ivory combs, broken amphorae, drowned fathers who have undergone sea changes into something rich and strange, whose bones are coral and whose eyesockets hold pearls.

Maybe the statue of a voluptuous goddess, its arms tragically severed. "Way down below the ocean," Donovan sang, "where I want to be, she may be."

As I was coming in, a rogue swell hoisted and then summarily dropped me on the beach rock, bruising my palms and taking some skin off my knee caps. Your imagination fairly shuts down when your knees are bleeding. Still, I was warm and tired and quite happy walking back along the beach—not another soul in sight—to the rock where I had left my shoes and t-shirt. I snuck back into the compound just as Conrad and Paul arrived with a load of sunburned students in the back of the truck. I showered in my room, picked up a lime and a full bottle of Meyers dark rum, and got pleasantly buzzed chatting up two lovely young women from the University of Colorado sitting prettily on a stone wall. "So you're a writer? I always wanted to be a writer."

The evening before we left San Salvador, I attended the final series of lectures of the week on Bahamian geology. Neumann presented his theory of rapid sea-level changes, complemented by Paul's description of chevrons pushed up by ancient storms on Eleuthera and Exuma. A structural oceanographer, John M. Bane, presented the last lecture on ocean currents that shape San Salvador. Just offshore from San Salvador, at the edge of the continental shelf, the Atlantic drops to many thousands of feet. Bane's lecture began with the first charting of the Gulf Stream, by Benjamin Franklin in 1770, and ended with satellite photos of a fierce cold front that swept southeast from North America to San Salvador—where the temperature fell into the mid-fifties—on January 28, 1986. That day the space shuttle *Challenger* roared into the sky above Florida and exploded, killing its crew, including the civilian teacher Christa McAuliffe. The rubber O-rings on its solid rocket booster had frozen and failed.

As I was checking out the next morning, Johnny's cousin who kept the books at the Field Station told me why I hadn't been able to find Ed at the bar. Ed had been rushed to the medical clinic at Cockburn Town: alcohol poisoning, fueled in part, I knew, by the money I'd given him. It was no consolation to imagine that he'd spent a long night of the iguana, fighting in delirium tremens phantom lizards that curled about his legs and bit him.

Later, with an hour to kill before our flight to Nassau, I strolled around Cockburn Town. I photographed headstones in the cemetery and the giant sculpture of an iguana—Iguana Don, I called him—that dominated the town square. I wondered whether this giant lizard had appeared to drunken Ed.

I fell into conversation with a young man named Donald Pinder who was carving a model of a Bahama boat in the shade of an almond tree. His only tools were a pencil, a machete and some sandpaper, but his finished works—replicas of various sizes and detail—were exact and graceful. Supported by a modest subsidy from the Bahamian government, Pinder crafted his model boats for sale to tourists. His current project was the trophy boat that would be awarded to the winner of the Family Island Regatta held every April off Great Exuma. An Exuma native, Pinder had a sorry story to tell of crack addiction, burglary, the theft and wrecking of a power boat, and a ruinous love affair. The cumulative impact of these experiences had driven him from his native island.

"So when this girl got pregnant," Pinder said, "her father come to me and say, 'Donald, you heavy-down my daughter and now what you gonna do? When you gonna marry her?' "

"Well I ain't gonna marry nobody I don't love, so I says back to him, 'how you know I the one that heavy her down? She sleep around all the time.' But he say she know I'm the father of the child and say he gonna kill me. So I go to my mama and explain the situation. And she say, 'Donald, you ain't got to marry dat sorry girl.' She say I take care of the child and you—meaning me—you get your rear part to Nassau."

But in Nassau there was more trouble with drugs, and Donald Pinder ended up doing time in the notorious Her Majesty's Prison at Fox Hill, Nassau, where the form of capital punishment, even today, is hanging—a ghoulish legacy of its pirate past.

When he came out, he brought his talents as a carver to the attention of the authorities who were impressed and packed him off to San Salvador where he would be more or less out of everyone's hair. Pinder hated the tourists from Club Med. "The fucking shit-ass French people come by here every day and don't even look in, ain't never bought one single goddamn thing from me." I could see why. He was shouting these profanities in the direction of a group of Medders cycling through the square.

"But people from the States, they different. They always stopping by to talk and sometimes they might buy one of my boats."

To change the subject, I asked if he missed the son he left behind on Exuma. "Yeah, he six years old now but, you know, me and that girl make up and she come here once in a while to see me. And when she come she always bring my son.

"But I still miss Exuma," he said. "It's the prettiest island there is in the Bahamas."

Ten thousand feet above Cat Island I made another decision. Paul was in the seat next to me. "Paul, my goat-footed, rock-hopping friend," I said, "I'm going to Exuma next."

Barataria
Settlement
•Rolleville
•Steventon
•Mount Thompson
Stocking Island
•Georgetown
Williams
Town
The Ferry •

EXUMA

N

Chapter 4
Heavy Weather, Sex and Death in the Exumas

BACK home it was another long season of teaching; more Chaucer and Shakespeare and Milton for other Christophers and Jennifers and Jasons, through the fall into the bitterest winter the East Coast had experienced in recent memory. In North Carolina, hoarfrost appeared in early December at the wet end of my yard where the newspaper landed in the morning. Later in the day, the sun faded into a vault where heavy, roly-poly clouds quick to open up and dump cold rain barreled along. On clear days it was arctic cold and the wind howled at midday. Most days it rained, and when it got colder, the rain froze on the trees, sheathing every branch and twig in a clear tube of ice. The dauntless cedars in our back yard, bent over under the weight of the freezing rain, swayed over the deck like weird hairy elephant trunks. Then it began to sleet and snow, filling in ditches and creek beds and curbsides, transforming the landscape into broad undulations, turning the steep hill beside our house into something from ski country down which squealing children and whooping parents tore on Flexible Flyers, inner tubes, garbage can lids, and sheets of plastic. We were sledding in the South.

It was fun for three days. But Southerners are unaccustomed to ten inches of frozen weather, and Durham came to a standstill. The kids were home for eight school days, long enough to try the patience of the most benevolent and devoted parents. Snowbound, I had a dream. I was standing on a mountaintop somewhere in the Bahamas, just before sunrise. There are no mountaintops in the Bahamas, of course, though there's one haunting promontory I'll take you to later in this book. In my dream, the island was arrayed beneath me, spits of land radiating out like the spokes of a wheel. The dusky top of the mountain was the hub of the island wheel, the view out along these spits was gauzy. Then I was on the ground, circling the base of the mountain in a Jeep, turning on to a single-lane dirt road running out to the cloudy blue water beyond. Speeding along between weedy canals lining the road I drove on and on, finally slamming on brakes and sliding up to a diamond-shaped sign that said "One Door City" in black letters. This was an actual sign I had photographed on San Salvador.

Next morning between classes, I called the travel agent and made reservations for Exuma

My conversation with Mabel Williams on San Salvador had changed something in me. Conrad and Paul were falling away. I knew next to nothing about rocks, though I had a rock formation—Marvin Gardens—named after me. But I wasn't really about geology. People interested me more. Talking to Mabel in that pretty living room in United Estates, something large shifted my Bahamian travels.

The Exuma trip started out badly. My first inkling of trouble came over Jacksonville, Florida. Beginning our descent into Ft. Lauderdale, the plane entered a cloudbank whose underside was blue-black. Water drops scudded across my window and we were flying over what seemed to be a washboard, bumping and grinding down through the clouds. We were twenty minutes late when the plane circled the airport once and approached the runway. I could see whitecaps scouring the Atlantic near the shoreline.

I got my bags and found the Bahamasair gate, five minutes before the Exuma flight was to depart. I wasn't really worried: Bahamasair flights were always late leaving. When I got to the gate, the Exuma plane was waiting on the tarmac, its cargo door open. I presented my ticket to a wiry, tanned agent who spoke with a very un-Bahamian Latino accent and evidently took a certain joy in some facets of his job.

"Too late," he said, smiling at me.

"But there's the plane," I replied numbly, pointing out the window.

"Yes, my friend, but look at your ticket. Check-in required."

I hadn't noticed that I would have to check-in. I complained, but the ticketing agent was unmoved.

"You think I can hold this flight up so you can get on?" he asked. "Forget it." I stood there, frustrated but implacable, while he diddled at his desk, pretending to be busy. He would drive home at the end of his shift. I was *en route* and angry. "Fuck this," I muttered under my breath.

"Look," he said, "come back in an hour and I'll get you on the next flight. Tomorrow."

"What? I'm gonna lose a day off my trip," I shouted. "Somebody's going to pay for this."

"Maybe," he replied. "But not me. This is the best I can do."

By this time, the Bahamasair flight to Exuma had backed out of the gate and was taxing for the runway.

An hour later the Bahamasair agent who said he would meet me was nowhere to be found. Then he mysteriously appeared behind the counter and went to work at the computer terminal. He looked up over his glasses: "I can get you on a flight to Nassau tonight at 7:30 and then on the 9:00 flight to Exuma tomorrow morning. Or I can get you on the afternoon flight from here tomorrow. Leaves at two. Your choice."

I called the Two Turtles Inn in George Town, Exuma, to tell them that I wasn't going to get there today.

"You turn back," the voice on the other end of the receiver said.

"What?"

"I know," he said.

"What?"

"I know."

"No, you don't know," I said, "I have a reservation for tonight at the Two Turtles, and I can't get there. I missed a flight."

"I know. Name?"

I gave him my name.

"Yeah, I got you. Long flight, yeah?" he said.

Long flight? What long flight? I explained myself again, this time slowly and entirely. Then I realized that he thought I was on the afternoon's flight to Exuma.

"Well, you lucky man, yeah?" He laughed. "The plane from Ft. Lauderdale turn back. Nobody get to Exuma today. Big wind here."

Nobody getting to Exuma today. "Hah!" I spat triumphantly into the phone. "Hah!" I stopped in the nearest bar to check on the weather and order a drink. A low pressure system had developed over Cuba, swept across the Florida Keys, swung north and was raking up the Florida coast. At present, the center of the storm, bringing torrential rains and wind gusts up to 40 miles per hour, was over Ft. Lauderdale. Given these conditions, I knew it would be nothing short of miraculous if our Nassau flight left on time. At 6:30 I checked my bags. Some time later, a rumor spread among the Nassau-bound passengers that our flight would be an hour late. Okay, I was tired and frustrated, but I had already waited five hours. Another brief delay would be immaterial. Go with the flow, I said to myself. Another hour passed and then another rumor of another hour's wait. This would get us in the air at 9:30, in Nassau at 11:00 P.M. At 10:20, the plane from Nassau touched down in a driving rain, and soon, a motley crowd of passengers filed down the concourse to the Bahamasair departure gate. The weather hadn't improved a lick. Wind gusts whipped rain in sheets and swirls across the tarmac.

At 11:00, the Dash-8, with not a vacant seat, groaned up into the black storm clouds. It was the flight from hell. As soon as we turned southeast toward Nassau, the plane started to shudder and rattle. She pitched and sank and soared, lurching forward in vagrant tail winds, seeming to come to a dead standstill in the air, her engines racing, in equally vagrant head winds. Most unnerving, she yawed, her tail threatening to slide around toward her nose. The doors to the overhead compartments clamored noisily.

During bad flights people invariably pretend to be sleeping. Everywhere I could see people's eyes were clinched shut. Their hands gripped the armrests. No one made a sound amid the terrifying din. Even the exhausted but neatly dressed and coifed flight attendant, strapped into her back-facing position, seemed frozen in fear. The cabin lights dimly illuminated the torpedo-shaped engine cowling out my window, but the rest of the world outside this noisy cocoon was impenetrable blackness.

An hour and fifteen minutes from Ft. Lauderdale the plane began to descend and soon the lights of Nassau appeared below us. We came in from the south and touched down as rain sheets blew in diagonal lines across the runway. It was a remarkably smooth conclusion to such a violent flight. We swept past the hulk of a rusting DC-3. The fronds of the stumpy palms lining the runway writhed in the wind.

It was nearly 1 AM when I cleared customs and walked out into the saturated air of Nassau. With no hotel reservations, but with the promise from my original airline to reimburse me for this brief night's stay, I decided not to economize. "The Radisson, Cable Beach," I told the taxi driver, directing him to the nearest large hotel. The Radisson had a "transient room" available for $175.00; the toll and resort levy was another $17.50; a $6.00 maid gratuity and a $4.00 service charge (for what?) brought the total for less than a seven-hour stay at Cable Beach to $202.50. Before turning in, I ordered a sandwich in the hotel lounge where corpulent, besotted middle-aged men drooled over the last of the tipsy, sunburned American coeds, then walked down to the beach. It wasn't raining but the night sky was starless.

I awoke just after sunrise at the Radisson and turned on the TV. There, to my momentary disbelief, the familiar faces of the morning news anchors from the Raleigh, NC TV station were reporting traffic conditions on roads I take to and from my office. Why the Raleigh station was broadcast here in Nassau, I couldn't figure. Outside, the faint rose color lining the far sections of the low cloud ceiling was a good sign that the storm was moving north. By the time I made it to the airport for my 9 AM flight to George Town, the sun was out, the wind up, and the clean-washed sky filled with racks of puffy clouds racing north over the Atlantic.

I checked in and took a seat in the domestic arrivals and departures waiting room. Its junky ash cans and broken plastic mold chairs were inviting. Light-brown children with soft, fleecy hair and gray eyes ran around in shorts, sandals and T-shirts, fidgeted and flitted about. A young man and his obese girlfriend hauled a crate sealed with duct tape into the waiting room. A spiffy businessman lingering over a copy of *The Nassau Guardian* sipped coffee from a Styrofoam cup. A young Japanese woman traveling alone read her novel. Two well-dressed women with briefcases, probably government officials, sat apart from the rest of us. We were all bound for the Family Islands— for Exuma and Abaco and Eleuthera and Cat Island and Mayaguana and Great Inagua. This morning there was an added presence to the domestic lounge: a strapping policeman in a fine black uniform with red-accented insignia, his shirt sleeves rolled up to highlight his pumped-up biceps, his forearm resting on the stumpy muzzle of an Uzi.

Nine o'clock came and went with no sign of our plane to Exuma. Some time later a Dash-8 taxied up to the domestic terminal and waiting passengers began to collect their bags and shuffle toward the departing gate. But the ticket agent picked up the microphone dangling from the wall and read a list of delays in crisp, perfectly enunciated statements. My Exuma flight, with continuing service to Long Island and Mayaguana, was rescheduled to depart at 10:30.

"Geez," I said to myself, "here we go again. Hurry up and wait."

The Exuma flight departed at 11:30 and an hour or so later began its descent over the long line of cays—one of these was Norman's Cay, the former stronghold of the Lehder drug cartel—stringing off the north shore of Great Exuma, and soon we were on the ground. The eight-mile cab ride into George Town took me through familiar features of the Bahamian landscape—bush and brittle limestone outcroppings, Casuarina-lined beaches. The cuts made for the roadbed were deeper here than on Eleuthera and San Salvador, the hills higher and forested in places. George Town was larger and better provisioned than any Family Island settlement I'd seen, with a bank, two markets, several hotels and a variety of shops. Dominated by a school and a cluster of ancient almond trees under which women sold souvenirs, its main square flanked a magnificent harbor protected by Stocking Island two miles over the water to the east.

Just off the main square, the Two Turtles Inn was a cut above places I'd stayed on other islands. My room on the second floor had satellite TV, comfortable beds and a tidy bathroom. Below was a courtyard bordered by a restaurant where women chopped cabbage and peeled potatoes in the shade of an awning. Attractive tourists, young married couples, seasoned and well-dressed yachties, sat at tables in the courtyard. On the patio fronting the street was an outdoor bar with a thatched cabana roof where I sat down to erase the flight jitters with shots of rum, congratulating myself on having survived a thirty-hour trip that should have taken only six.

Across the bar sat a thin brown man wearing a tightly wrapped yellow bandanna. His bandanna and glittering earring gave him the look of a pirate. He was complaining about the weather to a fat sailor with leathery skin. Eavesdropping, I gathered that it had been blowing a gale for three days and tomorrow was not likely to be much better. Nobody was sailing.

I walked out to Regatta Point at the end of a short peninsula across from the hotel. The slanting sunlight suffused every view, penetrating the clear water, soaking into the wet brown algae that clung to rocks, recomposing as a lighter shade the swaying greens of a neat row of palm trees at the end of the point, lighting up the hulls of the hundred or so yachts straining anchor in the harbor, their hulls as white as aspirin tablets. Conch shells at the water's edge seemed lit up from the inside, translucently beautiful. Ubiquitous in these islands, conch is something like the national dish of the Bahamas. Harvested in deeper waters, they're brought quayside, and dispatched with a single blow to the crown of the shell. Brained, the slick-sticky mollusk slides out into buckets. Wherever boats put in, discarded conch shells accumulate in large numbers. In the old days these shells were collected into mounds, doused with gasoline and set afire, burning down to a fine lime powder used as fertilizer and a main ingredient in mortar.

I had eaten conch frittered and cracked, saladed and chowdered, and had collected shells from every island I visited, including the cream and pink Queen Conch and the smaller, tawny West Indian Fighting Conch. But until now I had never noticed how feminine and sexy conch shells were, how much like the vulva, the outer labial fold of the shell spiraling inward in smooth pink volutions to a narrow vestibule at the entrance to some dark tidal secret. Venus herself might have stood on the enormous Queen Conch whose shell can grow to a length of three feet.

The wind was stiff and it was cool when I got back to the bar. In my absence three Venuses—beautiful bodies, teeth, hands and feet— had drawn a cohort of attentive men. Two were leggy blondes and the other a lovely woman with sad green eyes, patrician features and hair black as a starless night. The blondes might have stepped off the set of BabeWatch 90102, or whatever, and so might the black-haired woman if the casting director had an eye for subtle, compelling beauty. They were clearly enjoying the attention.

A rotund man, like a hairy pregnant old woman, in shorts and weathered topsiders, stood up and drew a quarter from his pocket.

"A game," he said with his chin raised, staggering slightly. He tried to say more but "a game" was all he could get out. He took an empty highball glass from the table and placed it on the floor with the slow concentration of a seasoned drunkard. Then he waved the quarter before the crowd like a magician showing that nothing was up his sleeve. He reached behind him into his shorts and drew back empty-handed, waving both hands before us as if he'd made a whale disappear. The drinkers howled wildly, pretending to fall off their stools. The drunk took three pooky steps, squatted over the glass, grunted, and let fall the quarter from his butt crack. It clinked into the glass, a dead ringer. The bar rioted. A line formed and it wasn't long before the quarter was passed to the California girls. Flashing squirrelly looks at their devoted audience, they took turns clutching the coin between their buttocks, squealing and waddling over to the glass. They weren't very good—not one scored a clinking hit—but they were fun to watch.

They teased the crowd. "Remember that boy you fucked at Laguna Beach?" the green-eyed woman said accusingly to one of the blondes. "Jail-bait. Or maybe he just shaved his legs." Everyone laughed.

"I got to him before you did," the other coolly replied and drained her glass. The parliament of horny men pressing in on these women hooted.

I struck up a conversation with a tiny, cricket-faced expatriate from Massachusetts who was missing his left ear. I wanted to explore Stocking Island, the six-mile long barrier island that formed the eastern shore of George Town's harbor, and I asked him how I could get there. "Well, you got two choices," he said. "The Peace and Plenty Hotel takes a group over twice a day. They're just up the street. Or you can call only one."

"Only one what?"

"Just only one."

I was confused. "Just only one?" I asked. "What are you talking about?"

"The water taxi. Calls himself 'Only One.' You can get him on the marine radio. Channel 19." I called Only One and arranged to meet him the next morning at 9:30 at the dock behind the supermarket.

The next morning, a thick-set, muscular young man the color of mahogany was waiting for me in his boat, a stubby, V-hulled 14-footer powered by a Honda 85 h.p. four-stroke engine, expensive but powerful and efficient. Only One was a man of few words and serious facial expressions. He charged four dollars per person each way and there were three others taking the trip—16 dollars out and another 16 back. The fare seemed steep to me, affording Only One the luxury of three gold chains that hung from around his neck nearly to his waist.

With a trailing wind we ran out toward Stocking Island along a choppy avenue lined with an armada of yachts uniformly bow-on to us. Overhead were even ranks of white cumulus clouds sailing through the high wind and bright sunshine toward the northeast. Only One cut the motor and rode us up on the beach. I walked north in the shade of Casuarina trees along the shore toward a narrow point where an aged yacht had broken from its mooring and was turned broadside, hoved up near the beach. Men working from dinghies, others chest deep in the water, were trying to turn her bow into the wind. Farther along, two hand-carved headstones under a palmetto bush marked the final resting place of family members: Jennifer who died March 29, 1991 at 17 years and Sam ("R. I. P."), age not given, who died November 34, 1992. A bit farther was another memorial, to Rebecca, *aetat* 23, who was "Here in Spirit." I wondered if these could possibly mark human remains. Maybe they were pets.

I walked toward a point which turned out to be the mouth of a cove that swung inland toward the south, blocking my advance. More yachts swung at anchor here; there was a volleyball net set up on the beach and the blackened remains of campfires. I followed the cove inland for several hundred yards. Here, the cove opened up into a lagoon 300 yards wide. A skate fanned along in the shallows and bonefish thrashed their fins out of the water. It was a beautiful estuary, but the farther I walked along it the more difficult the trek became. I climbed over a rotten pier and menacing ledge until I came to a thicket of red mangrove where an impenetrable mass of arching inch-thick roots dipped into the shallows. I was hoping there might be a shallow place near the head of the cove where I could wade across to the foot of the ridge separating me from the ocean on the eastern flank of the island. But the tide was rising and the mangrove was a massive tangle of roots that stretched into chest-deep water. It would be impossible to cross here. Besides, on the other side was nothing but thick bush running up the ridge, no sign of a trail. Attempting to pick my way up the ridge would be wasted effort. This was the end of the line. I could hear the ocean beyond the ridge but couldn't possibly make it through the mangroves and up the brush over the ridge to the beach. It was a moment of unusual and intense frustration, being this close to the beach but unable to get there, left to wonder what the shore was like on the other side.

Trapped, my attempt to reach the ocean thwarted, I continued around the cove and found a stone path leading up a steep rise. It led up to a cluster of resort cottages at the top of the hill. Signs warned that trespassers would be prosecuted, but there were no cottagers hereabout, indeed no one in sight. The buildings seemed vacant, the office was closed, and even the thatched bar near the harbor beach was empty, though a chalk sign promised an afternoon happy hour. It was an eerie feeling walking among the neatly-kept cottages where I could scan the view from the lagoon on one side and on the other across the harbor to George Town two miles away. The wind was raising scandal in the stumpy trees.

I continued down the far side of the hill and struck out south along the beach on the harbor side of Stocking Island, hoping to make it around the point to the Atlantic side. There was hardly any beach to walk here. The westerly gale was driving waves up under ledges which were high enough to require some careful climbing to get over. Crossing one of these moonscapes—they were the same formations I had seen in Eleuthera—I stumbled backwards in my wet sandals, my foot slipped down in a jagged depression of limestone, and a blade of rock cut an inch-long gash in my heel.

I limped back in the direction of the Casuarina trees where Only One had dropped me off, walking in the water to clean the wound.

On the trip back to George Town my heel was still bleeding and I felt no inclination to chat with the others. Sitting in the bow of the boat pounding along in a head wind, I thought of conchs and the California girls dropping quarters from their butts, and of the memorials to Jennifer and Sam and Rebecca I had seen on Stocking Island receding behind us. The ancient siblings Eros and Thanatos, sex and death, it seemed, had convened on Exuma. I thought of Shiva the Blessed One, Hindu lord of procreation and destruction, with his enormous phallus and demon-crusted necklace of skulls, and the English folk belief that every orgasm took a day off your life. Sex and death. Sex, and the bow pitched down into a trough; death, and the bow bounded down again. Sex, pound, death, pound, all the way to George Town, in numbing repetition synchronized to the throbbing of my heel.

That afternoon I hobbled off to the rental car agency. On the way I stopped at the N and D Fruit Market and struck gold.

Danzella Rolle who ran the market was a woman in her early forties, her hair pulled back into a knot at the back of her head; her features reminded me of Diana Ross. Danzella was petite and beautiful, quick to laugh, but she was also prosperous and knew it, blunt in the way successful people are. I told her I wanted to interview old Exumans.

"You want to talk to old people?" she asked with mock incredulity.

"Yes, I do."

"Why you want to talk to old people?"

"I want to write about them. Their stories, the way things used to be in the old days." I replied.

"Well, honey, you come to the right place." She dropped the interrogative mode and then seemed something more than friendly to this stranger. "I know everybody on these islands, both Great and Little Exuma," she said. "I live here all my life, and I see most of the old ones every day when they bring their produce here. I know those that can tell you all about the old times, I know them from all over, honey, them that remember the spongin' and turtlin' times. When there was nothing but a path where this here road is, I mean, when they wear cut-out tires for shoes. Come back later and I'll give you a list."

"Today?"

"Yes, honey, today."

Two hours later I returned. Danzella Rolle unfolded a packing envelope on a table in the shade of the awning at the N and D Market. On it she had written in a neat hand the names of almost every settlement on the two islands: The Ferry, Forbes Hill and William Town on Little Exuma; on Great Exuma, the Hermitage, Moss Town, Ramsey, Mount Thompson, Steventon, Stuart Manor, Rolleville and Barattara at the northern end of the big island. Under each of these entries she had written the names of people—forty of them—she wanted me to meet, many more than I would be able to interview in my remaining days. It was a bonanza.

The next morning I drove south to the Ferry Settlement on Little Exuma, stopping just across the narrow bridge linking the two islands. I was looking for Gloria Patient, known locally as The Shark Lady. Everyone seemed to know her, or at least to know of her, because for 20 years she had hunted sharks alone in her little skiff. At 80 she was still at it. And there was naughtiness in her past. For many years she provided an eye-catching finale to the Family Island Regatta, for which Exuma is famous, when she and her all-girl crew would cross the finish line dead last and drop their shirts, sailing topless up to the dock at George Town before adoring crowds.

Knowing she was a native of Exuma I had expected Gloria Patient to be black, but the robust woman who came to the door at the little house set back in a grove of sandalwood trees—a road-sized sign on her front porch said "Tropic of Cancer"—this woman was white with close-cropped silver hair, wearing a simple black shift and a single strand of gold around her neck. She was barefooted, her toenails and fingernails and lips painted candy-apple red. Her face was deeply creased and tanned but she hardly looked her 80 years. Had I fallen in behind her at a check-out line in Miami, and she were wearing shoes, I would have thought her a well-to-do widow, living comfortably off her dead husband's annuities.

"I'm looking for Gloria Patient," I said.

"Well, you've found her, Bucky Boy," she replied cockily.

She invited me into the front room, which was set up as a shop with a central table covered in driftwood branches strung with necklaces and earrings. Other tables were strewn with pearls and bleached shark vertebrae and sand dollars and sea fans. Hung over the doorway leading back into other rooms was the enormous gaping jaw of a shark.

"I'm afraid this isn't the best of times," she said. "I lost my husband of 45 years two weeks ago."

I mumbled condolences and turned to leave, but she didn't want me to go. "No, no, I'll talk to anybody almost anytime." I asked about her childhood. Born of Scots-Irish parents in a house just down the road, she had been expelled from schools at Forbes Hill on Little Exuma and in Nassau, both times for fighting. She married, had children and moved the family, as so many Family Islanders did, to Nassau. For 35 years she worked as a masseuse in the capital before coming back to Exuma in 1969 when the last of her nine children left home.

"In Nassau I did all your presidents and all your Canadian prime ministers." She laughed slyly and resolved the ambiguity—"Gave them massages. And all your movie stars, like Sean Connery when he was making Thunderball. I saw them all every night almost, Terrance Young and the rest. I did them all." She spoke deliberately in an almost Bostonian accent with subtle inflections, flattening out long vowels.

I asked about shark hunting. "Well, if you don't know anything about sharks, don't try catching them. I'm afraid of sharks but I know how to handle them."

How long did it take to land a shark? "Well, it's according to how big he is. A big shark, like an 18-footer, would take me about an hour. An 18-foot tiger shark, that's a big mother." She rattled off a list of sharks found off Little Exuma: bulls, makos, lemons, black-tips, white-tips, silkies, tigers, leopards, hammerheads. She never took the nurse sharks or sea turtles: The nurse is harmless and the turtles are endangered.

She said that even great whites sometimes made their way into these waters. "They caught one last year. They didn't know what it was, but they brought me the jaw and the tail. The great white's tail is like a half-moon instead of a triangle. You can identify him if you see him in the water because he swims with his mouth open all the time. He's an eating machine. Very dangerous. The one they caught last year was only ten feet long, and it was the first great white caught in the Bahamas. But they're down to the northern coast of Florida."

And you just go off the reef to catch these sharks? "No, I go out into the Atlantic. They're all around. Sharks would never be depleted here in the Bahamas for the simple reason that nobody's interested in catching them, except me. Now, they did start setting the big, long five-mile nets off Nassau. But we put a stop to that, Bucky Boy. Yessir, we went to Nassau and had a protest. I told them that if they ever came to Exuma and put a net here, I would chop up every piece of the net and shoot them."

From underneath a table she drew two orange flare guns and pointed them like six-shooters.

"That must have put the fear of God in them," I said.

"I'm going to tell you, it sure did. I was very serious, Bucky Boy, deadly serious. I didn't give a damn what the police said, but the police don't mess with me. I let them know I'm a pistol-packing mama, and when I go down to sea, you can hear those daddies talking, 'don't turn your gun on me.' If you don't want to smell my smoke, don't monkey with my gun!"

I laughed out loud, but Gloria Patient thinned out her grandmotherly smile menacingly. She picked up a rusty hook the size of a grapple from the floor. It must have weighed five pounds. "I bait this baby with a grouper head."

"And you just dangle that over the side?"

"No, Bucky Boy, you dangle your what-you-call-it over the side, but I don't dangle nothing over the side. I throw my line overboard and when he takes it I haul him in with elbow grease."

How do you kill the shark? "I get his attention with a magnum shell at the end of a bang stick, Bucky Boy."

This old woman of the sea led me into the back rooms of her house that had once been the post office at The Ferry Settlement. Tables were covered with neat rows of glassware and china plates hung from every space on the walls. An enormous Wedgwood vase dominated a table in the living room. On the other side was a picture window which gave a view of a clearing dominated by a bird bath on a pedestal where ground doves and mocking birds and several species of ducks fed. "I have a hundred pounds of feed brought in every two weeks for these birds." Bahamian hummingbirds called woodstars darted around feeders hung from the eaves.

Passing back through the middle room, she took something from her dress pocket and sat down on the bed: two pearl-adorned elastic bands which, one after the other, she looped behind her heels, pulled them over the tops of her feet, crossed them once, and hooked them over her red-nailed middle toes. Shadow shoes, a metaphor of shoes, a hologram of shoes. "I haven't worn a real pair of shoes for 40 years," she said. "This is what I wore at my audience with King Gustov of Sweden."

As I was leaving, she mentioned again that everything in the front room was for sale. I bought a small pair of shark-tooth earrings for my wife.

At The Ferry settlement I took the Queens Highway south through Forbes Hill toward William Town. Used to the rubble of other Out Island roads I was surprised that the main road on Little Exuma was in such good repair, evidence, I supposed, of the prosperity of the Exumas compared to other Family Islands. In William Town I had directions from Danzella ("top of the hill, straight up, no twist and no turning") to the house of Racey Stiles ("He knows everything and everybody; he's old and sick but still sharp, very smart man"). I found his house with no trouble—a low cinderblock building on a hill across the road from a spanking new church with a belfry topped by a white cross. There was a magnificent fig tree in Racey Stiles' front yard and a goat tied to a stake. Down the hill behind the house the calm water of the southern bank shone a translucent greenish blue. I knocked at the door and waited but no one answered. I knocked again and called Mr. Stiles' name. There was still no reply, so I walked around back where a decrepit leaf house stood surrounded by rusting machinery.

Racey Stiles wasn't at home. I loitered for some time in the yard hoping he'd return, but the people who stared at me from passing cars made me uncomfortable. I crossed the road and walked down a little street to where it ended at a squat bluff above the Atlantic. From a clothesline a naked doll hung on a noose.

The sky had fewer clouds today, the sun was high and blistering, but the wind blew steady still. It was cool and hot at the same time, and the moist air seemed to contain more oxygen than I needed to breathe, leaving me slightly lightheaded.

Back in George Town it was late afternoon when I finished taking notes on Gloria Patient, showered, dressed my heel, and ambled down to the Sunshine Bar. I took a seat beside the piratical-looking fellow I had seen early in the week. He was in his forties, lean, clean-shaven, fine-boned and fit. Without his yellow bandanna he looked more like the all-American male you'd see on a golf course than someone from the 17th century who might board your vessel uninvited. He also looked familiar. I asked where he was from.

"I sail my boat down here in the winter and spring," he said. "Live on Martha's Vineyard the rest of the time."

"Yeah? I've got a friend that's a native of Martha's Vineyard. Still spends his summers there."

"What's his name?"

"Conrad."

"Neumann?" he asked. "My God," I said, "you know Conrad Neumann."

"Everybody on the Vineyard knows Conrad. He's a legend in his own time."

"In his own mind," I laughed.

Small world. In the span of a few seconds the world contracted to an outdoor bar on a remote Bahamian island where two strangers discussed a mutual friend, the Beluga of the Bahamas. And things got more curious quickly. I was wearing a UNC T-shirt.

"You from Chapel Hill?" he asked.

"Durham."

"I went to high school in Chapel Hill. My father was head of the medical school back in the sixties."

He introduced himself. "Hugh Taylor." We shook hands, and I realized why he looked familiar. The resemblance to his famous singer-song writer brother, James, was unmistakable. I had met James Taylor's brother on Exuma. He asked how long I was staying in George Town.

"A couple more days," I said

"I'm leaving day after tomorrow. But I'm sailing over to Long Island if this blow passes tomorrow. Ever been there?" I hadn't, though some years later I would visit Long Island. I still consider it the most beautiful island in the Bahamas.

"Great place to sail, Long Island," he continued. "Some of the best water in the Bahamas. Wanna come?"

"I don't know. Let's see how things go."

"Coming to the party tonight?" He asked. I said I didn't know there was a party tonight, though I had noticed three oversized grills set up in the courtyard of the Two Turtles where women were peeling potatoes and grating mounds of cabbage.

"Dinner starts about five-thirty and music after that. You don't want to miss it. With this wind and these people hold up on their boats all week, they'll be ready to break out."

Indeed, they were. At four o'clock people began to drift into the courtyard, wealthy retirees, honeymooning couples, handsome young men and beautiful women from foreign lands, local expats, long-tressed surfer types, wizened salts, a few well-appointed children. The California girls arrived with two teenaged boys, the menage chaperoned by a silvery patriarch and diamond-studded matriarch. The nautical theme was prominent. One man wore a captain's shirt with epaulets, another was dressed as a buccaneer. After dinner—barbecued chicken, potato salad and cole slaw—75 party-goers readied themselves as the band fronted by Hugh Taylor set up in the courtyard. I suppose all parties are fractured events, small groups of people trapped in their own small circles, resisting whatever temptation there might be to break out and meet someone new. But this crowd of well-to-do boat people seemed especially fragmented. Boats bring people together in very intimate circumstances but they also segregate you from other people on other boats. Having no connection with yacht life, I stood around at the margins of the party with a tipster from Kentucky and an epicene boy called Carlos who worked the crowd for a john.

Hugh Taylor fronted the band, which was tight and favored Motown songs. I sat in for a couple of Sam Cook numbers, playing a borrowed Martin. It was as if we'd been playing together for years.

Afterwards, I walked out into the darkness behind the hotel. With the party rocking away behind me ("I can't get no saa-tis-faak-shun") I sat under a starry sky next to the lagoon. The Big and Little Dipper framed the sphere of the heavens, the thick flank of the Milky Way pressed down upon me, stars shimmered on the lagoon. Out here I felt comfortable again and, released from the vague desire to meet someone new, I was soon drowsy. I went back to my room, watched an old film of Mohammed Ali in his prime on ESPN for a while and went to sleep.

The sailing trip to Long Island didn't materialize, and I never saw Hugh Taylor again. The next morning I drove back to William Town to find Racey Stiles. When I knocked on the door, a startled voice said, "What you want?" I glimpsed in a window and saw an old man mostly bald with a white goatee lying in bed.

"Mr. Stiles?" I ventured.

"What you want?" he asked again in a crackling voice.

"Danzella Rolle in George Town said you might talk to me. I want to find out what it was like on Exuma in the old days. Could you spare a few minutes?"

"Danzella sent you?"

"Yes, she did."

"I can't hardly get myself out of this here bed. Hurtin' kinda bad this morning."

"I can come back later if you don't feel up to talking."

"And what is it you want to talk about?"

"The old times on Exuma." I was talking through the window.

"I'll get up. Come on in that other room."

The main room of the house held a low freezer, a faded vinyl sofa strewn with books and papers, and a matching chair. The far wall was pine paneled, with snapshots taped around a poster of a candidate for political office. The caption at the bottom of the poster said "We Care About You." A noisy floor fan whirred.

Racey Stiles made his way into the room, tall and bony with long almond-shaped nails and milky eyes. He wore a faded t-shirt and boxer shorts. In one hand he carried his trousers, in the other a cane on which he leaned heavily. With great effort he hoisted himself on top of the freezer and tried to put his pants on, one leg over one foot, but couldn't. I helped him with his pants while the old man stared out the window. Time and labor had nearly broken Racey Stiles; his fixed stare was the composition of pain and fear and mustered dignity.

"I was born 74 years ago in that leaf house behind here."

I asked if he had worked as a fisherman. "Oh, well," he said dismissively, "not so much of that. It was in the time when you could do the spongin' and turtlin'. I used to scull the boat, no engine, just sculling and catch the turtles and sponges like that.

"I used to go spongin' out on the bank there, and you check around the nubs, the black places in the water. And you had a sponge hook—some hooks," he said, counting on the thick twigs of his fingers, "some hooks you got have three prongs and some four. And you got a staff, sometimes about 50 feet long. You see the sponge down there on the bottom and you hook it and shake it and loosen it till you can pull the sponge up. It was a big job in the sun and all that. Sculling the sponge and turtle, it was hard work, I'm telling you, and dangerous too. A lot of them back then drown doing that work."

Any money in it? "Well, now, very little money, but in those days there wasn't any big money. You could buy a horse for 15 dollars, or a lamb, or something like that, for five dollars.

"Now the turtles was better, well, yes, fairly good. I catch the turtle with a rod and a net and a iron ring. My father could do all of that, and he teach me. You make the net that go wide at the bottom and smaller at the top. And you used to scull the turtle, and whenever you got the chance you used to drop the rod down and put it over him, and shake the net and he would fly up into the net and hook up hisself. And then you pull him up.

"The meat wasn't for anything. You kill the turtles and take the shells off. And you sell them shells." Owing to the type, he said, you got a good price for it. Stiles pointed to my faux tortoiseshell glasses. "The hawksbill, that was the most expensive. Good money for him. But the loggerhead, he was not good for his shell, just his meat. Same for the green turtle that people like the steaks from. Their shells bring no money. But you might sell the meat to somebody for a little something.

"The loggerhead, he was the biggest."

"But everything gone down now," he said. "They got all the chemicals to make that stuff, the shade and the spoon handle and knife handle, and they don't use the turtle no more."

Of the seven species of sea turtles—flatback, green, hawksbill, Kemp's ridley, leatherback, loggerhead and olive ridley—none is common today, and five—the Kemp's and olive ridley, the pelagic leatherback, the loggerhead and the hawksbill—are threatened or endangered. Only the green turtle, highly prized for its meat, seems to have gotten a finhold and then, mainly, because the animal is farmed, and no longer taken with impunity in the wild. But it wasn't men like Racey Stiles who brought sea turtles to the brink of extinction. Indiscriminate trawling by commercial fishermen and developers who have destroyed their breeding beaches are to blame for that. Yet, efforts to protect sea turtles are impressive, enough so to warrant a hopeful prognosis. Beach communities throughout the developed world are aware of the threat to turtle habitats. But it's ironic and perhaps unjust, I think, that while sea turtles may come back from the edge of oblivion, turtlers like Racey Stiles are fast and irretrievably headed for extinction.

I asked what happened when somebody in the old days fell ill or was injured. "Well, now, in them days, whenever you wanted to see a doctor, you had a sailing boat—one mail boat used to come from Nassau once every two weeks. And then maybe the mail boat can't dock because of the bad weather, and you have to scull out to the channel or take a dinghy boat out. And then it take eight days to get to Nassau. But that was your only choice, if you was real sick. Wait a long time or die. And a lot of them, they die on the boat before they get to Nassau."

Twice Racey Stiles was put on board the mail boat for Nassau with serious injuries. Both times he was hurt breaking the horses his father bred. The first time, at 20, he was roping a wild horse when the rope "hitched" around his leg and the horse bolted, dragging him "near a quarter mile" along a ditch and then across the road, which had just been paved. "I doubled up and took the thumping." Stiles put his arms across his face and tried to hunch over, imitating his posture behind the horse. "He took me up the street here where there was a well just on the side of the road and a wall next to it, just a little space between them. He slow his speed and I managed to take the rope and throw it over the well. It caught, and he couldn't get me between the wall and the well. So I managed to stop him then.

"Well, he had me scarred. My mother she greased me down and covered me with a table cloth. She cut out some of that [table cloth] and made tape. And she got a piece of plywood and greased that down so I could lay out on that with just my shorts on until it harden up some. When the scabs got hard, it was pitiful to see. They throw the sheet on me and sometimes it stuck," he said, wincing and blinking. "In the morning time, to get that off, and it bleeding and all that kinda stuff. Whew! It hurt me. When it did get hard enough, I took the boat to Nassau. I had three broken ribs."

Later, a horse fell on him and crushed his leg. "That was the worse time, when the horse go down on me. My mother think I was going to die. I did think that too. Oh, yes, that's a lot of pain now. I was in Nassau with my sister after my leg was broke. In a cast up over my middle part for three months. Oh, man, couple of times I asked my sister, I asked her to kill me. Give me something, let me die."

I asked about bush medicine, and Stiles added nicely to my growing list of remedies: leaves of the hardhead tree, chewed or brewed in a tea, for diarrhea; jackmedac, boiled, for high stomach pains; goombay beans for heart failure; salt, butter and lime juice for a bad throat; hard rosin, grated, mixed with flour and boiled, for venereal diseases; spoonwood for coughs; the milk of the crucifixion bush for cuts; big sage for pox; boiled pear leaves and green bananas for diabetes. The green banana, he added, posed a threat to livestock. "If you feed your cow green bananas, in two or three days there'll be no milk in the pail. Dry him right up. You can't do that. That's the reason why Haitians not so healthy. They eat a lot of the green bananas."

Early in 1945 Racey Stiles came to the United States as a migrant worker. He remembered being in Ocala, Florida, on April 12 when flags were lowered to half-mast at the death of President Roosevelt. In Florida he cut sugarcane and picked fruit. As the summer accomplished he cropped tobacco in Georgia and the Carolinas, moving with the camp north through Maryland to New York where he picked beets and beans. He did this for four years, sending money to his mother back in William Town.

"When I went to the States, I sign a contract, and they used to pay me three dollars for eight hours work. Eight hours, three dollars. And hard work too." Cropping tobacco seemed to stand out in his memory as the most difficult work of his migrant life. "Now that was some hard work. You pick it green, now, what they call it the lug leafs, to the bottom of the stalk. You got to be bending down to get the lugs. And you put them leaves in your arm and your arm break out in blisters all up and down it. And then you put the leafs in the sled pulled by a mule and take it to the tall oak barn like that." He lifted his arms toward the ceiling to indicate the height of the barns. "And when you get to the barn you have the long sticks and some twine. An you bunch them leafs and turn them around with twine and hang them over the stick. And then you hang them sticks up on the poles in the barn to cure.

"Sometimes I go up in the top of that barn to hang the sticks, and man, I tell you I was sweating tar. I done that all around in [North] Carolina. In Grifton and Kinston and Winston-Salem. All round them places.

"And you know, when I was in Carolina some of the people over there live like the people in the Bahamas. They got to draw the water from the well with a bucket at the end of a rope."

Winston-Salem, Kinston and Grifton were towns I knew well. I grew up amid the poverty of the rural south. In the early sixties, the son of a minister who served rural parishes in Virginia and North Carolina, I had worked fields like those Racey Stiles described. As a gesture of community spirit, my father hired me out as a field hand during the tobacco-cropping season in July and August. For two months in high summer I picked tobacco, arriving in the field with a group of men and boys, most older than I, before seven A.M. when the tall, sticky, broad-leafed plants were wet with dew. We wore long-sleeved shirts to keep tar exuded by the wet plants from coating our skin. We "primers" chose a row and waded in, bent over, to pick the low rung of leaves, usually two or three at a time, the ones that had faded ever so slightly toward yellow from their rich green color.

The rows were sometimes a quarter mile or more long, and by the end of the first—the first of many before we quit priming at noon—my back hurt and I was soaking wet. As I worked my rows, invariably lagging behind the others, I heated up and began to sweat and ache, my hands and wrists turning black with tar. It was the most grueling labor

I've ever endured. Every moment in the fields was a waking nightmare, and sometimes not just subjectively. I was 14, now a veteran of the long rows. One day I was working in a field next to a highway with six or seven other laborers under a blistering sun when just at the end of the row a terrible blasting crash split the air. I walked to the edge of the field and looked down on to the highway below. Two cars had crashed head-on and a woman with blond hair was lying in the road. Her head was nearly severed and her clothes were torn off above her waist, exposing her breasts, the first I'd ever seen. She was bare footed. My knees weakened and I sat down and vomited on my shoes. The lovely breasts of a dying woman—Eros and Thanatos came to me again on Exuma.

Just before I left I asked Racey Stiles about the good times he remembered.

"Well, now, I had many good times," he laughed and rubbed his eyes. "The best was the son I had in 1957. He still live around here. At the time I had a girl daughter with my wife. I used to work very hard, and an old lady came to me one day and told me, 'why you working so hard.' So I says, 'I got to work hard to make a living.' And so she say, 'how many children you got to feed?' And I told her, 'I got one daughter.' And she say, 'you shouldn't be working so hard,' she say, 'Whenever you die your name be gone. You just be forgotten.' And she say, 'I tell you, I'm going to pray for you to try to have a son. Someone to call after you when you done died, whenever you dead.' I did try it and sure enough I had a son."

When we finished talking, Racey Stiles followed me out into the yard. Talking seemed to have limbered his joints and he walked with more ease now. Perhaps his memory had been lubricated too; he seemed a happier man for it. But the sour smell of urine and soiled bed clothes hung in my nostrils, and the mental image of the waning life that would haunt that house, haunt me too, for perhaps a few more years put me in a funk. The farther I drove toward George Town, the worse I felt. I had a version of his life that I would use for my own purposes, but I had given him nothing lasting in return, only a twenty-dollar bill I left on the table, and that seemed a paltry, condescending gesture. I remembered La Rochefoucauld's maxim, *Les virtus se perd dans l'interet, comme les fleuves se perd dans le mer*, the virtues converge in self-interest the way rivers converge in the sea.

Documentary work had always seemed especially laudable to me —pure, detached, archival. I had seen Titicut Follies, Frederick Wiseman's 1967 documentary about life in a Massachusetts mental institution, in an undergraduate psychology class. It brought home to me the power and authority of documentary studies. And I admired it greatly. But now I was nagged by the feeling of having exploited Racey Stiles, the way a photographer who captures a tragic moment must feel when, knowing that he'll sell his photograph for high dollar, he watches but doesn't act. I seemed a voyeur of this man's pain. But I could do nothing to slow his crawl toward death. I would certainly never see him again, except in my mind's eye. I would return home to my normal life in North Carolina and carry on teaching and writing, within easy walking distance of decrepit barns and tobacco fields like the ones that had helped to break him.

As a documentarian, moreover, I was a rank amateur, asking the same questions over and over, and there was every chance that many of my questions were pointless or ill-conceived. I used them merely as prompts in what inevitably became conversations rather than interviews. I was doing much that was wrong, and what I sensed I was doing right seemed of questionable merit.

North of George Town, I slipped a Patsy Cline tape into the car's cassette player, but the Queen of Country did nothing to lighten my mood. Her whining ("I've got your class ring, she's got you") seemed fruity, idiotic. At Mount Thompson I turned west on a rubble road leading up the hill in search of pastor Thomas Rolle, another source Danzella had identified for me.

I found Thomas Rolle at his stone house, having just finished his noon meal with his wife, son and two grandchildren. He had been pastor of the Baptist church at the top of Mount Thompson—not a mountain but a hill—for 11 years. But the majority of his adult life— he was 71—Thomas Rolle had spent farming onions. He remembered the sponging and turtling times when he was a boy. His grandfather had drowned when a squall blew up while he was sponging. Rolle knew bush medicine and remembered when farmers burned conch shells and stones to render lime from which to build church walls. Later in my Bahamian travels I would discover the greatest church architect in Bahamian history, a Franciscan monk, Father Jerome Hawes, the Hermit of Cat Island.

Pastor Rolle was not particularly enthusiastic; he talked more about onion farming than preaching. It was only when I drove him up to his church at the summit of Mount Thompson that he began to engage questions about religion with any passion. He led me into the sanctuary, a cavernous room, dark and cool with blood-red stained glass windows, rows of oak pews, and a simple pulpit, lectern and altar on a raised platform. On the wall behind the altar were two framed photographs of recent bishops, both askew, flanking a chalkboard on which last Sunday's attendance and hymn numbers were written. Nearby was a banner that read "No Chewing Gum." I noticed both hymn and chant books and asked the difference between them. The blood-red windows combined with the moldy smell of Bibles and song books cast a spell in the sanctuary, and I began to sense the passion that must fill this building on Sunday mornings when it was crowded with bodies in crisp shirts and flower-print dresses, no one chewing gum, and the old hymns, "Just As I Am" and "A Closer Walk With Thee" being raised. I remembered the Easter service attended by Dilsey, Frony and Benjy Compson at the end of Faulkner's *The Sound and The Fury*, and imagined worshippers in this church on Mount Thompson bathed in red light from the windows, aneled like Dilsey in the recollected blood of the slaughtered Lamb of God, ravished by the passionate vision of the crucified Lord who was dead, buried and on the third day rose from the grave.

Ten miles north along the Queen's Highway which hugged the white line of deserted beach and the aquamarine water visible through stands of palms and casuarinas, I came to the settlement of Steventon, where nurse Lydia Rolle worked at the medical clinic. Born on Cat Island and trained at Princess Margaret Hospital in Nassau, nurse Rolle had been posted first to Long Island and then to Exuma in March 1958. She had been here ever since. She and three other nurses worked with the only physician on Great and Little Exuma, to care for the several thousand Exumans. Lydia Rolle was a round woman wearing a simple uniform of pale blue, her hair pulled into a tight knot at the back of her head. She had lively eyes, a broad flat nose and a large gap between her front teeth. She spoke in a manner familiar among Bahamian women of her age, softly, her lilting voice rising and falling on the final syllable of words like Nassau, almost as if her sentences were song lines.

106

"When I first came here," she said, "there weren't no proper roads. You could count the cars what was here. And the motor bikes and the bicycles. You knew exactly who they were.

"And in those days the government find a bicycle for me and I have to ride from settlement to settlement tending to the sick and dying. Those times was very hard for me." Infectious diseases were often epidemic in her early years of nursing. "Here they had tuberculosis, and the most important settlement which was infested with it, it was Rolleville. Well, you see, the water supply wasn't good then, and so we have many cases of gastroenteritis too, especially in the rainy season when the wells fill up with bad water.

"Years gone past, they had only one doctor, he was at George Town, a senior nurse to George Town, and I was the senior nurse out here." "Out here" meant in the northern part of Great Exuma, the region of Steventon, Rolleville and Barattara. "The doctor in George Town, he would come visit me once a week at this clinic, and then once a month when I would go around with him to every settlement. The clinic here was very small, you see, and the people could not afford to come to the clinic, so we have to go round to them." Even then, the Bahamas being a British holding, medical care was free to the people.

"But medical conditions on Exuma have improved greatly now. Most of them back then they take the bush medicine." Nurse Rolle was the only person I'd met in the Out Islands who rejected bush medicine out of hand. "With me, you know, I wasn't interested in it because I stick to my medical training."

"I bet you've seen a lot of babies born."

"Oooooh, you know it," she said laughing. Suddenly, her professional guard was down and she was instantly happy. "All my babies then, in those days, they are like men and women now." She said this with well-rehearsed, well-deserved pride. "Over a hundred."

"On police force," she said, hammering the frontal consonants in a slow rap, "and school teacher. And politician and commissioner and like that," she said.

"And you brought them into the world," I said, proud of her. She laughed like a girl and clapped her hands. "Yes, that is truth, I did."

Were the midwives helpful to her? "Oh, yes, they were very helpful." This was her first and only concession to traditional medical practice. "They know what to do, but they want to see what the nurse would say. And so they send for the nurse and let the nurse come. But the midwives they did a very good job," she said making her point again. "They learn it from the old ancestors."

"Most of them, the midwives, they now die out." In the sixties the government had begun requiring the signature of a nurse or physician on every birth certificate. "In the late years we have had some card that came from the Commissioner in Nassau that, [for] all babies that was born, we would have to sign this birth card. Now, most of the midwives they could not have signed nothing like that. So they just bring me on to help them, and then I could sign the card." This policy no doubt helped to reduce infant mortality, but it also superannuated a valuable traditional practice, all but eliminating midwifery on the islands. Nurse Rolle knew only one remaining midwife, an old woman who had recently moved to Nassau.

In her years she had helped as many people leave this life as come into it. "Oh, yes, I have seen a lot of them die very bad. But all things pass—trees and people too. I comfort the families and trust in God for all things."

Every other Exuman I met, it seemed, was surnamed Rolle. There's a Rolleville settlement and a Rolletown. Rolle is such a big name in the Exumas, because of the past: slave times. In 1784, at the conclusion of the American War of Independence, Denys Rolle (1720-97), a wealthy Devonshire squire, who owned large estates in Florida, was, like many other wealthy loyalists, granted promisingly fertile lands in the Bahamas. Rolle's lot was four plantations on Great Exuma, totaling 2300 acres. From his Florida estates he transported 150 enslaved people to work this hardscrabble land. The ruins of slave quarters still exist on Exuma.

In time, ownership of the Rolle plantations fell to Denys's son, Lord, John Rolle (1750-1842), a querulous dullard best known for taking a tumble at Queen Victoria's coronation. The Queen noted in her diary that "Poor old Lord Rolle, who is 82 and dreadfully infirm, in attempting to ascend the steps fell and rolled quite down, but was not the least hurt; when he attempted to re-ascend them I got up and advanced to the end of the steps in order to prevent another fall." Richard Harris Barham's doggerel paean "Mr. Barney Maguire's Account of the Coronation," versifies Rolle's roll.

Then the trumpets braying, and the organ playing
And the sweet trombones, with their silver tones

> *But Lord Rolle was rolling; t'was mighty consoling*
> *To think his Lordship did not break his bones*

As I've mentioned before, the geology of these islands isn't suitable for plantations. By the time they came under Lord Rolle's ownership, the cotton fields were already failing. This meant that the Rolle slaves had far more time to devote to family life and the cultivation of their own land, to fishing and hunting. The Rolle slaves were only nominally property now; they were what Craton and Saunders call "proto-peasants."

Given a rare degree of autonomy, nowhere enjoyed by slaves in other parts of the Caribbean, the population of Rolle slaves had increased to 357 by the official end of slavery in 1834. Africans were thriving in the Bahamas. But by 1830 it was apparent that the Rolle plantations—and so the Lord's expectations for steady profit—were inevitably failing, for geological and geographical reasons I described earlier. True slavery was obviously on its way to oblivion. Sensing this, and aware of the loose surveillance and oversight they experienced, they rose up.

Rolle employed several overseers to manage his holding, which was a futile gesture.

The Rolle slaves used benign neglect to grow and strengthen, to feed off the wonderful fish in the waters, to cultivate the vegetables and fruit in their gardens. Ripe mangoes that dropped like mulberries. The sweet and juicy pineapples (effectively banned from US markets today), the starches and breads they enjoyed. Exuman slaves, while nominally slaves, were healthier and more stable than those in the lower Caribbean. The failing agro-economy plus the increase of people he was responsible for feeding and clothing meant that Lord Rolle was losing more and more money. In 1825, he complained that he had lost £500 yearly since 1818. To make matters worse, Lord Rolle attempted to turn a profit from his slaves—supervised by only one agent—by transferring some of them to Trinidad. This was his colossal failure from his point of view; from his "properties'" point of view, in retrospect, it was a blessing in disguise, in that it ignited fire that would—with surprisingly little bloodshed—bring freedom to the ancestors of the free Exumans I had spent the week with.

Rolle's plan to transfer his slaves to Trinidad, where he thought they would be profitably employed, occasioned the most important slave uprising in Bahamian history. Enjoying relative autonomy, the

Exuman slaves refused to allow themselves to be relocated. Adopting a strategy of passive resistance, they simply stopped work altogether. They had reason to think of themselves as free Exumans, after all. Not only did they rightly sense the end of slavery was near, they believed they occupied a special status among slave populations of the Bahamas because Denys Rolle had decreed in his will that his Exuma slaves "should never be sold or separated or otherwise severely dealt with."

News of Rolle's plan to deport them reached the slaves late in 1828. One Sunday afternoon in November, forty-five of them, many armed with muskets, gathered in an area they called "the parade ground" and began firing their weapons in a threatening, paramilitary exercise, led, ultimately, by a 32-year-old slave named Pompey—his classical name indicating, perhaps, that he hadn't been baptized, at which time he would have received a Christian name. Pompey was fierce, brave and determined. The overseer, Thomas Thompson, feared for his life. "I never in my life saw anything to equal it," he wrote. On Monday only a few slaves went to the fields, and on Tuesday night an angry crowd surrounded Thompson's house, protesting that "they want the land to maintain themselves, and they won't be flogged by any white man, neither will they remove from this place."

The outgoing Governor, Lewis Grant, sent a regiment of soldiers to quiet the rebellious slaves. Arriving on December 8, the officer in command, Captain Thomas Ferguson, gathered what slaves he could round up—most had fled into the bush—and heard their grievances.

McPherson reported that the slaves were refusing to work, but that was because of the threats to deport them. He also noted that more than three hundred enslaved people were being overseen by one agent—an impossible task. He recommended establishing a small permanent garrison of soldiers on Exuma to maintain peace. But his recommendation was never implemented. Instead, Rolle's Nassau agent hatched a plan to transport the most troublesome slaves, including their nine leaders, to virtually unpopulated Grand Bahama. His order gave these unfortunate men, women and children only a few days to gather their crops and belongings. Again, the slaves balked, and twenty of them were forcibly taken off the island. Making an example of these twenty only further enraged the remaining Exuman slaves. A second plan to transfer many of the remaining slaves to Cat Island sparked a major uprising.

In response to this outrage, forty-four Exumans seized a boat belonging to Lord Rolle and set sail for Nassau, where they hoped to gain an audience with the sympathetic new Governor Smyth. But Rolle's agent caught up with the fugitives near Harbour Island, tried them as runaways, and most, including breast-feeding mothers, were viciously flogged. When Smyth learned of this treachery, he was appalled and ordered that the captives returned to Exuma. Back home the Exuman adventurers were received as heroes, with much singing and rejoicing. Newly emboldened, the increasingly defiant Rolle slaves again refused to work.

Open rebellion seemed imminent. In response, the sympathetic Smyth sent two ships carrying fifty soldiers to Exuma, arriving at Steventon on June 20, 1830. They rounded up what slaves they could find in the bush. But most of the slaves had dispersed inland to hiding places. Other soldiers were sent overland to another plantation, now Rolleville, five miles north of Steventon. Another slave village. But Pompey escaped from Steventon and ran along the beach to Rolleville, arriving ahead of the soldiers. Alerted to the coming danger, the Rolleville slaves disappeared into the bush.

For this act of defiance, Pompey was given thirty-nine lashes in public, as his friends and family watched.

Subsequent interviews with the enslaved men and women revealed again, however, that they had grounds for thinking themselves free people, and had every reason for resisting deportation as well. With the evidence apparent that the slaves were unjustly treated, and that the government—short of committing to a permanent armed garrison on the island—was hopeless to force slaves to work the Rolle plantations, orders were given for the soldiers to return to Nassau, leaving Exuma to the Exumans.

Pompey's "miniature rebellion," write Craton and Saunders, "was the first substantial victory for Bahamian slave resisters." It sparked uprisings on Cat Island, Eleuthera, Crooked Island, Ragged Island, and even New Providence before August 1, 1834, when slavery was officially abolished, and the Rolles, like slaves throughout these islands and the rest of the Anglo-Caribbean, began their liberation. On that date they became officially apprentices rather than slaves, a transition to full freedom that came on August 1, 1838. Pompey's uprising, like the others, hastened this inevitable outcome. "By 1830," Craton and Saunders conclude, "Out Island slave owners could expect little cooperation from their slaves unless they treated them humanely, gave them generous allotments of land, and issued them their full quotas of food and clothing as provided by the law."

Which brings me back to the surname Rolle. With the abolition of slavery, all of Rolle's former slaves took his surname, which meant that, by law, they were now owners of Rolle's former lands. To this day, in theory, any of the five thousand or so Rolles living in the Bahamas can "claim a house lot or provision grounds on Exuma." However, Craton and Saunders dispel a legend, widespread even today, that Rolle himself was responsible for this distribution of land, having generously deeded his plantations to his slaves in his will. "In fact," they write, "no such deed has ever been traced." They continue: "Rather than giving credit to a querulous and self-serving absentee, it should surely be argued that by their uncooperative behavior and actual resistance the slaves Lord Rolle ostensibly owned virtually won independence and land for themselves—setting a proud example for all Bahamian blacks."

From Steventon I drove north on the Queen's Highway through the Rolleville settlement, a cluster of little pink houses scattered over a hillside, and then west down the escarpment to Alexander where the map showed the end of the road. But it didn't end at Alexander. The road turned north again, carrying across a salt flat and two bridges toward Barattara. The highway was empty here, so I stopped in the middle of the road to pick up a dead boa constrictor and hung it from the rear view mirror. Soon Barattara, the last settlement on Great Exuma, appeared on a rise ahead. It was an isolated village, forlorn in the slanting sun of late afternoon. The street hugged the top of a bluff from which one could see the water and a line of cays trailing off north toward Norman's Cay, Carlos Lehder's former stronghold. At a dock at the bottom of a dead end side street a ferry was loading passengers bound for the Cays. I drove along the main street, drawing stares from old men sitting outside faded buildings and kids on bikes, stopping at the top of a ridge which afforded a 360 degree view from the cays to the east and north, south across the flat and west to the Exuma Bank. I parked the car and walked down the slope to where the Queen's Highway terminated in a paved lot that had been converted to a basketball court. It was empty; someone had painted the image of Michael Jordan, wearing number 23, on the asphalt under the netless rim of the basket in this far, forgotten corner of the Earth. Even here Jordan had his adoring fans who no doubt dreamed of a rich life in far away Chicago the same way that back home I had dreamed of the end of Exuma and a sign that said One Door City.

I had reached the end of the highway, the end of the island. It was an eerily lonely feeling standing on this court in the lengthening shadows, with the wind stiffening out of the east. "I wouldn't want to die here," I said to nobody.

I was much happier on the way back to George Town. Listening to James Brown on the cassette player, driving with the windows open, cool and tired, I dropped off the car at the rental agency and walked back to the Two Turtles. The place seemed vacant. The bar and restaurant were closed. I hadn't eaten all day, so I walked halfway around the lagoon to Tino's, a shotgun shack where the food was reportedly very good. The California girls were there, eating with their well-heeled chaperones. A German couple in their seventies, dressed in matching crisp whites, were drinking and chatting amiably with Tino at the bar. I ordered a drink, and Tino's wife brought out a tumbler nearly full of rum. Then I had another. I ordered a green-turtle steak—I persuaded myself they were farmed-raised—and mashed potatoes. The steak was delicious, the texture of beef and the flavor of oysters, and the heaping mounds of creamy potatoes were the perfect complement. By now the restaurant was noisy, and I was grinning. The California girls laughed and the German couple at the bar issued drinking challenges in the general direction of the diners. Then, above the general din I heard a discordant sound of clacking and a raucous laughter. I turned to see Tino's face plastered with a toothy grin. A plastic wind-up penis, stumpy and pink, was hopping across the bar in front of him. The German couple pointed and howled. On the TV screen above Tino's head a naked woman lay spread-eagle on a beach, the foamy lacework of waves frothing up between her legs filling her crotch. She threw her head back in mock pleasure. Raw Eros, I said to myself, lacking only the entry of Thanatos—the oversized silvery patriarch clutching his chest and falling to the floor, say, to complete the theme.

Back at Two Turtles I walked out to the lagoon and sat down to clear my head. The wind was nearly dead, and the neon-white arc of the quarter moon was shattered on the surface of the water. A chorus of Hallelujahs from the Church of God of Prophecy across the lagoon reached me. I took it as a sign of affirmation, the passion of the singers carrying over the still, quiet lagoon, and the star-fretted canvas of night sky above me. I didn't know where next in the Bahamas I would go—maybe pristine Great Inagua in the south; certainly at some time Great Abaco and Andros—but I knew I would come back to this island nation, these children of the sun, as soon as I could.

The shadow of Thanatos arrived the next morning in the banner headline in *The Nassau Guardian*: WAVES WASH MAN OFF N. ELEUTHERA SPAN; FEARED DEAD. It was a rage at Glass Window, an enormous wave driven up by the same swirling low pressure system that had trapped me in Ft. Lauderdale and yachties all week in their boats on Exuma. The victim, a salesman in his fifties, had gotten out of his car and walked onto the bridge when he was "toppled over" by a wave "70-80 feet high." According to an eyewitness, the man was standing in the road when "one wave came and washed him overboard." Attempting to save the unnamed salesman, I read, police constable 1934 McCoy had miraculously escaped death when "waves of over 50 feet washed him off the bridge." Constable McCoy had been airlifted to Nassau; the salesman's body had not been recovered. Glass Window Bridge had been closed.

The fraternity of salesmen working in North Eleuthera was small, I supposed. Could the victim be Ted Goldsmith whom I had met at Cambridge Villas in Gregory Town the year before? My flight was direct to Ft. Lauderdale, so I would have to wait to find out the name of the corpse that floated in the green water of the Bight of Eleuthera.

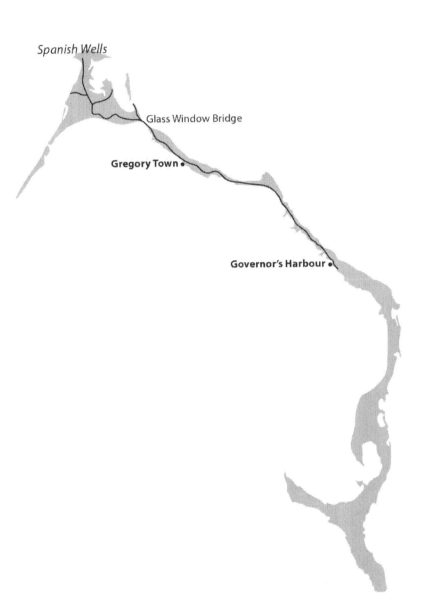

Spanish Wells

Glass Window Bridge

Gregory Town •

Governor's Harbour •

N

ELEUTHERA

Chapter 5
Sam Pedican and the Rage at Glass Window

"One child home, and one to the fold—"

~Camalo McCoy

H IS name was Sam Pedican. He was fifty-five, a salesman, husband, father, brother and a dead mother's son. He lived in the Bluff settlement at the north end of Eleuthera, and on March 12th, 1996, a windy, overcast day of chilly squalls, Sam Pedican set out for Gregory Town, fifteen miles south on the Queen's Highway, a route that would take him over Glass Window bridge. It wasn't a sales trip, something he could postpone until the weather improved. He had to get to Gregory Town to arrange for a coffin to carry his brother who was dying—who, in fact, unknown to Sam Pedican, was already dead—in Nassau. Had Sam Pedican seen the future he would have ordered two coffins.

Pedican parked his truck at the north end of Glass Window and made his way on foot across the bridge in heavy weather, arriving wet and barefooted in Gregory Town some time later. Presumably, he took care of the coffin business; he made some stops around the village, and hitched a ride back to Glass Window. By this time, mid morning, the rain had stopped but the wind was higher. Small groups of people had gathered at both ends of the bridge, their progress blocked by the rage: waves 70 and 80 feet high sweeping in ranks over the bridge. No one was getting across Glass Window.

At about this time Constable Camalo McCoy, a seven-year veteran of the police force, got a call in Lower Bogue six miles north of the bridge. Someone had been washed over in a car. With two fellow officers, McCoy arrived at the north end of the bridge twenty minutes later. Whoever had been washed over was nowhere to be found, but the car was chassis-up in the Bight of Eleuthera on the west side of the bridge. Among those waiting to get across was a tourist from the Midwest who photographed the scene.

Two years later, when a version of this story was posted on the internet, this tourist sent me sequential photographs of the rage crashing into and over Glass Window Bridge. They were enormous.

Another observer was the shoeless Sam Pedican, who was about to make a fatal attempt to cross the bridge between waves.

A year after Sam Pedican died in the rage at Glass Window Bridge, I sat in Constable McCoy's living room at Lower Bogue listening as he remembered that day. McCoy was a robust, muscular man of 27, with close-cropped hair and a broad smiling face that exposed a gap between his front teeth. He had just arrived home from church and was seated on the sofa in his Sunday clothes, sans his tie. His wife Portia sat with us, from another room the cackling admonitions of a televangelist.

"On arrival at the scene," McCoy explained in police talk, "I could see the waves two, three miles away. I, along with the two officers, we went over to the south side of the bridge because that's where the vehicle had gone over, and while on the south side, we met Sam Pedican who wanted to come back over with us. So on the return, coming over, we waited for the waves, because normally you're supposed to wait five minutes to let the waves come in sequence, before they die down.

"So we waited to come back across—the two officers, we all waited together, and I waited for Mr. Pedican. He was moving slowly, looking down at his feet. When the time came to go I held my hand out to him and said, 'Sam, the waves will be coming, we got to run.' But Mr. Pedican kept looking down at his feet. Then he looked up and said something I didn't hear.

So there was a lag in time. We made about ten, eleven strides, and we were smack dab in the middle of the bridge when the wave come and hit us full force. It was the first wave of a sequence, which is normally the biggest one."

I said that the Nassau paper reported the wave was 70 feet high. Was that possible?

"I believe it was higher than that. Maybe a hundred feet. We got tossed up in the air and then dropped down on the slope, on the stones, on the Bight side. I was holding on to the stones after the first wave, and before the second wave hit I saw Mr. Pedican down below me. I reached out to get his hand, and I called him—he was on a rock below me—and I shouted his name, but he didn't answer me. He must have been unconscious. I also looked up and saw the other two officers who was shouting down at me, trying to tell me that another wave was coming. And when I was holding on to the rocks I called on the Lord and asked Him to help me, but this next wave come over and pulled me off that rock"—he showed me his scarred hands where the force of the blow had ripped him from his hold, tearing flesh from his palms and fingers—"and then I got knocked down straight down to the bottom."

"And as I came down I could feel the waves knocking me back and forth between the rocks, the stones hitting my head all that time. I must have been unconscious for, oh, probably five seconds, something like that. After a while, I came to the surface and started swimming away from the current around the point north of the bridge, to get away from the waves. From there I waded into the shore. The waves had tore my jacket off, and some of my pants. The two officers climbed down from the road and helped me get up the rocks. I never saw Sam Pedican again."

Constable McCoy had narrowly escaped death. "In that ordeal I suffered a broken coccyx bone, a chipped spinal cord, injuries to my knee caps and hands, plus numerous superficial injuries."

McCoy was taken first to the clinic in Lower Bogue—Portia was told that he was dead—and then air-lifted to Nassau where he spent a week and a half recuperating in the hospital. The next day, Tuesday, Sam Pedican's body was found floating face up south of the bridge near a small outcropping called Goulding Cay visible from the highway. He was naked.

The experience left McCoy with a dread of the bridge: "Even now, every time I reach that certain spot on the bridge and have to slow down, something in the back of my mind say that wave is going to come again and knock me over." It also made a Christian of Camalo McCoy. Before I left, he unfolded a sheet of paper and read me a

poem he'd written one restless night after the rage that killed Sam
Pedican.

It was a cool and windy Monday morning;
I left home for work a few hours after dawn.
In route to the Glass Window Bridge to render some help,
I never even thought of endangering myself,
I saw a crowd gather as we drew nigh,
The waves looked like they were reaching the sky.
Above the roaring waves and the air full of mist
I saw the gentleman we needed to assist;
My two comrades ran across the bridge quickly
As I waited for the man who had stopped suddenly.
He was saying something that I could not understand.
He then looked up at the sky and I reached for his hand;
I then heard a rushing wave, and the last thing I could see
Was a huge white wave crashing down on me.
I was afraid, I did not know what to do.
I felt I would never make it through.
My heart trembled with a fear that I could not confine,
My mama always told me that God is by my side.
I never thought that I would make it,
After being dragged and knocked about with rocks.
I heard someone say it was only good luck,
But I called on the Lord. Oh, there is power in that name
And from that day on my life is not the same.
On that day He took one child home, and brought one to the fold,
He gave me a new life, and for Him I am bold.
Only God knew that I would make it that day.
What the future holds, no man can say,
For each of us God has a master plan;
You may run like Jonah, but you can't shun His hand.
God, He has seen what we all do.
When I was in sin, He saw me too.
He could have left me there to die,
Or even let the waves pass by.
God used the swelling tide to show me I cannot hide.
God could have done anything He wanted to do,
He let me live so, that I can tell you
He let me fall and fixed me back upright

And wrote my name in the large Book of Life.
I will keep holding, to Him I will hold strong,
Because it is my God that keeps me living on.
We can always make it through this life one way,
And not have to go through what I did that day.
God is willing if we only be faithful and true.
He brought me out of the waves, and he'll do the same for you.
We can all make it, and make it we will.
There is love in Jesus Christ; find Him and get your fill.
In all things put Christ first, I say
And whatever the trial may be, we will make it His way.

So many years later, and after so much coarsening of life in these islands, it's Constable McCoy's words I look back to as the voice of the Bahamas: doing his job, daring to help, believing, learning so much that he wrote a poem in the middle of the night.

Still under the spell of McCoy's account of the drowning of Sam Pedican, I left the McCoys to their Sunday routine, and drove north from Lower Bogue along the Queen's Highway past the airport road to Harbour Island, turning left on the road to the Bluff. I drove past the rock pillar where three years before Conrad Neumann, Paul Hearty and I had encountered the Jehovah's Witnesses, and on into narrow main street of the Bluff, stopping to ask the first person I saw where Sam Pedican's widow lived.

"The blue house just there behind the church," said the toothless old man from under his ball cap.

I turned and turned along the narrow streets, all the while in sight of Pedican's house but ended up at the public dock. I doubled back and parked at the church and walked to the neat, royal blue house where Sam Pedican's widow lived.

Pedican's daughter Madeline, 20, beautiful, barefooted, wearing a simple blue shift, answered my knock. I was so taken by this lovely girl that I stumbled over my well-rehearsed greeting.

"My mama's not here," she said, "she's in Nassau, visiting."

"Well, I wanted to talk to someone about her husband's death. I'm an American, and I want to write his story, how he died."

"He died in the water," she said. Inside the house I could see a young man—her boyfriend?—sprawled on the sofa in front of the TV. He was watching the NBA playoffs.

"Well, would you talk to me?" I asked. "I know you loved him very much."

"Yes."

"Could you tell me how he died?"

"He died in the rage last year," she replied flatly. "His brother died the same day."

"Really?"

"Yes." She closed the white door behind her and looked down at the ground. I remembered McCoy's poem where, seconds before he died, Sam looked down at his feet. Was she saddened, I wondered, or did the Pedicans have a familial habit of staring at the ground.

"Daddy was just coming back over from Gregory Town that morning where he went to get my uncle's casket, and when he was coming back over the bridge, the wave washed him into the ocean. That was Monday. They found him Tuesday, and brought him back up here in a body bag."

Her lower lip quivered and her eyes suddenly welled with tears, and once again I felt wretched for having invaded someone's life for my own selfish reasons.

"I'm sorry," I said, and touched her bare shoulder. She tolerated my hand briefly, until I realized I'd made a mistake and withdrew. I asked where her mother had been at the time of Sam Pedican's death.

"Moma been in Nassau then. She was sick in the hospital with stroke blood." My touching Madeline's shoulder had, it now seemed, softened her a bit. She wiped her tears with her finger and went on.

"I was there with her too, at the hospital, when my sister-in-law called and asked to speak to me. She said to me, 'Your papa gone down in the ocean. Your daddy gone. No more daddy.' Well, I had to be so brave because mama was so sick. I went into the bathroom and cried."

She was beautiful, her full lips and dark eyes and lovely breasts outlined by her shift, especially in this sad moment, crying in the hot shade under the afternoon sun. She wiped her tears again.

"They found him naked by the rocks. The waves had torn all my daddy's clothes off him. And they brought him back here in a bag."

I asked if she had any photographs of her father.

"Yes, we kept them."

She came back with a photo album opened to double pages of Sam Pedican lying in his coffin. The image was unforgettable: a barrel-chested man in gray pin-striped suit seemingly squeezed into the white silk lining of the body box, his hands folded just above his crotch, his eyes and mouth drawn tight toward the corners of his puffy face, his oval head covered with tight pills of white hair. Sam Pedican looked like a dead man, not like someone at rest. I assumed the day he spent in the water, not a mortician's clumsy work, accounted for the ghastly distortions of his appearance.

I asked where her father was buried and, half-sickened by the heat and the sight of this lovely girl holding images of her starkly dead father, I offered my condolences to Madeline Pedican and said good-bye. Following her directions, I drove past St. Paul's Anglican Church where Pedican's brother is buried in the public cemetery at the end of the street where Sam reposes. Circled by a white cement wall waist high, the cemetery was overrun with dry weeds and vines. A pile of rubble stood beside an empty grave, freshly dug. Sam rested under a concrete slab near one corner.

I'd come a thousand miles to find Sam Pedican, and now that I'd found him, I wanted to know why he had been barefooted coming back over the bridge. It was what had killed him, that lag time McCoy spoke of, the looking down at his feet. But Sam Pedican was silent under that concrete slab blazing hot white in the sun.

Just as I was leaving, Sam Pedican, Jr., the dead man's son, pulled up in a huge Oldsmobile. We talked for a while and he told me that he had a copy of the video tape shot by the tourist who had been at the bridge the morning his father was killed. But he'd lent it out. It clearly showed, he said, his father and Constable McCoy being washed over. The tape had been shown on TV stations in south Florida. I gave Sam Junior my mailing address in the States and offered to pay COD for the tape if he would send it. He promised but I doubted, correctly, that I would ever see that tape.

On the way back to Gregory Town I turned north on to Whale Point Road in search of Marvin Gardens and Neumann's Pool, places we'd discovered along the cliffs during my last visit to Eleuthera. I passed a house I didn't remember from before set on a flat slab cut out of the limestone at the top of a ridge a couple of hundred feet back from the cliff line. A fierce dog roaming the front of the house snarled and growled as I drove by. That house, I thought, was in exactly the right place to be blown away by a storm, its owner courting disaster.

Farther along I came to an embankment that looked like the place we had climbed before to make it out to the cliffs. I parked and climbed up through the sea grapes and past termite mounds out onto the moon rock. It was four o'clock, cloudless, the air filled with a fine mist from the spray that, filtering the slanting rays of the sun, cast a thin patina of rainbow over the scene. I walked to the cliff edge and looked down at the waves thundering against the wall seventy feet below me. Startled, I stepped back from the ledge and nearly tripped over a blade of limestone behind me. Only the sure grip of my new hiking shoes saved me from serious injury falling on the rocks or worse—a tumble over the cliff into the ocean. Moving north, I gave the cliff edge a wide berth as I searched the western escarpment unsuccessfully for the rhizomorph I had found three years before.

Two hundred yards farther along, I heard the ocean thundering loudly, too loudly this far back from the cliff. With every step I took the thundering intensified. Another twenty yards along I saw a jagged-edged depression in the rock ahead of me. The noise was deafening. I stooped and crept along, my heart pounding, to the edge of the trough. I peered over the rim into a hole wide enough to swallow a large man's body. As my eyes adjusted to the darkness of the hole, I saw a tumult of white water crashing and frothing far below me. The ocean had eaten a narrow tunnel into the base of the cliff here over hundreds of years of wave action. This hole, lying in wait to drop the unwary walker to a sudden and terrifying death, was graphic evidence of what Stephen Jay Gould—who did his earliest work in the Bahamas—called "deep time." Eons ago, it had been a blow hole. Now it was a death trap.

Another two hundred yards I topped a ridge and looked down at Neumann's Pool. It was just as placid and inviting as I remembered, with the waves periodically cresting above the lip and flooding the pool. I thought how much Conrad would enjoy seeing this place again, remembering that wave that caught him, laughing, from behind and sent him tumbling butt and heels over head, his white hat surfing toward the pool's edge. I made my way down to Neumann's Pool, but I wasn't tempted into the water this time. When I sat down for a moment looking out on a scene I had witnessed several years ago, I was anxious at being alone out here. I wanted no more of Neumann's Pool or Marvin Gardens or any of the Whale Point Road cliffs.

I wanted to get out of here alive, as quickly as possible.

On the way back to Gregory Town I pulled off the highway on the south side of Glass Window, walked back up the road to the bridge and climbed the rocks up to the cliff top on the east side, where someone had cemented the wheel cover to a Cadillac into a boulder the size of a Volkswagen Beetle, and looked down into the gorge beneath the bridge. Far out, the ocean appeared flat but close in the swells heaved up against the stubby platform of rock beneath the bridge, were sucked back out, exposing more of the rock face, and heaved into the wall again. On the other side of the bridge, the Bight was flat and calm. I climbed back down, crossed the road and made my way down to the base of the bridge. I climbed north over the strewn-about boulders where Sam Pedican had died, until I was standing on twenty yards of limestone directly beneath the bridge. I looked up at the underside of the span; its steel reinforcing rods, snapped and twisted, jutted out from the sides like the whiskers of a giant mangy cat, evidence of the damage done when a rage struck Glass Window on Halloween day, 1991, and shifted the entire bridge seven feet to the west. I stood in the middle of this flat-top rock and thought, if I took a few steps east I could dive into the Atlantic; a few steps west I could jump into the Bight of Eleuthera.

But I did neither, and didn't stay long. I had a bad case of the creeps.

It was still daylight when I got back to Cambridge Villas. I drained a tall glass of rum, collected my snorkeling gear and walked north out of town along the Queen's Highway, taking a left on the Road to Paradise, a half-mile dirt track overhung with hibiscus and banana trees that led out to an empty, smooth-stoned beach. Along the way I spooked a Bahamian boa that slithered off into the bush a few feet in front of me. Just before the beach the track rose up a small but steep hill and past an abandoned house which had been ruined by hurricane Andrew. Coconut palms had scattered fruit all over the grounds, and there were rusted chairs and a washing machine lying about. This was a shame. The ruined house afforded a wonderful view of the cove, especially at this time of the day, with the declining sun glinting off its three remaining window panes. You could probably buy this lot on the Road to Paradise for the proverbial song, I said to myself, sink fifteen grand into restoring the house and have a magnificent place to retire.

I put on my fins and mask and walked backwards into the warm water. Fifteen yards out, the bottom dropped off and I snorkeled west along the ledge almost to the point and back in pretty deep water. On the way back I paused over a huge lurking grouper beneath the ledge. I was tired and unambitious, floating effortlessly face down in the water, mesmerized by the small coral heads and fish and swaying sea fans that passed beneath me.

Back at Cambridge Villas I feasted on cracked conch and mashed potatoes in the restaurant, and went upstairs for a snooze. Well into the night, I woke up and walked downstairs to the bar, refreshed, joining Mr. and Mrs. Cambridge who were talking among friends.

Soon the conversation turned to Sam Pedican. I recounted my interviews with Camalo McCoy and Madeline Pedican, mentioning my surprise that Sam Pedican had attempted to cross Glass Window barefooted. That terrible image had haunted me all day. As my drink arrived, someone tapped me on the shoulder—a young man with a finely sculpted face, soft curly hair and a single gold stud in his ear— and whispered that he had been one of the people who had found Sam Pedican's body. By now, the conversation was developing faster than I could keep track of and I turned back to Mrs. Cambridge who was talking about Sam Pedican being barefooted.

"Why is it you think, Marvin Hunt," she was saying, "why you think Sam Pedican show up here in Gregory Town without his shoes? He come right in here that morning without his shoes. Now, why you think he come here that way?"

I didn't have an answer.

"Well, Marvin Hunt, I'll tell you why that stupid man come over here barefooted." She stood with her arms akimbo, a towel over her shoulder, and lectured me. "He come to Gregory Town that way because he got washed over that bridge coming down here that morning. That's why he's dead, the only reason why he's dead."

"Do you mean that Sam Pedican got washed off Glass Window twice in one day!"

"That's just right what I mean," she said.

"That's it" I said, clueing in. "He lost his shoes when he was washed over the bridge the first time coming down from The Bluff. Why didn't someone tell me this? Probably cut his feet climbing back up top, lucky to be alive. Yeah, I'll bet that's what happened."

"That be a good bet, Marvin Hunt."

"No wonder he couldn't keep up with McCoy," I said. "No wonder he was looking at his feet." And McCoy's poem mentions that Pedican said something that he, McCoy, couldn't understand just before they ran, or rather tried to run. Probably said he couldn't run because his feet were cut to pieces. I shook my head and said "Poor stiff." It hung in the air while Bernard Lowell, retired from the Bahamian telephone company and bearing a striking resemblance to another Bahamian, the actor Sidney Poitier, nodded and wiped his face. Harcourt Cambridge sitting beside me smiled at the floor.

"When he showed up here, yeah, his clothes were still damp," he said in a deep weathered voice, stammering a little as he sometimes did.

"I'll be damned," I said. What was old news to them hit me in the head like a wet newspaper. "That's got to be a record. Wiped off Glass Window twice in a single day. Gawddam!"

"You know," Mr. Cambridge went on, "you know, Sam Pedican did some strange things. When they found that man he was naked."

"I know. I heard all about it today. His daughter cried when she told me that they carried him up to The Bluff naked in a body bag. The waves beat his clothes off him."

"That never happened," Mr. Lowell said with quiet authority.

"He wasn't naked when they carried him to the Bluff?"

"No, that's not what I mean. The waves didn't strip Sam Pedican's clothes off."

"That's the Caribbean side over there" he said. "No waves on that side of the island are powerful enough to tear a man's clothes off. No, no," he shook his head slowly side to side, drew a deep breath and sat up in his stool, planting his elbows on the bar. "And besides, where are his clothes? If waves beat them off, something—his shirt, his underwear—something would have been found. But not a stitch of Sam's clothes were found, and somebody would have found his clothes if the waves had beat them off."

"What do you mean?" I asked. "They found none of his clothes?"

"Not a stitch," replied Mr. Lowell.

"But then, where did his clothes get to? He wasn't naked when he went over."

"No, he wasn't." Both men chuckled and looked at Mrs. Cambridge. "No, he had his clothes on when he went over."

"He had only one cut on the back of his head," Mrs. Cambridge interjected, adding to the mystery. "His body wasn't torn up."

I've got to trim back on the pop-skull, I thought, looking befuddled at my half-empty rum and tonic.

Then Mr. Cambridge dropped the other shoe. "Everybody knew," he said under his breath, "that Sam Pedican carry between six and seven thousand dollars on him everywhere he go. Cash money."

I spun around in my barstool and stared at the empty chairs behind me. The dining area was vacant. The young man with the gold stud in his ear had slipped out.

So that, I realized, was the sorry end of Sam Pedican. Whoever found him stole his cash and stripped his body, perhaps to cover the theft or just for meanness' sake. I hoped the full story hadn't, and wouldn't, reach Madeline Pedican's pretty ears.

With no concrete evidence to say that a crime had been committed, what many suspected no one could prove, and the matter had been forgotten until I came along to dig it up. I was shocked. I hadn't thought Eleutherans capable of such treachery, and I understood why people would want to bury the episode.

I realized that I had carried around the tacit, unchallenged assumption that Family Islanders were better than other people, incapable of heartless crimes, even though I knew that drug dealing and other nefarious activities went on in these islands. I had never seen an act of violence in the Bahamas, though I had heard reports of them. Confronted with an ugly reality, I was saddened that these children of the sun were some of them as desperate and greedy and evil as people anywhere.

I was still in a funk the next morning on the drive from Cambridge Villas to the airport at North Eleuthera—at least as far as Glass Window. Approaching from the south, the highway tops a hill lined on both sides with Casuarinas and then drops steeply below the ridge behind the cliff top to the right before rising gently up a long slope. The approach to the bridge is beautiful and menacing, with a slate-colored wall of rock to the east stopping a killer ocean that you can hear but can't see. Below and to the left the sweep of the Bight's electric green water takes the eye ahead down the hill and up over Glass Window bridge and then gently to the left a mile or so out to the point. The sand under the Bight's clear and shallow water is rippled and pale as a shark's belly.

Anyone topping this hill, especially anyone piloting a dubious rental car, is sure to recognize the potential danger of this crossing.

Even if you know nothing about the history of this stretch of road, your instincts tell you to run like hell. So that's just what I did when I crested the hill. I put the pedal to the metal and was half way down the slope when the engine gave off one muffled pop and died. I shifted into neutral and, coasting to top speed at the bottom of the hill, faced the decision whether to pull off the road to the left and slide to a stop in the rubble, or to carry on and hope my momentum would take me up the slope and over the bridge, trusting to the gods that no one would be crossing from the north at the same time.

I aimed the car toward the bridge, losing speed as I drifted up the slope. All the while, as I wrenched the ignition key and feathered the pedal, the engine whined but wouldn't crank. The car rolled up onto the bridge and the ocean came into view. I braced myself and glanced to the right, fearing I would see a wall of water, a rage, bearing down on me. What an ironic end to an untold story that would be. The ultimate victory of Glass Window. In an eerie silence the car crept on across the bridge as I thrust my shoulders forward and back and forward again like a kid on a swing, trying to coax the dusty Buick across.

It came to a stop, its rear wheels still on the bridge. I left the shift in neutral, threw open the door, ran to the back of the car and pushed it off the road on the north side, in the shadow of the rock wall towering in the east.

Heart pounding, stomach turning somersaults, I got back in the car just as Bob Marley was singing "Everything gonna be all right/ Everything gonna be all right. / No woman no cry" on the tape player. I waited a few minutes in the stillness until my breathing returned to normal. I had a plane to catch. Resisting the temptation to try to restart the engine too soon, and flood it again, I waited several more minutes before feathering the gas pedal once and turning the ignition key. The car started on the first try.

Forty-five minutes later, I sat in the co-pilot's seat of a twenty-year-old twin engine Cessna. The pilot, half my age, his crisp white shirt rolled up to show his thick biceps, climbed up the wing and came feet first through the open window. As he settled in and checked his instruments, I looked behind me at the other passengers: three mournful Haitians with stunned looks on their faces and one very large Bahamian woman in a flower-print skirt. It was ten AM; pancakes and

Sanka churned in my stomach like clothes in an overloaded washing machine. Too early in the day for so much trouble and anxiety, I thought. As the engines fired up, I noticed the tachometer for the right prop wasn't working, and the pilot was penciling notches on the throttle housing whose markings had long ago peeled off. I don't need this, I said to myself, I'm too old.

With the engines blowing a concussive wind behind us, we taxied to the end of the runway, swung hard to the right and came to a stop facing the glare of the sun and the full length of asphalt ahead. The pilot brought the engines up to full bore, released the brake, and the plane whined and shook violently as we raced down the runway, giving one final thud as she lifted off and climbed out over the end of the island. Out over the water, the plane dipped once and my breakfast threatened to spew out my mouth as Dunmore Town and Harbour Island come into view. We banked left over the island and climbed into the wild blue yonder.

The Abacos, and a very different set of adventures, lay ahead somewhere in the shimmering water beneath the morning clouds.

N

ABACO

Chapter 6
The Abacos: Loyalist Brogues And the Birth of a Nation

Polonius: *What do you read, my lord.*

Hamlet: *Words, words, words*

Polonius: *What is the matter, my lord?*

Hamlet: *Between who?*

~Hamlet 2.2

"HI" I said.

"Hoi," the old woman replied.

I almost fainted. I had come to the tiny settlement of Cherokee Sound in a remote stretch of Great Abaco after a long drive down from Marsh Harbour, the island's main settlement. I wanted to test a hunch that there might be a connection, long forgotten, between my part of the States, the South, and the people of this island, 60 miles east of Nassau.

In more than a decade living in eastern North Carolina I had been to every village and town along our coast from Corolla in the north to Calabash in the south. You probably recall that I spent summers in my young manhood on the Pamlico River. I knew Ocracoke and Harkers Island, where descendants of the earliest Scots-Irish settlers still speak with a thick brogue—"hoi" for "high," "toide" for "tide," "aout" for "out," "soond" for "sound" and so forth—that closely resembles what I was now hearing in the speech pattern of Suzanne Pinder, the woman who had greeted me at the door of her small white home with green trim just back from the beach in Cherokee Sound.

The name itself, Cherokee Sound, had piqued my interest. I doubted that "Cherokee" was a corruption of "Cherry Cay" ("cay" as "key"), which has been suggested, simply because the settlement isn't a cay. And cherries aren't indigenous to the Bahamas. So the spelling "Cherokee," the same as the Indian tribe that still inhabits the western part of North Carolina, seemed not coincidental. I knew, of course, that the Bahamian islands were consolation prizes for the wealthy, landed losers of the American Revolution. How, I wondered, did this settlement get the name Cherokee Sound? Was there a connection between the tribe of Indians that inhabited western North Carolina at the time of the Loyalist diaspora and this remote settlement fifteen hundred miles to the southeast?

A bulwark of the northern range of the Bahamian archipelago, Abaco was easy to reach with eighteenth-century sailing vessels. The pirates favored it. And so did Loyalists, who descended upon Abaco from all parts of the east coast of America at the end of the War. There are a half-dozen loyalist settlements on Abaco, all of them better known than Cherokee Sound—Hope Town on Elbow Cay (settled by South Carolinians) and New Plymouth on Green Turtle Cay (settled by New York refugees) among them. Just minutes from mainland Abaco, both are major tourist destinations. But I was intrigued by Cherokee Sound, where for more than ten generations the villagers built and sailed their distinctive single-masted wooden "smack boats," living almost entirely off the sea.

Suzanne Pinder, eighty years old, stooped, her blue eyes milky from cataracts, was saying "hoi" again in what seemed to me the same Scots-Irish accent I knew from once isolated communities in extreme eastern and western North Carolina.

Mrs. Pinder—Pinder or Pender is a common name in eastern North Carolina today; there is even a Pender County—invited me into her tidy living room whose walls were lined with photographs of children and grandchildren, its low central table and a corner curio filled with mementos gleaned from eight decades of life in this tiny settlement of 167 people, almost all Caucasians. Her husband, Whitney, was lounging on the sofa, a copy of "The Upper Room," a daily Methodist guide to prayer and meditation, lying beside him. At eighty-six, Whitney was still a large man, with wispy white hair, a perpetual smile, and pale skin covered with crusty lesions, the legacy of a lifetime spent in the sun.

It immediately occurred to me that I should record Suzanne and Whitney. My friend and colleague, the socio-linguist Walt Wolfram, specialized in the brogues of eastern North Carolina. If I recorded the Pinders, Walt could analyze their dialect and speech patterns. Perhaps the dialectical similarities I was hearing pointed to a common ancestry, dating to the period of the American Revolution when, with the defeat of Cornwallis at Yorktown in 1781, Loyalists were granted large tracts of land in the Bahamian Islands.

The Colonial migration patterns of the Scots-Irish down from the middle colonies was two pronged. One branch spread down the spine of the Appalachians. The other came down the coastal regions, settling in islands like Smith and Tangiers in the Chesapeake, and Ocracoke and Harkers in North Carolina. Historically, hardscrabble mountain villages and windblown coastal communities go back to the same origin, so west and east share many dialectical characteristics.

I hit the "play" button and the tape began to wind. As I chatted with Suzanne and Whitney, I tried to nudge the conversation so that one or the other might say "sound" and "tide" and "high" and so forth. We talked of the decline of boat-building and of hurricanes and Whitney's building this house with his own hands at their marriage fifty-six years ago. I asked how Cherokee Sound got its name. They didn't know. I asked where their ancestors had come from.

"Well, from your country," said Mrs. Pinder softly. "The United States."

"Where in the States, do you know?"

"No, I don't know where they came from, what part of the country exactly. But it was a long time ago, in the depression after your Civil War."

I wondered how anyone, even in this remote settlement, could mistake the Civil War for the Revolutionary War. Later in the conversation I realized that Suzanne Pinder wasn't confused at all, but white Abaconians had a very different perspective on the events of 1776-1785. For modern Americans steeped in the glories of the

Jeffersonian revolution, the War of Independence pitted a nation struggling to be born against a tyrannical foreign power, the New World versus the Old World. But for Loyalists it *was* a civil war, one that pitted neighbor against neighbor, father against son, in the struggle for the character and soul of the nation. For Abaconian Loyalists, like Southerners after the Civil War, a legacy of loss had shaped their view of history. Their ancestors had been dispossessed, displaced, hounded, vilified, maimed and killed by the victorious militias of the United States, formerly their countrymen, in the aftermath of Cornwallis's loss at Yorktown. Persecuted, despised, they fled *en masse* from New York and Charleston and East Florida, then to parts of the Out Islands, where they settled in, lived and died, generation succeeding generation, all the time maintaining their allegiance to England.

With these early settlers might have come a number of Indians, who had sided with the Loyalists. I was hoping that the name reflected a connection between the founding of this settlement and Cherokee Indians who migrated south with the White Loyalists.

Just before I left I asked Suzanne Pinder for her maiden name.

"Pinder," she replied without a trace of drollery. "I been a Pinder since I was born."

Owing to their isolation, some degree of inbreeding was common in the Loyalist communities of Abaco in earlier times. Proud and separatist by nature, they were loathe to miscegenate and so developed, it's been reported, a variety of curious and rare physical and mental aberrations as a result of marrying close relatives. Widespread jokes play upon the alleged dimwittedness of Bahamian Loyalists. One has a Cherokee Sounder warning his neighbors that when the road to the settlement was completed, strangers would come to rob the women and rape the men. Another tells of a man who, taking the mail boat home from Nassau, packed a block of ice in his suitcase to give to his girlfriend. Arriving home, he became enraged and accused the crew of stealing his ice and soaking his clothes.

There is also documentary evidence—some of it admittedly biased and anecdotal—to support the belief that genetic deformities resulting from inbreeding have occurred in the loyalist communities of the Bahamas. In 1905, the Baltimore Geologic Society published the results of an expedition which undertook the first comprehensive survey of life in the Bahamas. Under the heading "Degeneracy" the authors reported that "Individuals who had evidently reverted to conditions both physically and mentally lower than that of their immediate ancestors, were frequently met with throughout the Bahamas; but there were two settlements where these conditions seemed particularly well marked." Those settlements were Spanish Wells off the coast of Eleuthera and Hope Town on Elbow Cay, south of Great Abaco. On Spanish Wells they noted "that the acumen of many of the inhabitants was rather low"; they documented abnormally large percentages of "locomotor ataxia, and eye diseases, including cataracts, pingueculae and pterygium-growths"; and they interviewed a sixty-nine-year-old dwarf woman. At Hope Town, the Geographic Society traced the lineage of the widow Wyannie Malone, "a Tory sympathizer [who] not wishing to remain in the United States after the close of the Revolutionary War, changed her residence from Charleston, South Carolina to Hopetown." She brought with her no husband but four children. Her daughter, Sarah, perhaps sensing what was to develop, soon ran off with a whaler and was never heard of again, but Wyannie's three sons took wives from other loyalist settlements and remained on Elbow Cay. The Society reported that from Wyannie Malone's three sons descended several healthy generations of people but that, owing to the close intermarriage of only four families—Malone, Russell, Albury and Key—high instances of malformed and dimwitted offspring began to appear in the population of Hope Town. The degeneracy culminated in the presence of "five idiots" in one generation of the Sawyer family, it reported. The mother of two other other girls "seemed to be a sensible individual, in spite of the harrowing fact that so many of her children were born idiots." Two of the four children of William and Elizabeth Albury were found to be deaf mutes. Benjamin C. Malone, one of Wyannie's boys, "was another congenital idiot" who was also cursed with "flaccid paralysis of the left arm and hydrocele of the scrotum."

Needless to say, the present descendants of Wyannie Malone in Hope Town reject out of hand any claim that the Malones are subject to higher than normal genetic disorders. The day before going to Cherokee Sound, I had visited Hope Town and spoken to Vernon Malone, 60, the grandson six times removed from Wyannie Malone, at the Upper Crust Bakery on a narrow street in the center of Hope Town.

"That's rot, simple rot," said Malone in reference to the Baltimore report. "Mere words." A wiry man wearing an apron, his hands covered with dough, Malone had taken time out from baking savory loaves of bread to talk to me. His speech, which tended to flatten vowel sounds the way New Englanders do, in no way resembled the speech of Suzanne and Whitney Pinder, suggesting that the two populations came from very different regions of eighteenth-century America.

"Those people from Baltimore," he said, "came here with an agenda. They came to find something wrong with us, and they found it. No surprise there. None at all. They ignored the fact that the people from Hope Town regularly married people from Harbour Island—and other settlements too—so that they weren't marrying their close kin at all. That's just rot."

Remembering that Wyannie Malone had come to Abaco with only her children, I asked what became of her husband.

"Nobody knows for certain, but we think her husband had been killed by the militia in the States. She was from Charleston in Carolina, and when she first came to Abaco she settled over at Carlton on Treasure Cay—that was the first Loyalist settlement—then she came here to Hope Town. Everybody—all the natives, that is—on these cays come down the generations from her sons."

Vernon, who had spent all but eighteen months of his sixty years on Elbow Cay, introduced me to his twenty-something son, Brian. A drop-dead handsome man six feet tall with fine brown hair and piercing blue eyes, deeply tanned, wearing a salmon colored tee shirt, shorts, and Top Siders, Brian showed no signs of genetic corruption. But he did complain of "losing everything Bahamian" with the influx of tourists to Hope Town, and of incidents of rudeness in his father's bakery.

"Last winter," Vernon interrupted, "we had people pushing and shoving here in this shop. This very shop. I'd never seen anything like it since I opened this place in 1962. Too many people—and some of them are the wrong kind."

Brian added: "At least we got rid of the damned jet skis. That was the worst problem, buzzing boats, crashing into each other in the harbor."

I asked Brian if he too wanted to remain in Hope Town all his life.

"Well, I can't say that I will. But I'm still here. For somebody my age, or anybody under thirty, it can be hard living here all the time. You get 'rock fever,' and you just gotta get off this cay for a while. I deliver yachts between here and Florida, so I get to travel some, and that makes it easier. And I went to high school in Annandale, Virginia. And I lived for a while in Princeton, New Jersey."

"Going to school?" I asked.

"No, chasing a tourist."

"Let me guess: a girl."

"Right. But I learned my lesson. Let them come to me. Don't follow them. That's my rule."

After leaving Suzanne and Whitney Pinder to their Bible study, I walked out to the end of the long dock at Cherokee Sound with dark squall clouds gathering in the south, sat down and read a pamphlet a friend had given me that morning in Marsh Harbour. Written by Patrick J. Bethel, a prominent Abaconian I hoped to meet later in the week, it was called "Growing Up in Cherokee, 1935-50." It answered some of my questions about the history of the settlement. Mr. Bethel had "no doubt" that Cherokee Sound was founded by Colonel Thomas Brown who commanded a battalion of King's Rangers first in the Carolinas and later in East Florida. "The King's representative to the Cherokee Indians," Brown had taken at least one Cherokee, a woman, with him in his flight from the Carolinas to St. Augustine some time after 1781 and before 1783 when the Spaniards, then in control of East Florida, gave the Loyalists eighteen months to convert to Catholicism or leave. Brown and several hundred followers sailed the Straits of Florida, passed through the Northwest Providence Channel, rounded Hole-in-the-Wall at the southeast tip of Abaco, and sailing north, stopped in the first "reef harbour suitable for small vessels" they came to. Brown presumably named the settlement he founded after the Indian or Indians he brought with him, Bethel reports, but he didn't stay long in Cherokee Sound. Finding the location difficult, he moved to one of the southern islands, leaving several hundred Scotch-Irish settlers and at least one Indian woman of childbearing years behind.

I left Cherokee Sound just after noon believing that I had found a cultural and linguistic connection between North Carolina and Abaco. The early settlers of Cherokee Sound came from the western mountains rather than the Outer Banks. The similarities between the brogues of Cherokee Sound on Abaco and North Carolina's mountains and barrier islands might indicate how widespread these linguistic commonalties were at the time of the Revolution.

From Cherokee Sound I drove back to the Great Abaco Highway and turned south toward Sandy Point, the last settlement on the island, at its extreme southwest corner an hour south of Cherokee Sound. In forty miles, I passed one roadside bar at the entrance to a fishing resort, two cars traveling in the opposite direction, and a rusted crane near Crossing Rock. The road seemed to take you down some enormous, very hot throat. Though I had the windows down and the wind was whistling through the cab, I felt anxious and claustrophobic, as if the landscape were swallowing me.

Yet the landscape was familiar. Here was none of the usual Bahamian scrub brush, no Casuarina pines, only one fleeting view of the water to the right in the entire drive to Sandy Point. Instead, the road was lined on both sides by vast, unbroken forests of young pines like you see in the eastern Carolinas, tall, skinny trees whose acidic needles prevented a dense undergrowth from developing. Unknown in islands to the south, these piney woods are evidence of fresh water, a compelling attraction to early settlers of Abaco. Along several stretches of the road, stands of pines bore scorched trunks where lightning-sparked wildfires had raced through so fast that the trees weren't consumed. And above in the brightening sky, turkey vultures, one of the most common birds of the Carolinas, wheeled and soared on thermals high over carrion.

Just before Sandy Point the road turned sharply to the right and the emerald waters of south Abaco came into view, just below tire level, it seemed, as the road hugged the water line for another mile into the village. I drove down the main street at five mph, passing one very neat house at the edge of the settlement, and then a line of shanties and the police station and the school to the end of the road. I stopped the car on the last inch of the Great Abaco Highway in the shade of a coconut grove. Ten yards ahead was the white sand beach and the green water as far as I could see. Nine miles off shore, out of sight, was Gorda Cay.

Conch boats were coming in with the morning's catch. I kicked off my sandals and walked up the beach, around the point, to where a young black man was unloading conchs. His stomach was hurting, he said; I presumed from the depths he'd had to dive to gather his catch. The conchs squirmed and banged about the fiberglass hull of the boat, using their obscenely slick, tongue-like foot, or operculum, to flail themselves about the boat.

I walked back south around the point—six feet from the water, at the top of the beach, spiny clumps of prickly pear grew alongside the sea grapes under the palms—to the car. It was now cloudless and hot as Hades. The cool water, with the current running around the point into the harbor, was irresistible. I put on my snorkeling gear (Italian-made fins I had bought that morning in Marsh Harbour) and slipped into the sea. Twenty yards out I caught the current and floated face down around the point into the harbor. In deeper water there was little aquatic life to see, only a few fish, no coral, but in closer I came upon schools of yellowtail snappers and small angel fish, especially at the end of streets where concrete slabs had fallen in the water creating a shelter for the fish.

The sudden thought of sharks startled me, and I looked back out into the darkness of the deeper water, imagining that a bull or hammerhead lurked just out of my vision, his eyes on me. That was enough.

I came ashore near a dock where local conchers were preparing their catch for transport to restaurants in Marsh Harbour and Treasure Cay. They were all men but not all black men. Some were freckle-faced with tawny skin. And walking back along short streets to the car I saw other people of a similar hue, men and women sitting on porches who waved and said hi to this lone white man in a bathing suit, carrying fins and snorkel.

They might be the descendents of Cherokee Indians, I thought, who interbred with Africans in the distant Abaconian past. The white population was clustered in the central section of the island, in Marsh Harbour, Treasure Cay and the outlying cays. Below Cherokee Sound I hadn't seen a single Caucasian, except myself in the side view mirror. I knew, also, that the settlements north of Treasure Cay were entirely black—"Black Abaco," someone had called the area of northern Great and Little Abaco, referring to Cooperstown, Cedar Harbour, Mount Hope and Crown Haven, places I would visit later in the week. The pattern suggested that black slaves—and perhaps that Indian or those Indians at Cherokee Sound—had escaped from their owners in the white communities in the middle of the island and taken shelter in the inaccessible areas of the extreme south and north where they couldn't be retrieved. A similar demographic pattern existed in Exuma. Perhaps here in Sandy Point at the southern end of Abaco black people and Indians had intermarried and produced descendants, some of them strikingly beautiful. It was pure inference, but it did explain the remarkable complexions I passed on the walk back to the car.

But its inhabitants weren't the most outstanding sight in Sandy Point. That dubious distinction belonged to a cluster of industrial-sized trailers and a lot with a half-dozen cars parked in spaces reserved for drivers with their names blocked out on concrete butts. The entire area, which took up a large vacant lot in the middle of the settlement, was surrounded by a chain-link fence ten feet high. I assumed it was a government engineering project, perhaps a new water supply system or microwave tower in progress, but that wasn't it at all. This was the staging area for men and material for the Disney Corporation's transformation of Gorda Cay, just over the horizon southwest of Sandy Point into Castaway Cay, "your own Bahamian island," to serve as a stopover for Disney cruise ships touring the Caribbean.

Every major cruise line owns or leases a piece of the Bahamas, small cays and remote stretches of beach which they convert into private "island paradises." I had always found the practice of selling chunks of the Bahamas to foreign corporations despicably unpatriotic, though I know that foreign interests own prime real estate in US cities, and that, owing to our staggering national debt, China virtually owns the Land of the Free and the Home of the Brave.

But given the history of Gorda Cay, it's probably a good thing that Disney purchased Gorda. During the heyday of drug trafficking in the 1980s, an American, Frank Barber, leased Gorda from the Bahamian government, put in a landing strip, and, in cahoots with other shady operators, ran a major drug transshipment operation from the tiny cay. For several years, while the Bahamian authorities, their palms outstretched behind them, looked the other way, drug money poured like honey into Gorda. Barber's caretaker, hired at a salary of $500 per week, was paid more than a million dollars in eighteen months working for Barber.

When the DEA busted Barber and jailed him in Texas, his operation fell into disarray, a circumstance that was quickly exploited by Sandy Point fishermen and "a renegade boat operator from the ultra-conservative and respectable all-white settlement of Spanish Wells," of all places. For generations Sandy Point fishermen had cultivated land on Gorda Cay and fished its waters. One day, a boatload of them found a hidden cache of drugs on the island and, being an enterprising lot, ransomed the drugs back to the dealers, becoming instantly rich beyond their wildest dreams. But they weren't willing to leave well enough alone. Denied a formal piece of the drug operation on Gorda, a group of them, armed with cutlasses, brazenly hijacked a plane loaded with cocaine and sold the loot for $25,000. Instantly they were hunted men, some of whom lived like kings for a while in Florida "carrying suitcases of cocaine and hundred dollar bills," snorting their stash in a paranoid frenzy.

When Frank Barber was arrested in 1982, Abner Pinder of Spanish Wells purchased the cay and soon more drugs and money than ever were passing through Gorda, with Pinder reportedly taking $1,000 per kilo of coke and $20 per pound of ganja. The operation continued for several more years until the major crackdown of the late eighties. Never formally charged, Pinder—that "renegade boat operator"— retired in splendor to his native Spanish Wells, living openly and without recrimination in "the reputedly law-abiding and God-fearing community."

Early in my preparations for the Abaco trip, I had called up a search engine and typed in Abaco. What came up on the screen were some advertisements for island villas, an on-line edition of the *Abaco Journal*, and the e-mail address of the improbably named Sinclair Frederick of Treasure Cay. I wrote Sinclair, who pinged me back saying that he had passed my name along to Jack Hardy, editor of the *Abaco Journal*, who had included my notice in the next issue of the journal. Within days, names, addresses and phone numbers began to arrive by e-mail. I wrote directly to Jack thanking him for his assistance. "Call when you get here," he wrote back, "I'll show you around. Just now, I'm off to the bone flats for some fishing."

On Maundy Thursday 1967, a bleak day of scudding clouds and a chill wind raking down from the north, the remarkable Jack Hardy finished his teaching duties in the cathedral city of Durham, England, and caught the number ten bus four miles to Eaglescliffe where he changed for the ride home to his flat in Billingham. Waiting for his bus at Eaglescliffe, he picked up the *Times Educational Supplement* and read an advertisement soliciting teachers for the Bahamas. Newly married and sick to death of the "miserable weather" and "sterile life" he was enduring as an English teacher in Durham, Jack, who'd never been out of the British Isles, decided immediately to respond to the ad.

That summer he accepted a position as an English teacher in the Bahamas. In August he was posted to the school in Sandy Point. In thirty years since coming to the Bahamas, Hardy had returned to England on only three occasions, two of those for funerals. Two years later he had become a Bahamian citizen.

On the evening of my trip to Sandy Point, Jack and Valerie invited me to dinner at their home in Murphy Town. We drank rum and ate stuffed grouper baked in lemon-butter sauce, conch fritters, peas and rice, tangy cole slaw, fresh tomatoes from the Hardy garden (itself a wonder to behold), fresh bread and butter, and sweet fried plantains for desert. With us were the Hardy children—son John, teenage daughters Melissa, Vanessa, Serena and Cassandra, a toddler grandchild, as well as a steady stream of in-laws, boyfriends and neighbors who stopped by during the course of the evening.

With a full mane of fine white hair, red-faced with a nose like Peter Sellars', cornflower blue eyes and a deep booming voice, Jack sat at the head of the table and held court amid the din of screen doors slamming shut, clanging dishes, the chatter of girls and the laughing and grunting of the toddler we passed around the table. Sipping rum and Coke, wearing a faded William Butler Yeats t-shirt, smoking like a chimney, Jack covered his early years as the only white man in Sandy Point—"the honkey man in town," his wife Valerie said. He told of the disintegration of his first marriage culminating in his wife's leaving him for a woman; his courtship of Valerie, a former student, and their marriage. He told of children coming, of their reassignment to Ragged Island for several years, and of more children being born, and their return to Abaco where Jack now headed the English department and edited the *Journal*. In addition to being an editor and teacher, Jack was a poet and story writer, as well as being perhaps the best-known gardener in the Bahamas. His column on gardening was a popular weekly feature in the *Nassau Tribune*.

"I'm an icon in my own time," he mockingly announced, folding his arms across his chest, sitting up and trying to look down his nose at me, "an absolute Abaconian icon."

"Say that three times fast," I said, and he couldn't.

Jack and I recited what we could remember through rum-fog of Yeats' poetry, Jack favoring the later mystical works, "Sailing to Byzantium" and "The Second Coming"; I the earlier romantic lyrics "The Lake Isle of Innesfree" and "that lovely poem that begins, 'When you are old and gray and nodding by the fire—' "

I was starting to gush. Too much good food and drink.

"No, listen, Jack, listen, isn't this the most exquisite lyric?" I said, climbing on my soap box. "And it goes, 'and some will. . . some have. . . how does it go, Jack?"

"How the bloody hell should I know how it goes? It's your poem."

"Yes, now I've got it. Here it goes: 'How some have loved your moments of glad glee. / And some have wanted you—no, needed you, no, loved you—with a love floss or true"—I paused to reconvene speech and memory—"But one man loved the pilgrim soul in you / And loved the sorrows of your changing face," ending the stanza with flawless accuracy and great depth of emotion, I thought.

"You do that respectably well," Jack remarked, "for a man dripping mango juice from his chin."

The mangoes were delicious. And Jack was a man after my own heart. I couldn't remember a time when I'd more enjoyed getting to know people, this family gathered around the kitchen table after dinner, the kitchen heavy with the aromas of cooking, the rum flowing, the conversation lively and learned, ranging over topics from British comedy to bone fishing to Irish poetry to cricket to the subtle magic of gardening to computers to local custom and lore.

For a moment I stepped mentally away from the table and observed the microcosmic rainbow coalition. Jack and I were pale skined, Jack's son John black as mahogany, Valerie a light-skinned Sandy Point woman, the Hardy daughters paler and beautiful with lovely complexions, soft hair and gray eyes. Vanessa Hardy reminded me of the actor and singer Vanessa Williams. The beautiful child we passed around was black. Where, I wondered, in this spectrum of color could racism ever gain a foothold? If you were a Hardy you couldn't be prejudiced on the basis of skin color because someone in your immediate family was that color.

It's only in such an environment that you can really talk freely about racism, of course. And yet I had been advised that race and politics were subjects to avoid on Abaco. Friends in Nassau had warned me of Abaconian racism. And I had read an anthropologist's bleak account of race relations on Green Turtle Cay during the early seventies when the Bahamas gained its independence from Britain. I had prepared myself mentally for what I thought might be ugly encounters with people who considered themselves victims of the changing political complexion of the Bahamas.

For most of its history the Bahamas was governed as a Crown Colony by Britain, but for most of the twentieth century it was effectively ruled by a powerful clique of white investors and businessmen collectively known as the Bay Street Boys, after the main street of Nassau where most of the Colony's wealth was concentrated, many of them hailing from Abaco. This was, for the most part, a happy arrangement for white Abaconians who dictated government policy through their political proxies. House of Assembly seats from Abaco, and other Out Islands, were regularly held by Nassau business men who voted in the interests of their constituents. Abaconians went about their lives trusting the powers in Nassau to work on their behalf. But by the 1950s dissatisfaction with the status quo was festering. As tourism grew during the 1960s, Abaconians complained that they sent three times more money collected from import duties to Nassau than they received in services. At the time, there were no paved roads on Abaco, very little electricity and no high school.

Stresses created by the overall inequities in the Bahamian system of representation, moreover, couldn't be endured indefinitely. With the post-war influx of black Family Islanders into Nassau to fill largely menial jobs in the support sectors of the tourist industry, the Bay Street Boys worked to preserve their interests by resisting calls for redistricting that would provide a more equitable representation of the black majority. The white people of the Bahamas, comprising 15% of the population, effectively ruled the 85% of Bahamians who were black or colored.

The status quo was intolerable. In 1953, the Progressive Liberal Party (PLP), a black nationalist party, was formed to challenge the white grip on Bahamian politics. The first political party in Bahamian history, the PLP was modeled after Michael Manley's Popular National Party in Jamaica and took its moral tone from the Southern Christian Leadership Conference. It supported greater government expenditures in health care, education and transportation, the creation of a social security system and the sharp reduction of foreign interests and labor in the Bahamas. Lynden O. Pindling emerged as the PLP's leader.

The Bay Street Boys, whose power was so secure that they hadn't even formed a political party, were caught off guard by the formation of the PLP. For the first time the clique of powerful whites had to deal with a small but influential group of black Bahamians who were committed to politicizing their constituents. As a response to the formation of the PLP, the Bay Street Boys formed their own political party, The United Bahamian Party (UBP) to shore up their power. Yet events of the 50s and 60s served only to strengthen the PLP at the expense of the UBP. The PLP grew steadily as more and more black people, as well as some white Family Islanders who felt themselves betrayed by the power structure in Nassau, joined the party. In 1956, Sir Etienne DuPuch, Editor of the *Nassau Tribune* and a member of the Assembly pushed through an anti-discrimination bill that outlawed segregation in public places. For the first time in Bahamian history the black majority had free access to restaurants, hotels and public transportation.

Two years later, when the government awarded white-owned firms the exclusive rights to ferry passengers between the new international airport and Nassau, the largely black taxi union went on strike, followed by hotel and construction workers, and a general strike that paralyzed the nation's economy ensued. With Pindling and the PLP now a force to be reckoned with, the government withdrew the contract and the strike ended. As a concession, Pindling demanded and got four new Assembly seats in the Nassau district, all of which were taken by PLP candidates. Now the PLP held nine of the thirty-three seats in the Assembly. Clearly, times were changing, a hard rain seemed poised to fall on the white power structure.

White Bahamians were further alarmed in 1962 when women were granted suffrage, a move which doubled the size of the black electorate. Yet the results of the 1962 General Election were disappointing for the PLP. Owing largely to inequities in districting, the PLP won only eight of thirty-three seats while carrying 44% of the vote; the UBP took nineteen seats with only 36% of the vote.

The growing tensions between the hunkered-down UBP and the upstart PLP came to a crisis three years later when Lynden O. Pindling chunked the 165-year-old Mace, a gift from loyalist sympathizers in South Carolina, out the Assembly window. It was the definitive moment in Bahamian political history. To the PLP and its supporters, Pindling's was an act of heroic defiance in the face of a wicked and intransigent minority regime. To the UBP it was an act of cowardly vandalism by a reckless upstart. The lines were clearly drawn now and tensions were running high as the threat of black majority rule in the Bahamas grew through the mid-sixties into an inevitability. In the General Election of 1967 the PLP won eighteen seats, the UBP won eighteen and one independent candidate, reading the handwriting on the wall, sided with the PLP. The UBP had been toppled, Lynden

Pindling became Prime Minister, and the Bahamas for the first time in its history had a black government.

The political developments of 1967 were observed with dismay by loyalist Abaconians. While all three Abaco seats had gone to the UBP in the 1967 General Election, white Abaconians were clearly swimming against the current. As much as they feared black majority rule, they feared even more that Pindling and the PLP would work to gain independence from Great Britain, a move which would betray the deep-seated loyalist sympathies of white Abaconians and subject them to "a racist and incompetent black government in Nassau."

But independence from Britain was exactly what Pindling and the PLP were committed to achieving. Immediately upon taking control of the government, Pindling engineered more redistricting so that by the following year the PLP held twenty nine of thirty eight seats in the House of Assembly. With its power base securely in place, the government instituted its "Bahamianization Plan" which severely restricted the role of foreign capital and labor, expanded educational and health programs and otherwise set about remaking the political and cultural landscape of the Bahamas. All the while the Bahamian economy, built almost entirely on tourism, continued to grow at a robust rate. The healthy economy in turn strengthened the black majority government's hold on political power. It was hard to argue with success.

But while the Bahamas moved toward full independence, Abaconians were not sitting on their hands. They launched a series of serio-comic efforts to secure Abaco's secession from the Bahamas. In 1970 the Greater Abaco Council (GAC) was formed, and in July 1971 the GAC submitted to the British government a petition signed by 75% of the adult population of Abaco endorsing separation from the Bahamas. The following year a new political party, the Free National Movement (FNM), was formed to put up white candidates for seats in Grand Bahama and Abaco. With this new political power base, influential Abaconians would lobby Great Britain to grant Abaco Royal Crown Colony status separate from the Bahamas.

1972 was a watershed year. The GAC had everything at stake in that summer's General Election, which the PLP had called for as a mandate on independence. On Abaco the PLP countered the GAC's efforts by carving out a gerrymandered district consisting of Cooperstown in the north and Dundas Town and Murphy Town, the black suburbs—if that word can be used in reference to a one-stop-light island—of Marsh Harbour. The result was disastrous for the GAC and the FNM. The PLP took both seats on Grand Bahama and the PLP candidate from the Cooperstown district, Scherlin Bootle, defeated the FNM incumbent Leonard Thompson by four votes. The Greater Abaco Council had been defeated, losing three of four coalition seats, even though the FNM had garnered 62% of the popular vote on Abaco.

Even as Pindling issued his White Paper on independence on 18 October 1972, the Greater Abaco Council was petitioning the British government for separate status. It soon disbanded, however, only to be replaced by a new and more radical Council for Free Abaco (CFA), led by Errington Watkins and Chuck Hall, which submitted to the English House of Lords and the House of Commons a petition signed by half the Abaconian electorate asking for Crown Colony status. The petition fell on deaf ears in Britain, however, and the House of Commons passed the Bahamas Independence Bill on 22 May 1973 by a vote of 74 to 4. A devastated Watkins complained that England had betrayed its loyal subjects on Abaco. In a series of speeches delivered in the white settlements of Abaco, he asked, "Why are we who have been so loyal for 200 years trying so hard to stay with them when they fight so hard to kick us out?" He concluded that Abaco had "no other choice at this stage but to go along with an independent Bahamas. I don't mean that we must join the PLP—God forbid—but we must do everything we can to make Abaco a success in an independent Bahamas."

Others were not so quick to concede defeat. If Abaco couldn't achieve separate status through formal channels, then Chuck Hall was willing to pursue other means to break from the Bahamas. He enlisted the support of Mitchell WerBell of Defense Systems International, a Georgia firm that dealt in second-had arms, and Lt. Col. Colin "Mad Mitch" Mitchell, a conservative member of the British House of Commons, to engineer a military-styled revolution. It was alleged that WerBell was recruiting armed mercenaries.

In May 1973, the Abaco Independence Movement (AIM) was formed with the covert purpose of forcibly resisting union with the free Bahamas. AIM pushed to make Abaco a free trade zone, a libertarian paradise, a free-for-all island nation of no taxes and a bare-bones government. AIM founded a newspaper, the *Abaco Independent*, framed a constitution, designed a flag and attempted to purchase, it was rumored, a 90-foot patrol boat and a number of single-engine Italian fighter planes. The revolutionary plan called for rounding up the police force on Abaco, shipping the helpless constables off to Nassau, and simply declaring independence from a fledgling nation that had no standing army, air force or navy, and therefore no ability to reclaim the island.

The revolution, scheduled for 1 January 1975, never happened, of course, and the whole affair took on the character of farce, a couple of swashbucklers allied with a few harebrained ideologues in the effort to create an offshore paradise under the benign protection of Great Britain. It was laughable. In responding to the veiled threats of AIM, Prime Minister Pindling reminded the rebels that half the island's population was black and that a PLP candidate held one of its two seats in the House of Assembly. He also knew that support for an independent Abaco had declined precipitously in the wake of independence, the feared recriminations, confiscations, and oppressions having not taken place, the transition to full independence moving along smoothly, the nation's economy continuing to grow.

As a British citizen, Jack Hardy watched the developments of the late sixties and seventies with anxious detachment. He had no dog in this fight for an independent Abaco, having come to the Bahamas at the invitation of the PLP-led Bahamian government. He had no ties to the loyalist tradition of Abaco either, though as a white British citizen he was probably regarded favorably by the loyalists. Further, since he was not yet a Bahamian citizen, he could in no way directly affect the course of Bahamian politics. Yet, he worked in continual jeopardy during those years. At the end of his annual contract the government might at any time give his position to a Bahamian and deport him, despite the fact that he was married to a Bahamian woman.

"I was nervous, scared what might happen," he said, "but there was really nothing I could do, except keep my head down, cultivate the right kind of friends, stay out of trouble, and do my job well."

The next day at New Plymouth on Green Turtle Cay I sat in on a live, remote radio interview at the Albert Lowe Museum featuring two of the Cay's most senior and revered citizens, eighty-eight-year-old Charlie Lowe, a white descendent of South Carolina loyalists, and seventy-three-year-old Paul Curry, a black man whose ancestors had come from Eleuthera. The two life-long friends huddled around a single microphone in the main room of the museum for the interview conducted by Silbert Mills, owner and principal disc jockey for Radio Abaco, 93.5, "The Sounds of the Abacos," the island's only radio station. I'd met Mills on the ferry over from Treasure Cay, and he'd asked me to join him for the interview.

Mills addressed the men with condescending paternalism, as "Uncle Charlie" and "Pa Paul." His questions were often clumsy— "Uncle Charlie, can you tell us how Green Turtle Cay got its name?"— and he sometimes struggled to come up with the next one. There were problems with the remote feed to start with and then ten-minutes of dead air time in the middle of the interview when the electricity went off. But for all these problems, Mills managed to take the two men back over their long lives, their origins and schooling, years of turtling, sponging and wrecking, shark hunting, logging and boat building. They talked of the pineapple and sisal plantations that once existed on Green Turtle Cay, of the hurricanes and harrowing voyages they endured separately and together. Lowe told of a "Chinaman" who had come to Green Turtle in the fifties to harvest sea cucumber or "sea dog," had grown rich selling and shipping the long, flaccid, penis-like creatures gutted and dried to China where they were a soup delicacy; and had later opened the first Chinese restaurant on Bay Street in Nassau. He is buried in the main cemetery on Green Turtle Cay, which he considered his home.

Lowe was a loquacious man with a thin, almost gaunt face, elephant ears and cloudy blue eyes; Curry, a handsome dark-skinned man with gray eyes and white hair, was taciturn, not good radio material. I admired these two old friends in their Sunday clothes, Lowe wearing a cream-colored shirt buttoned to the top, Curry in a sportier blue pinstriped shirt opened at the neck. The two of them hunched up together at an awkward little table in front of the microphone, sliding it back and forth, forgetting to speak into it and having to be cued up, exchanging nervous glances, speaking in soft, raspy voices. Their accents weren't the same as I had heard in Cherokee Sound or Hope Town. Their speech reminded me of New Englanders, Lowe flattening the "a" in "rather," and saying "aunt" rather than "ant." Curry seemed deferential to Lowe, perhaps owing to Lowe's seniority—Lowe called Curry "Paul" while Curry addressed Lowe as "Mr Charlie"—but they were clearly two men who shared a common past, one less defined by their different races than you'd expect. They had attended the same school, been taught by the same teachers, played on the same vacant lots, fished the same waters. Even though they were brought up in segregated neighborhoods of New Plymouth, they regarded each other with warmth and respect, and clearly always had.

But Lowe depended upon Curry's memory throughout the interview. He often asked Curry for clarification and kept his eyes on him much of the time he was talking. Lowe was difficult to silence once he got started. Mills concluded the interview by asking each of them what he hoped for the future of Green Turtle Cay.

Charlie Lowe took the mike. "I would like for people to be more loving to each other. I think that's why things are what they are today. People have forgotten how to love each other. When I was a boy, on Sunday you could see those plates goin' cross and cross the street to each other. If you had some kind of food, and I had something different, why, we'd exchange those plates." He shook his head. "Now, you don't see those plates going across the street anymore. And that's what I think we've got to get back to, loving each other more than we do now."

He slid the mike over to Paul Curry. "Well, for sure, what Mr. Charlie said is true. And that is what I would like to see. People getting together, and living together here as one. And building Green Turtle Cay as one place, one people."

That afternoon I went to the Hardy's again for drinks. Valerie explained the racial epithet "Conchy Joe," used by blacks to refer to especially loathsome white people, a reverse counterpart of "nigger," only if anything more inflammatory, if that's possible. She speculated that the phrase derived from the early days of the Bahamas when white conchers came in to shore with their mouths foaming, a reaction to the conch's slimy skin which the conchers yanked off with their teeth on the trip in from the sea.

"Use that word in a local bar," Jack warned, "and they'll carry you out on a stretcher."

Drinks not surprisingly carried on into dinner time at the Hardy's and we ordered a very un-Bahamian pizza delivered from Marsh Harbour. I answered the delivery man's knock and was shocked to see Silbert Mills framed in the porch light, his vaguely chic radio outfit replaced by a Pizza Hut uniform, two large pizza boxes perched on his upturned hand.

"Silbert Mills," I said. "My, this is a small world."

That morning I had detected a superciliousness in Silbert's attitude toward me. Now he was standing in front of me playing the role of a servant, a delivery boy. He was keenly embarrassed.

"This is my other job," he said glumly. "It's my franchise, and I have to do the work. $22.50, please." I paid him and Silbert Mills faded into the darkness.

"You'll never believe who delivered the pizza," I said back at the table.

"Probably Silbert Mills," Jack said. "He's doing a lot of his own deliveries these days. Poor thing."

It was a very odd juxtaposition, I said, radio man and delivery boy.

"Odd, indeed," said Jack. It was an apt description of Silbert Mills whose career had been marked by notable ups and downs, booms and busts. "Some years back he was caught flying drugs to Miami," Jack said. "Did two years in prison. Banned from returning to the States. He didn't speak fondly of America in your interview, I suspect."

A stretch in the Big House had done nothing to dampen the entrepreneurial spirit of Silbert Mills.

"Yeah, well, Silbert has friends in high places," Jack said, "which is how he gets franchises and licenses. Nothing like having the right friends if you want to get along in the Bahamas."

I spent the next morning trying futilely to reach Patrick Bethel, author of "Growing up in Cherokee, 1935-1950" at his home in Marsh Harbour. Supposed to return to Abaco early in the week, he was still in Miami receiving treatment for skin cancer. Since I had to leave the next day, I wouldn't get to talk with Bethel, who by all accounts was an extraordinary man, at least not on this trip. It was the major disappointment of the week.

That afternoon I drove north along the Great Abaco Highway past Treasure Cay to explore Black Abaco. South and north of Treasure Cay there were "No Hunting" signs posted along the road. What could you hunt out here, I wondered. The answer: wild boars. Feral hogs roam the nearly impenetrable Abaco bushlands, descendants of animals dropped off on the island by the British navy. It was a common practice throughout the Caribbean hundreds of years ago, meant to insure that food would be available to ships passing through the islands in the future. Now the boars are a source of meat for local people and sport for foreign hunters.

In Cooperstown, the largest settlement in the north, I passed the modest home of Hubert Alexander Ingraham tucked in behind needle-shaped evergreens—Norfolk Island pines—along the main drag. It was from this house in the gerrymandered Copperstown-Dundus-Town-Murphy-Town district that Ingraham launched his remarkable political career. Running as a PLP candidate, Ingraham easily won a seat in the House of Assembly in 1977 and again in 1982, becoming Minister of Housing and National Insurance as one of the rising stars of the PLP. But as the Bahamian economy slumped in the early eighties, and as charges of corruption and involvement in drug trafficking began to taint the Pindling administration, Ingraham emerged as an opposition voice within the PLP. A 1983 NBC report implicating Pindling and several government ministers in a scheme of drug payoffs further alienated Ingraham. With the only viable opposition party, the Free National Movement, calling for Pindling's resignation and a general election, the Prime Minister established a Commission of Inquiry into the matter of drug-dealing and stonewalled the election through 1984, as news of the Inquiry dominated the headlines. At about the same time, late 1984, Pindling dismissed Ingraham, by this time a staunch critic of the Pindling government, from his ministry posts and the following year cashiered him from the PLP.

Undaunted, Ingraham ran as an independent candidate in the 1987 General Election and won easily. The FNM didn't bother putting up anyone to oppose him, and Ingraham defeated the PLP candidate by a margin of two to one.

Clearly, Pindling would have to continue to deal with this bulldog who tormented his government with relentless attacks on its integrity. For the next three years Ingraham was, Dodge reports, "an amazingly effective one-man opposition." In April 1990, the leader of the Free National Movement died a week after Ingraham had given up his independent status and joined the FNM; the next week Ingraham became the party's new leader. Ingraham immediately began crafting a campaign to topple Pindling in the 1992 General Election. The PLP failed to put forward a platform, running instead on its record. The PLP had won every election since 1964 by a smaller margin than the one before, and by 1992 it was more vulnerable than ever. It was clear that Bahamians were ready for a change. On Abaco, long stretches of the main highway were still rubble, many settlements didn't have electricity, and there was no telephone service to much of the island.

Yet Abaco was pouring $25 million annually into the national treasury. Abaconians were being shortchanged.

When the election was held on 19 August 1992, the FNM culled nearly 56% of the vote to 44% for the PLP. Hubert Ingraham had won the election by a landslide. Pindling announced that "the people have spoken, and the voice of the people is the voice of God." Ingraham held his position as Prime Minister from 1992 until 2002 when he was defeated by the PLP candidate, Perry Christy, but won again in 2007. He's still, as I write this, the Prime Minister of the Bahamas.

Driving past Hubert Ingraham's house in Cooperstown the irony that the current Prime Minister of the Bahamas came from this black town on an island settled by white separatists was not lost on me.

Until the second half of the twentieth century Northern Great Abaco was virtually undiscovered. In 1948, before there was even a rubble road north of Cooperstown, Jack Ford, an Englishman freshly posted to Green Turtle Cay as superintendent of the Abaco school system, had sailed in a locally-built schooner, the *Star*, north along the coast of Abaco visiting settlements and schools from Cooperstown to Crown Haven. He wrote a fine little book, *Reminiscences of an Island Teacher*, in which he recounts the trip. Cooperstown was then a place of unpainted wooden houses and a ruined school house.

The situation in Cooperstown and the rest of northern Abaco is very different today. There is a government health clinic in Cooperstown and the highway is smooth and wide. North of Cooperstown, the landscape became hilly, and the highway was lined with old growth forests of pine and hardwoods that sheltered huge ferns growing by the roadside. There was nothing at all tropical in the scenery here, no palms or Casuarinas, where the highway traveled inland in a straight line to Angel Fish Point, then turned sharply to the west and the water came into view at last as I crossed onto Little Abaco Island. Below Cedar Harbour, government workers were stringing power lines from huge wooden spools along the highway. To make way for utility poles the forest had been pushed to one side, and I saw dozens of mahogany trees uprooted and apparently left to rot where they had fallen. Rolling through the sleepy-hot settlement of Cedar Harbour, I passed groups of black children dressed in gray striped uniforms eating mangoes on their way home from school.

At Cedar Harbour, Ford found a "very poor" settlement of huts. The local constable was a well-known moonshiner who bragged to Ford of having children "in every settlement along the shore," fifty or sixty of them. Ford also noted in Cedar Harbour "relics from the bad old days of slavery" when folks "escaped to a life of seclusion" at the back of very awkward channels where the way through the mangroves was so devious that strangers would either become lost or be ambushed.

"When strangers approached Cedar Harbour," he added, "the whole population took to the bush, a habit that still continues today."

At Mount Hope I passed more school children walking along the road, these wearing bright red striped uniforms, and still more children in colorful uniforms at Fox Town, which looked out on Hawksbill Cay. The small, brightly colored houses of the settlement were adorned with porches where old men and women sat in the heat of the afternoon, waving at me as I passed. Clothes fluttered on clotheslines in a light breeze and a young white man, an unusual sight this far north, was swabbing a boat at the dock. Ford described Fox Town as "a beautiful place in a rugged sort of way, standing on a raised rocky shore overlooking myriad tiny green cays which were scattered for miles." Long ago, Mrs. Fox had come with her husband from Long Island in the south. In 1948 she was "still alive and very proud of the fact than she had founded a settlement." Today the settlement has a population of 600, and with the only deep harbor on Little Abaco, is in a position to attract the yachting crowd as a stopover for traffic between Florida and points south, though the facilities at Fox Town are still rudimentary.

In Ford's day, the houses of Crown Haven, the most primitive village he'd seen on his voyage, were built of driftwood with thatched roofs, the wooden church doubled as a school, and children ran about naked. The bar specialized in brewing the local liquor which was sold "hold-sail and rat-tail." One of the *Star's* crew members went on shore at Crown Haven to visit family. Several hours later, to the dismay of the captain, he showed back up knee-walking drunk.

At Crown Haven, still little more than a cluster of shanties and a bar at the foot of a hill, the road jogged sharply to the right and came unceremoniously to its finish at the top of a rise. It was a poor, hard-bitten landscape. Even the Casuarina pines looked scraggly and underfurnished here. There was no sign marking the end of the Great Abaco Highway, just the rusted cab of a pick-up truck off in the bush and an abandoned concrete hut at the summit of the hill. I walked to the top of a rock ledge and looked out at the sea, which was flat smooth, slightly rounded like a blister and dotted with small cays that looked like black mushrooms in the haze. There was no beach, so I walked along the top of the ledge for a hundred yards east to an impassable cut. A lone barracuda hung motionless in the shallows. A mockingbird fussing in the bush and the gentle sloshing of water beneath the ledge were the only sounds. The rest was silence. The feeling was eerily melancholic and threatening at the same time. Crown Haven seemed a forlorn place, desolate and forgotten at the end of the road, inhabited by vaguely desperate but unreadable people who were watching you in shadows from their windows. I was overtaken by the same strange feeling I had standing on Michael Jordan's face in Barattara, Great Exuma, a sad loneliness in which a nagging hint of danger lurked.

Crown Haven seemed like the end of the world. Nowhere in the Bahamas had I been physically closer to North Carolina than here on the northwest coast of Little Abaco, yet nowhere and never had I felt so far away from home.

BOO!

It was Halloween night and I was back in Abaco, my second trip to the island in less than a year, dancing down rain-slick Queen Elizabeth Street in Marsh Harbour, belly full of turtle steak and rum, with a crowd of black children in white face. Goblins and ghouls were everywhere. There were skeletons waving cutlasses, Darth Vaders threatening people with laser wands, and one child wearing a pig's face. Despite the rain I was happy to be back on Abaco. After my first trip, I'd played the tapes of the Pinders for Walt Wolfram who found the evidence of linguistic similarities between Cherokee and North Carolina enticing enough to send me back, this time with a graduate student in linguistics looking around for a subject for his Master's thesis. After this day's interviews he was already sensing he'd found one.

And I had finally met and interviewed Patrick Bethel, whom I'd missed the first time around. Bethel—a freckled and energetic man in his sixties, with high forehead and wavy red hair, an elegant manner, wearing shorts and sport shirt, speaking an immaculate British English—made the case for Carolina connections with lively enthusiasm as we sat in deck chairs under a sour orange tree outside my hotel.

"Cherokee stands out as a very different settlement from Hope Town and other loyalist settlements on the island, for two reasons. You see, it was far and away more isolated than other Abaco settlements. All communications, all exchanges were made by boat, of course, in those times. You didn't go anywhere by land but only by water. So Cherokee Sound was more often in contact with Nassau and especially Spanish Wells and Harbour Island, fifty miles across the water at the northern tip of Eleuthera than with Hope Town or Green Turtle Cay. The Bethels, my family, seem to have come originally from Harbour Island. Even when I was a small boy it was quite common at Christmas time for a sloop full of men to come across for the holiday, and quite frankly, all looking for a wife. And that was in the early forties. Even so, contact with the outside world was limited.

The second reason is that the people who settled Cherokee Sound were different, came from a different part of the United States. I mean the New York Rascals are the ones who settled Marsh Harbour, and the families in Hope Town and Green Turtle come from Wyannie Malone. But Cherokee is different. I presume it was settled by [the well-known Loyalist commander] Colonel Brown, who was very influential with the Indians, and the Indians were very influential during the [Revolutionary] War. And this Brown seemed to have done something—I put it down to his personality rather than his ability—to convince the Indians to come with him, down from the Carolinas—or Georgia perhaps—to East Florida, and from there to Abaco. This migration took only a few years. These people had surely been pushed south, pushed south swiftly, so many who came to Abaco in their forties were born in the Carolinas.

Brown is known to have kept an Indian girl in East Florida, and it makes sense that he would bring her with him to Abaco, doesn't it? Certainly, there were Indians in South Abaco from the earliest times. I could take you to some Sandy Point roots people whose ancestors were clearly Indians. The connection is quite unmistakable once you see them. The name Cherokee alone suggests as much, of course."

I wanted to be persuaded by Patrick's reasoning, though he was himself less than confident that his theory of the origins of Cherokee

Sound was correct. "I have no proof of any of this," he confessed, "but it makes a good story."

My hope was that where the historical record came up short, the linguistic record might be more complete and telling. Over the next couple of days we interviewed Cherokee Sounders, and each of them, especially the women, shaped vowels in ways that reminded me of the brogue of North Carolina. Far and away the most interesting were old people, for their speech as well as their stories. At eighty five Katie Bethel was the matriarch of Cherokee Sound. A distant cousin of Patrick Bethel, she had lived in her house, built by her husband for their marriage, up the gentle rise from the Pinders, for sixty-five years. She lived alone now, her husband, a smack fisherman long dead, and their children scattered about, in Nassau and Ft. Lauderdale and Los Angeles. She was lively and acute, though sometimes the rush of thought and memory overwhelmed her and she fell speechless. Then she would make a sound somewhere between a sob and a laugh and cover her mouth with her hand. At other times, talking back over her life, she laughed out loud and then reached to touch my leg confidentially, as if to say, "Could I tell you some stories, sonny boy!" Her eyes were the deeper blue of the sea beyond the bone flat.

"I'm been here in Cherokee eighty-five years. Some things I can remember now, keep it in remembrance longer than the young ones. In those days there was no lights, except kerosene, and later some have a generator. There was no doctor. We had to work harder, too, in them days than what they do today. I did, because my father was a cripple thirteen years before he died. All that time, he crawled on his hands and knees same as a baby. This father, his body, just his legs, perished right away."

"What crippled him?" I asked.

"We never could find out. He used to go on the fishing smacks from here to Nassau, like they doos."

"Something happened at sea, maybe?"

"I don't know. Some people told my mother—you know in them days they used to have a lot of superstitions—said somebody may have worked obeah on him." She laughed.

In the old days, life in Cherokee was indeed difficult for Katie Bethel. Her husband was out on the smack boat for six, eight weeks and longer in the fall, when she was left with three babies to care for alone, with no grandparents alive to help. She faced the constant perils of life on and near the sea, the unheralded storms and hurricanes, and the loss of boats and men from the settlement. She told the gruesome story of her husband being bitten by a barracuda. "He had a barracuda on the line, and when he went to lift it in the boat, the barracuda swung around and catched him right here." She pointed to the back of her arm, above the elbow. "And don't say he didn't have a gap in his arm when he got home. He given him a bite that day. But we get them barracudas back, I'm telling you."

"How's that?"

"Fried," she laughed again.

Neither she nor her husband ever went to the doctor, she said, and, surprising for a woman her age in remote Abaco, she had never practiced bush medicine. "No. Thank the Lord," she said, "I go on from day to day and just wouldn't say one thing. One of my grandmothers, she was ninety-one when she passed away, and never went to a doctor." Katie Bethel bore two of her three daughters in the corner bedroom of her house, attended only by a midwife. Hers was the last generation of Bahamian women to have been attended by midwives. The improvement in health care delivery systems in the Bahamas has completely eliminated them. There are more midwives in trendy Orange County, North Carolina, than all of Abaco, I suppose.

Katie Bethel deeply appreciated the changes that made life easier in Cherokee Sound. She'd had a washing machine for two years. "All my life, I used to go to the washing board under that tree." She pointed through the bedroom window. "All my life," she said again, in measured syllables. "And the children wanting to give me a washer for a long time: I said, 'mama don't want it.' And I'm glad today that I'm got it." She appreciated the new road less than the coming of electricity in 1994. "I think it's wonderful. Look heah!" she nearly shrieked, "I'm got lights, I'm got phone. Never had it before. We got streetlights, we don't have to walk out now in the dark," she added, pronouncing her w's as v's. She had a new television but no antenna or dish, so she could only watch tapes her children sent her. She prized the telephone above any device. "I said to the one [her daughter] up in California, you so far away from me. If I get sick and I want you—she says, 'well, mama, you only the distance from your phone from me.'"

She hadn't succumbed to the sweet drug of nostalgia. Her life had been rich and eventful in this small, hard paradise, but she keenly remembered the trials of a long life spent in Cherokee Sound. Just before I left I asked if she ever locked her doors. "No, never. No fear.

No fear." Then I asked if it had been a good life. "Yes," she said. "And thank the Lord for it."

Would she like to live it again? "I don't think so," she replied without hesitating. "Once is enough."

Benny Sawyer, eighty-one, and his wife Viola lived at the other edge of Cherokee Sound by the creek in the neatest of the neat houses in the settlement. Its remarkable construction and efficient layout were accounted for by the fact that Benny designed and built it fifty-four years ago—and many other houses in Cherokee—by himself. Its location by the creek was not haphazard either since, along with building houses, Benny Sawyer had built boats for much of his life, twenty-four in all, ranging from 18 to 102 feet, every one launched here in this creek at the edge of Cherokee Sound. At one time there were a dozen or so boat-builders working in this settlement. Now there are none. But Benny Sawyer was without peer. In *Abaco: The History of an Out Island and its Cays*, 1995, Steve Dodge calls Sawyer "surely one of the finest master shipwrights and boat-builders Abaco has produced."

Benny and Viola invited us, unannounced, into a small room adjacent to the kitchen where Viola was baking bread. Though not a large man, Benny had obviously been robust and handsome in his prime, with watery blue eyes and a perfect jaw. Trained by his uncle, Benny built his first boat, a dinghy, in 1946 and retired after finishing his largest, a fishing vessel 102 feet on the deck and 90 feet on the keel, in 1968. All were made of wood. Now hard of hearing, Benny was precise in his description of the master craft of boat building. First, he would design the boat in his head and then execute a blueprint before constructing a scale model for her buyer. This was a phase Benny particularly enjoyed. Next, the wood was selected. In the early days, the various components of a boat's curved frame were selected from naturally crooked trees Benny found in the forests near Cherokee. Soaring, absolutely straight pines supplied the masts.

One of the factors that contributed to Benny's retirement was the arrival in south Abaco of the Owens-Illinois lumber company which denuded the forests of trees Benny used for his frames and masts.

"That's partly why I gave up building boats when I did. After Illinois come here and put roads all through the land, the timber got scarce." Before Owens-Illinois harvested the aboriginal forests of south Abaco, Benny had access to mahogany, horseflesh, corkwood, dogwood and Caribbean pine. Now there is only pine. "So I cut out building boats and went into house construction."

The planking for boats was bought at lumberyards in Marsh Harbour, and the housing, especially for smack boats, was often constructed by someone else and added later, typically in Spanish Wells where Benny sold many of his boats. As many as six carpenters worked nearly a year to finish big boats. In the early days, Benny worked without power tools. It took two and a half months to build an eighteen-foot boat in those days. "You see, the first of my boat building I had to use hand tools," Benny told me. "Everything was manual labor. I didn't have any electric tools or anything. Many hard labor. Many hard labor."

"They were good days, though," Viola added. "Happier then than what you are today."

Each boat was launched in this creek at spring tide under an almond tree across from his house, slid down on rollers into the water. The larger craft—*Blue Waters, Sea King* and *Pinocchio*—which drew more water than the creek held, were fitted with iron drums below the water line to keep them off the bottom. For Benny, launching the boats was the most anxious phase of the process; he worried that one would slip off her rollers before she reached the water, which would mean time and labor to right her, and possibly structural damage to the boat as well. For Viola, it was the most frightening time. She worried that someone, possibly her husband, would be crushed. "I didn't look forward to that," she said absolutely. "It was too dangerous, one of them men get up under that boat and oh, Lord. . . ." She couldn't allow herself to say what might have happened. "I just didn't look."

Benny Sawyer passed around photographs of the boats he had built. He paused at *Pinocchio*, ninety-two feet on the keel. "This one was a boat I built for a fellow in Palm Beach by the name of Dick Russell. She's name of *Pinocchio*," he said, his voice rising suddenly, choking with emotion. "She's been all about through the world, all about." Richard Russell of Palm Beach who commissioned the *Pinocchio* "had a disaster when I built it," he continued. "He estimated the cost on his own, and I told him, I say, 'Dick, if you carry that over there at that cost they gonna take your boat from you,' because he was underestimating, you know." Underestimating the cost of a boat amounted to tax evasion. Customs officials frown upon it. "And true enough when he got her over there, they taken her from him and auctioned her off. So it's a man up in San Francisco got her now. She was lying in San Francisco Bay in this picture."

Benny Sawyer had squeezed the remarkable career of the *Pinocchio* into a couple of sentences. Subsequently, I learned that she had been bought by William F. Buckley, Jr. and renamed the *Cyrano*. It was the trans-Atlantic crossing in this boat that Buckley described in *Airborne: A Sentimental Journey* (Macmillan, 1976). He called her "My beautiful *Cyrano*" (36).

Recently, the present owner of the *Cyrano* wrote Benny asking him to document what she was built from. "And so I did," he said. "I made up a list of everything I could remember and sent it to him. And he sent me fifty dollars." He laughed but he wasn't amused. He well knew that this was a paltry acknowledgment of his work. It symbolized his plight as a boat-builder, the undervaluing of his work. In his prime Benny Sawyer made ten shillings a day—less than two dollars—building vessels that would later sell, as *Blue Waters* (Benny's favorite boat) recently did, for hundreds of thousands of dollars. In those days "you didn't get nothing much for your labor. The wages was low then. You didn't get nothing much, just enough to live with. Couldn't save nothing. You only could live. And not in luxury neither."

His consolation lay in watching his work come to life: "You know what I used to like in building me boats, when I'd launch 'um off. I'd carry 'um out to the side of the channel and moor 'um where I could look at 'um from the side. Just stand up and admire 'um. I liked that the best."

I asked Benny about his own boats. "I never had a boat myself," he said matter-of-factly. "I had such little time to use one, it wasn't worth the money." When we left, Viola tucked a loaf of fresh bread, still warm, into a paper bag and gave it to us for the road. "Everybody say my bread is the best there is in Cherokee Sound."

So, had I found a community of Carolinians at Cherokee Sound? When I returned to campus I played all the video and audio tapes I had made over two visits to this remote settlement for Walt and several of his graduate students. They started work immediately analyzing the evidence and when I published a version of my Abaco travels in *The North Carolina Literary Review* (Number 7, 1998), Walt added a side bar in which he commented that in the case of Cherokee Sound "the clues are tantalizing because they raise the prospect that the distinctive voices of Cherokee [Sound] had their roots in the sounds of historic North

Carolina," while adding that "the identification of its dialect heritage is still difficult to establish precisely." He wrote that if you listened to "the vowels of older lifetime residents of Cherokee Sound and you might think that their fishing vessels, which have a likeness to those built in eastern North Carolina to begin with, took a Gulf Stream route from the Outer Banks of North Carolina and the Pamlico Sound." He noted, however, that while the pronunciation of the long *I* in high, tide and time, closely resembled the pronunciation of these sounds on the Outer Banks, other aspects of the Cherokee Sound dialect are common in other Bahamian dialects—"the alteration between *v* and *w* in words like *v*ell for *w*ell and some*v*ere for some*w*here" and "the loss of *h* in words like *h*ere and *h*orrible pronounced as 'ere and 'orrible."

"To muddy the dialectical waters even further," Walt added that "the common pronunciations of words like *aks* for *ask* in Cherokee Sound could have come from the well known pronunciation of this word in the African Diaspora, including slaves from the eastern seaboard areas of the United States who brought the pronunciation with them."

As for grammar (as opposed to pronunciation), Walt reported stronger evidence of a Carolina connection, noting that one of the residents said "I'm done forgot what your names were," a formulation "that we still hear in the isolated regions of eastern North Carolina." Similarly, constructions such as *I'm* for *I have* as in *I'm* been there for I've been there, or *I'm* got one for *I've* got one, common among the old speakers in Cherokee Sound, are characteristic of the dialect grammar of Lumbee Indians in southeastern North Carolina. Furthermore, Cherokee Sounders' unusual use of *be* in sentences such as *I hope it bes a girl* and *They be take their honeymoon* "could easily be added to our list of examples from North Carolina." Walt found a connection between the dialect of Cherokee Sound and the mountains of western North Carolina, moreover, in the use of *s* on verbs as in The boat*s* get*s* here or The Cherokee people eat*s* a lot of fish. These, Walt wrote, "could have come from the mouths of speakers living in the Smoky Mountains of North Carolina, where the Cherokee people happen to reside, as easily as it flowed from the lips of those [interviewed] in Cherokee Sound."

But, Walt exercised scholarly caution: "The parallels are undeniable," he wrote, "but we still have to acknowledge that none of the examples we have gathered so far solves the historical dialect mystery of Cherokee Sound by itself," since "many of these dialect items are found in other relic dialect enclaves scattered throughout

North America and England." Still, he concluded his essay on a more positive, if oddly phrased, note: "[W]hat we have in our sights"—a hint at future work by his students that would produce three Masters theses—"makes us willing to claim that a Carolina dialect connection for Cherokee Sound is more that a wanton potshot."

So, that was how I would leave the matter and get on to other islands, a strong possibility that the founding families of Cherokee Sound came from North Carolina but not a certainty.

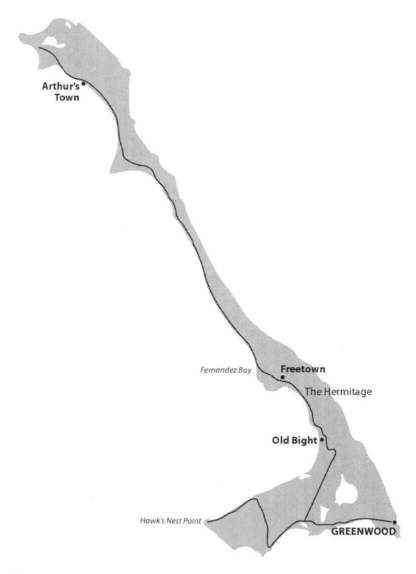

Arthur's
Town

Fernandez Bay

Freetown

The Hermitage

Old Bight

Hawk's Nest Point

GREENWOOD

N

CAT ISLAND

Chapter 7
The Spirit World of Cat Island

I T's rare that my inner child talks to me, so when it does I listen. This time it said jump, and I didn't ask questions. I flung open the door and leaped. The 1984 Mercury, its windows darkened by sheets of tinted plastic *appliquéd* with Free National Movement stickers, its interior festooned with stuffed animals, rolled through a cloud of blue smoke and hissing steam and crawled to a stop in the bush. I caught up to it, waited for the smoke to clear, pushed my way around to the front and checked the chrome bumper which had crushed a goat's skull half an hour earlier. The stupid animal had dashed from the bush into the road straight into my path. The bumper was undamaged.

The oil light began to flicker above Arthur's Town at the northernmost tip of Cat Island, 40 miles away. Anxious about being stranded that far from New Bight where I had rented the car, I had started back toward the middle of the island. Passing south through the villages at Tea Bay and Knowles and South Bay, once dodging a madman waving a machete in the road, the flickering oil light became a steady red glow. The valves started to clatter like timbales and I had no choice but to drive as hard and far as it would go before the engine melted down.

It finally exploded just north of New Bight. Now she was snug in the bush, smoking. It was hot and dry on Cat, and I was momentarily afraid the fuming car would set the island on fire, and we'd all of us

—50 or so tourists and the 1,700 permanent residents—have to be rescued from this harpoon-shaped island in the middle Bahamas. But the smoke and hissing steam were dying now. I took the ignition key and started out on foot toward New Bight, a mile down Queen's Highway.

I cursed Hazel Brown, Cat's most feared Obeah doctor. This was only fair. After all, she had cursed me yesterday, spitting at my feet as I started out her door, and today I had killed a goat and blown an engine. It seemed definitive: I had fallen under the spell of Obeah. You need turpentine, the entrails of farm animals, and plenty of salt to kill Obeah curses. I knew where to find a fresh goat carcass, but I hadn't any turpentine or salt.

I'd been told that pockets of Obeah still existed on Cat Island. Obeah came to the Bahamas from West Africa with the slave trade during the Diaspora, when Africans of the Horn—Ashanti, Biafra, Coromante, Mandinga and other tribal/cultural groups—were hunted down and trapped like animals, sold to European traders, chained below decks and shipped to America and the Caribbean. The spirit world of West Africa thrived in these new environments. On islands colonized by England—the Bahamas, Barbados, and especially post-Hispanic Trinidad and Jamaica—it retained more of its original character as a mysterious system of fetishes, talismans, charms and curses used to invoke retributive powers. In the Francophone Caribbean, notably Haiti, Obeah's sister Voodoo was infused with Catholic rituals and forms, and evolved more nearly into an organized and active "religion," and a potent means of resistance to the slave system. Voodoo culture was instrumental in the campaign of Toussaint L'Ouverture to win freedom for Haiti, the first successful independence movement in the Caribbean. On the eve of the 1791 rebellion, which led to the Haitian Revolution, a Voodoo priest called Boukman exhorted his followers to "throw away the symbol of the god of the whites who has so often caused us to weep, and listen to the voice of liberty, which speaks in the heart of us all."

Like its grander sister Voodoo in Haiti, in Jamaica Obeah found its most powerful expression, really its fulfillment, as a subversive device to terrify slave owners. The geography of the island provided a sanctuary, the Blue Mountains, where blacks could mass and mount a guerilla campaign against colonial authority. Jamaican Maroons (from the Spanish word "cimarron" for escaped cattle), led by the fierce

Coromante warriors, had always been effectively independent, simply because they outnumbered their supposed owners. They fled inland to the fastness of the Blue Mountains from which they fought the British for decades. In the prosecution of this guerrilla war, Obeah doctors applied spells to the bodies of warriors to create an invisible shield that bullets couldn't penetrate. Hundreds of Maroons were killed, but their fierce confidence was daunting to colonial planters. So desperate did the situation become that they imported dogs and Mosquito Indians from Central America to hunt down the Maroons. Eventually, inevitably perhaps, the Maroons were defeated. But they didn't give up their independence. The Blue Mountain Maroons remained a separate nation until 1962 when they were incorporated into the nascent Commonwealth, virtually on the eve of Jamaica's independence.

The English were fascinated by Obeah, becoming, in late 18th-century something like an intellectual fetish for the London *literati*. In reaction to the Jacobean movement for abolition, English audiences were provided a diet of Obeah spectacles in scores of popular poems of the time, also in Edmund Burke's *Reflections on the Revolution in France* (1790), and in lurid plays at Covent Garden such as *Obi; or, Three Fingered Jack*. As late as 1822 Thomas De Quincy was exploiting the fierce myth of Obeah in his *Confessions of an English Opium-Eater*. African spirit systems continued to fascinate writers for a century and a half. Perhaps the most interesting modern treatment of Obeah is Jean Rhys's *Wide Sargasso Sea* (1966).

Bahamians use the term "Obeah" to denote the instruments of the system as well as the system itself. Someone uses Obeah to curse you, and when you find cat entrails on your steps, that's Obeah too. Obeah doctors, as much like lawyers as physicians, are contracted by people, often jilted lovers, to intervene to right a wrong that has gone undiscovered or unpunished. Stripped of its subversive role in a slave culture, Obeah has not lost its social and political power. On Cat Island, I'd been told, Obeah and Christianity coexist in a peculiar way. Almost always a woman, the Obeah doctor, as I found out, might be a deaconess in the Baptist Church. Hazel Brown was both a conscientious Baptist and an Obeah doctor at the same time.

I'd met 67-year-old Hazel Brown the day before at her tiny pink bar north of New Bight. We'd talked on the back porch overlooking the electric green waters of the Exuma Sound. I drank a Kalik from a bottle; Hazel drank gin from a coconut she'd knocked the head off of. She was a stout woman who wore her cropped hair tied in tight rows under a ball cap. After asking about her childhood and family, I dropped my well-rehearsed question:

"Can you help me? Everybody says you're the woman to talk to. Back home, there's a man trying to take my wife from me. Everybody says you know the Obeah way to get rid of him. Can you help me?"

"Not without a shotgun." She laughed.

"No, I mean with Obeah."

"I don't know nothing about no Obeah. There ain't been no Obeah around here since Jesus Christ rose from the grave, praise God." She pointed up to the sky. "God up there put away the Devil down here long ago, I tell you."

I was prepared for this feint. I knew Obeah people put strangers off by copping straight Christianity. For two centuries Obeah has shared spiritual space with Protestant Christianity in the Bahamas. Daniel in the Lion's Den and Jonah in the Whale can easily be understood from an Obeah point of view.

"But I've prayed and prayed and nothing helps," I said.

"Do she want this man?" Hazel asked tentatively. I said I didn't know.

"If she do, then there ain't much else I can do but praise the Lord that works in mysterious ways," she said, and took another hit from the coconut. "What you should do is give me some money for the church. St. Phillip's Baptist up the road here. Twenty dollars. We want to buy some new pews."

I said I didn't have it.

"American man like you come to Cat with no twenty dollars!" She rose up in her seat. Hazel was suddenly angry. "You think I got the time to sit here and talk to you, and you nursing only one beer in your hand. Get yourself another one. They in the refrigerator."

I did, and sat back down. It was flaming hot under the awning overlooking the Sound, and distractingly beautiful. In the gentle slosh at the water's edge, a black-tip shark pup, three feet long, cruised the translucent water above the blanched limestone.

"But you're not being helpful," I pleaded to Hazel Brown. "I got trouble."

"I ain't studying your troubles," she said. "I got my own. The Lord be praised, I'm still alive."

"But you've had trouble with men in your life too, I bet."

"Me?" she asked incredulously, turning her head dismissively toward the Bight. "Trouble with men? I ain't never had no man troubles. Too sharp, too sharp for all them men. White and colored want me too, I tell you. I was a woman then."

I said she was pretty, but Hazel Brown was pissed: "Who send you up here to take up my time?" she demanded. I said I'd heard several people talk about her, said I should talk to her about Obeah.

"They don't know nothin' 'bout me," she said. "If I wanted to, I could make you freeze up right there in that chair. You want to move in that chair but you can't."

I didn't know whether this was a threat, a joke, or a *fait accompli*. I didn't move.

"You want to move right now but you can't," she said again, and I was still still. Then she abruptly broke the spell.

"Now, I got work to do. Get out, or give me some money—for the church." I got up, slipped six dollars under my full beer, and walked past her. She remained seated and stared through me as I walked, then spat wickedly at my feet just as I reached the door.

If that was a curse, its effect was now plain to see. I was legging it into New Bight under a murderous sun with the full expectation that, if I weren't run down by a car while walking, Betsy at the filling station where I had rented the Merc would charge me for it. I could have brought two of them at a junk yard in the States for what it cost to rent this one for a week on Cat. At the very least, I thought, I'd have to haggle with her over the towing cost and damages to the engine.

But when I got to the station and explained what had happened, Betsy was happily apologetic. Perpetually busy renting, repairing and gassing cars—hers was one of only two gas stations on the island at the time—she was a consummate businesswoman, ordering her employees around with authority, her every move natural as a dance step. Handwritten lists posted on the wall enumerated the virtues of the work ethic, and included a Customer's Bill of Rights. She was clearly successful, and naughtily happy.

"We give you the old one, anyway," she said in the middle of doing something else. "That might happen with that car. Where is it?" I told her it was up the road, and she sent her mechanic in a tow truck to the scene. When he return with news that the motor had burned up, Betsy surprised me again. "I'll make it up to you," she said.

Soon, I was tooling down the Queen's Highway in an immaculate, nearly new Dodge Caravan, feeling free of the Obeah curse. I purred south along the empty stretch of road from Old Bight toward the Greenwood Resort and Dive Center where I was staying, 20 miles away, at the end of a stretch of rubble road past Port Howe at the extreme southern end of the island. This remote stretch was a favorite haunt of eighteenth-century pirates, contemporary drug dealers, and home to a nudist camp.

Said to be named after the pirate Arthur Cat, Cat Island was virtually commerce-less. There was no bank on the island, no shopping, no movie theater, only one meager grocery in New Bight. There were two physicians and only a few scattered clinics along the island. But Cat's beaches, on both the Atlantic and Caribbean sides, were among the most beautiful I'd seen in the Bahamas. The island's six modest resorts seemed to be thriving, though sparsely occupied this time of year. Even the most remote of them, Hawk's Nest, which I visited that afternoon on the way to Greenwood, was well groomed and unguarded.

At the Greenwood resort, I had drinks with Waldemar and Anna Illing, its German owners. One of only three others staying at Greenwood in early June, I was already feeling more like an invited guest than a paying customer. The bar operated on the honor system. You poured your own and marked a chit. This turned out to be expensive, of course, especially for an honest *bonhomme* like me. But it was just my sort of place. Modest by resort standards, to say the least, the twenty-room motel was a pleasant refuge from the heat and my harried travels on Cat. The Illings successfully married European efficiency with the island's easy pace, so that whatever you might need you could get. Meals—breakfast and dinner—were served at a leisurely pace, and you ate along with the Illings and the other guests on the verandah facing the beach. Evening meals were delicious: spicy conch one night, baked grouper the next, spiny lobster, which Bahamians call crayfish, on another night. Cabbage, peas and rice, tangy coleslaw, new potatoes and tomatoes came with main dishes. Coffee and brandy after dinner.

I'd selected Greenwood because Charlotte Caffrey, a Florida-based travel writer I'd met on Abaco, had told me it was the most beautiful spot on the island. We'd met six months before in Hope Town on

Elbow Cay when, drenched by a sudden thunderstorm, we'd shared a lunch of conch burgers and coleslaw under the flapping awning of a restaurant overlooking the harbor. In quick succession during the 60s Charlotte was divorced and her only son drafted and sent to Vietnam. She was left suddenly alone.

"At the time," she said, her eyes dancing, "I had two choices. I could stay where I was and dry up and die, or I could do something. I chose to do something." She'd come to Cat by herself, spending 18 months living out of her VW van, camping up and down the island before there was a paved road on Cat, when it was truly pristine. Little Winding Bay, where Greenwood Resort is located, had been Charlotte's favorite place on the island.

Greenwood's setting lived up to Charlotte's advertisement. It fronted eight-and a-half miles of deserted pink-white sand and gorgeous water. Blotches of patch reef darkened the surface just off shore, north and south. The faint trace of history enriched the physical beauty of this setting. In the autumn of 1492 Columbus rounded the point on the island that bears his name, just south of here, sailing north windward of the Bahamas. Some experts believe that Cat rather than San Salvador to the southeast was the site of Columbus's first landfall in the Americas. The evidence is complex and difficult to assess, involving the conversion of Columbian nautical measurements to modern ones and deciphering sketchy descriptions of land features, made all the more difficult to follow because in Columbus's time these islands were covered in dense forests. Now scrubby and desiccated, its aboriginal woods long ago razed, the landscape of the Bahamas presents a very different view today than it did to Columbus.

To sit alone under the cabana on the sand at Greenwood and imagine square-sailed ships running up the coast just beyond the dark shadows of patch reef added something profound to the simple act of gazing out to sea.

As peaceful as Greenwood was, it shared with many places in the Out Islands a dark and violent past. The former owner was found floating face down in the resort's pool, the victim of a drug deal gone bad. By 1994, when I first visited the Bahamas, drug trafficking had long been a widespread and deadly enterprise in this island nation. By the mid-eighties, it had reached a horrific crescendo that, incredible as it may seem, involved Bahamians of virtually all ages and walks of life: national leaders, greedy and desperate commoners, old codgers and young thugs, even children were caught up in the business of drugs. In 1983, one local distributor testified to receiving the staggering sum, by Bahamian terms, of $90,000 for his part in a run-of the-mill transaction. Children on one island were being paid $500 to act as mules. Waldemar recalled sitting in a small Nassau bar when a nervous young man took a seat near him and ordered a brandy. He downed his drink, took out a hundred dollar bill from a briefcase stuffed with cash, left the hundred on the table and walked out. In those days, cash was so abundant that dealers weighed rather than counted their money.

Otherwise innocent islanders, finding bales of weed tightly wrapped and watertight washed up on their beaches, booty dumped by traffickers under chase, became instantly rich. This happened so regularly in the 80s that islanders took to calling this watery manna "square grouper"—a wry understatement since profits from selling grouper, the most valuable fish in Bahamian waters, can't compare to the bonanza that rolled up on the beach so often. The result was that some people in the Family Islands either by dumb luck or willing complicity became instant millionaires. Local people who had rarely left their homes in the Family Islands purchased mansions in Florida.

The Colombian drug baron, Carlos Lehder, was the godfather of traffickers in the Bahamas. In 1978, he purchased a small, gloriously beautiful little island called Norman's Cay in the northern Exuma chain, a couple of hundred miles south of New Providence, and made it into one of the most efficient and successful drug transshipment points in the world. He built a runway, and pristine Norman's Cay was instantly transformed into a bastion for Lehder's gang. Small planes flew in tons of pot and coke from home bases in Colombia, off-loading their cargo with impunity around the clock. Profits were staggering. One pilot, who made dozens of flights into Norman's Cay, testified to receiving $400,000 per flight. If you've seen "Blow" starring Johnny Depp, you have some sense of how it must have been in those days, when yachts cruising down the Exumas were fired upon for innocently passing Norman's Cay. So much air traffic passed through Norman's Cay that President George H.W. Bush declared it the "O'Hare of the Caribbean." Snowy Chicago in the sweltering tropics.

By the early eighties, involvement in the drug trade was so rampant that the entire nation seemed to have been co-opted. Gorda Cay, off the south tip of Great Abaco, as you'll recall, had become a rival of Norman's Cay in the drug trade, and tiny Bimini was deluged with drugs and money for much of the 1970s and 80s. In 1977, U.S dollars transferred from Bimini to the Central Bank in Nassau totaled $544,360. By 1983, that figure had escalated to an astounding $12.3 million.

The extent of the Bahamian drug problem was detailed in a January 1982 exposé in the *Wall Street Journal*. A year later an NBC Nightly News report alleged involvement by the highest officials of the Bahamian government, including Prime Minister Lynden O. Pindling himself. This was followed closely by a series of articles in the *Miami Herald* titled "A Nation for Sale: Corruption in the Bahamas" that leveled serious allegations against the Pindling government. Pindling, the father of the Bahamian independence movement and the country's first prime minister, was a *bona fide* national hero, and the accusations against him and his government were a stinging embarrassment to the young nation. Something had to be done. A Commission of Inquiry, convened in November 1983, spent four months gathering information on the problem of drugs and its report wrecked the Pindling administration. It found staggering corruption among government officials and police. Five government ministers with ties to organized crime were forced to resign, as were several senators. The deputy Prime Minister, Arthur Hanna, resigned in disgust. Though the Commission of Inquiry did not bring an indictment against Pindling, it did report that the Prime Minister had accumulated enormous wealth during his time in office—nearly five times his annual salary from 1977-1983. This income included "gifts" totaling almost 1.5 million dollars. One commissioner, offering a minority report, conceded that none of this money could be directly traced to drug lords but openly speculated that much of this money might have come from criminal sources.

The traditional means of flying or shipping drug cargos into the Bahamas has been curtailed, thanks largely to a sophisticated surveillance system of balloons tethered over Grand Bahama, Exuma and Inagua, that enables US DEA and Bahamian authorities to track virtually every movement in the air above or in the sea surrounding these islands. What one reads most often in the Bahamian papers today is the arrest of small time Bahamian street dealers and occasionally the nabbing of a larger supplier. But the international big players haven't abandoned these islands. They've merely found new methods of shipping drugs. In October 2008, police seized 311 kilograms of cocaine valued at $7 million from a container at the

Freeport Container Port, pushing the total amount of cocaine seized at the Freeport facility in 2008 to nearly one metric ton. Most of these containers were destined for south Florida, to be trafficked along the interstates north and west.

Given its proximity to the United States and its sprawling geographical nature—islands scattered roughly from a parallel with Ft. Lauderdale to just north east of Haiti—the Bahamas has and will always feed the American appetite for illicit trade—slaves in the earliest period, rum during prohibition, cocaine and pot from the eighties on.

Rather than to score coke or pot, people came to Greenwood now for the diving, Waldamer being the foremost dive master on the island. I took the next day off from the work of getting to know the island and, after years of snorkeling, went scuba diving for the first time. With two other neophyte divers (a couple from Cincinnati who worked for the postal service) I checked out gear from the shop—regulator, buoyancy control vest, lead weights and belt, and full air tank. I had my own mask, snorkel and fins.

We spent the next hour in the pool, where the previous owner had been dumped, learning to breathe under water, to remove, drop, retrieve and clear our masks, to buddy-breathe by taking our primary regulator out of our mouths and taking an auxiliary regulator called an Octopus from another diver. In an astonishingly short time, we were waddling backwards down the lovely beach in front of Greenwood and into the water. With forty years diving experience (his earliest work was on Phoenician and Bronze Age wrecks off the Turkish coast), Waldamer inspired confidence. The Cincinnati couple buddied up, and I was paired with Waldamer. I followed him at his leisurely pace, me sucking air madly, totally freaked, as we pumped into deeper water. At fifteen feet, circular coral heads the size of carousels cropped up. They were virtually pristine, no trace here of the shroud of brown algae that chokes reef systems not only in the Bahamas but all over the world. Conch littered the bone-white bottom. A hundred yards offshore we circled impressive mounds of brain coral and dramatic ledges under which spiny lobsters hid. Thirty feet down, there were narrow arches, and outcroppings of gorgeous elkhorn and dangerous fire coral, and caves penetrated by shafts of sunlight. Ten feet above us a lone barracuda looked on. Within half an hour, I had sucked almost all the air from my tank. When we made our way back to the shallows where my feet could touch bottom, my almost desperate excitement passed and I was overcome with an intense euphoria I had never felt before. This was great fun. Scuba diving could—and did— become my own magnificent obsession.

But diving was an unexpected diversion. I had come to Cat Island to lift the veil on its spirit world, and there was another side to that world I hadn't yet encountered—an orthodox, in fact high church world that would take me up rather than down. The next day I drove back to Old Bight and climbed Mt. Alvernia, at 206 feet the highest point in the Bahamas. Atop this bush-choked "mountain" sits The Hermitage, built in 1940-41 by Father John Cyril Hawes, the Hermit of Cat Island. Born into a devout Anglican family in Richmond, Surrey, in 1876, the young Hawes was trained as an architect, a profession in which he would achieve great distinction, especially as a church architect and builder. He was naturally attracted by baroque structures and ancient rituals of Catholicism. Added to this, his disposition was naturally and powerfully ascetic and nomadic. In his twenties, this gifted and well-trained son of privilege would dress himself in rags and set off on what he called "trampings," extended periods of time when he roamed the English countryside, from Surrey and Sussex to Oxford, Warwick and on to Hull, sleeping wherever he could and living on food provided by strangers. He never begged but took what was freely offered him. In the summer of 1907, as a novitiate on the island of Caldey, he lived for a time as hermit in a cave in a limestone cliff. Hawes was a curious work in progress, a nomad and hermit in the making.

On October 18, 1906, Hawes became a novitiate in the Anglican priesthood, taking the religious name of Jerome. In 1908, he learned that a hurricane had destroyed churches on Long Island in the Bahamas and Hawes, ever restless, appealed successfully to be dispatched to Long Island, just south of Cat Island, to rebuild the ruined sanctuaries. Hawes boarded the *Mauretania* bound for New York and then took a steamer for Nassau and another on to Long Island.

Hawes spent the next two years on this the most beautiful of Bahamian islands. He lived for a time in an eight-foot shack he put up from the rubble of a ruined church in Deadman's Cay while overseeing the rebuilding and expanding of the Church of St. John the Evangelist, which is still an active place of worship, as is his Church of St. Andrew. He also built during this period the Church of St. Mary the Virgin at

The Bight, Long Island, now in ruins. Then he turned his attention to Clarence Town, ten miles south of Deadman's Cay, where he undertook the ambitious design and building of St. Paul's Church on the site of the former church, flattened by the 1908 hurricane, atop a grand hill in the middle of the settlement. Over the next year, he and his Bahamian volunteers raised the splendid edifice of St. Paul's. Today St. Paul's—along with the glorious Catholic Church of Sts. Peter and Paul on the next hill over, which Hawes designed after an absence of thirty years from these islands—still dominate Clarence Town.

On November 17, 1939, the 63-year-old, sea-sickened Hawes returned to the Out Islands after an absence of three decades, arriving at The Bight on Cat Island aboard the steamer *Monarch of Nassau* where he beheld the derelict building in the middle of the settlement and the hill known as Mt. Coma rising out of the tangled bush behind the village. He decided immediately that he would build the people's church on the site of the collapsed building, and then turned his gaze up Mt. Coma. He must have thought something like: *On this rock I will build my church.*

But Monsignor Hawes spent only a few hours on Cat Island during this trip. He left that evening on the mail boat for San Salvador where he celebrated mass with the local Benedictine community, and then caught a steamer to Long Island where some of his aged former congregants fell to their knees and tearfully embraced their former pastor. It must have been an intensely gladdening homecoming for Hawes who beheld the wonderful baroque twin towers of St. Paul's— now called "The Pearl of the Bahamas"—rising above the village. But he didn't stay long in Clarence Town either. He was soon on his way to Nassau and then to Harbour Island where he spent Christmas, 1939.

After Christmas he returned to Nassau and began planning his future work on Cat Island and Long Island. He made arrangements to purchase Mt. Coma for £35, which he would rename Mt. Alvernia after St. Francis's retreat in Tuscany. But he struggled for a time with a peculiar conflict. As a Franciscan, he shunned material possessions —he had long ago given most of his estate to the charities. And this ascetic strain of character was more dominant and demanding than ever before. "The new life I am called to begin," he wrote, "must be more hidden-solitary. To preach the Gospel in silence, living not only as a priest but as a hermit [in] Solitude, Poverty, Abjection, Obscurity." In seeking spiritual enlightenment in a high place, Hawes was following a Christian tradition at least as old as Moses; in other religions, the practice is even older.

He could justify buying the highest point in the Bahamas, but he struggled with whether to buy a boat, which would be the most efficient way to reach his scattered flock. In the end, he resolved to purchase a sailing vessel on Abaco—long famous for boat building. He hired an accomplished sailor and willing first mate, a twenty-five-year old black man named Victor Fergusson he met in Nassau, and the two set out on the mail boat for Marsh Harbour, Abaco. For £45 he purchased a fine smack, which he christened the *Roma*, and soon the two men were sailing down the Abaco coast for Nassau. With unfavorable winds hampering their progress, Hawes and Fergusson put in at Cherokee Sound where they spent two days, Hawes celebrating mass aboard the *Roma* each morning. A terrifying and exhausting two-day sail across the storm-swept Northeast Providence Channel to Nassau followed and, after rest and repairs to the *Roma*, another perilous journey began on February 1, 1940, south to Cat Island. At sunrise on the fourth day of their voyage, the *monsignor* and his mate landed on the pink sand beach at Port Howe, Cat Island, only a few miles around Columbus Point from Greenwood. After a week of rest and recuperation, Hawes sailed around the southern reach of the island and up to the Bight. His cargo included "eight bags of cement, tools, shovels, picks and crowbars."

He and a number of local men, whom he paid with the remaining money and provisions he had, began carving the tortuous stone path up to the summit of the hill. Soon, construction of the Hermitage began. He slept on board the *Roma* for a time but then discovered a cave on the north face of the hill which better suited his monastic desires. Here he slept on a straw bed on the floor of the cave, tormented by flies and mosquitoes, his body aching from strenuous labor. Of this cave he wrote: "Anyone coming up and finding a dead hermit has only to put the body on a board and shove it right into the far end of the cave, and then wall up the same with stones lying ready at hand. No coffin, no undertaker or funeral cortege, no trouble or expense to anyone." In his diary, he left a ghoulish contemplation of the fate of his mortal remains worthy of Hamlet himself:

> When the time comes and my soul is in Purgatory (if my body is walled in here) worms and maggots will be ceaselessly at work on it—until the bare white bones lie in the form of the cross and

perhaps a snake will wiggle through the empty eye sockets of the skull, and crabs, no longer dreaded, walk under the ribs. But close by overhead beyond the rough arch of natural rock is the holy altar of God: even now it stands prepared, the chalice with its black veil and burse and the black missal and cruets.

Lurid in its detail, this passage is also curiously depersonalized: "my body" becomes "it," "the" bones "bare white"; a serpent slithers through "the empty eye sockets of the skull," a dreaded crab tours "the ribs."

This cave, under a ledge on the western face of Alvernia, would be his final resting place.

Over the remaining months of 1940 and into 1941, the Hermitage rose steadily atop the rocky summit of Alvernia: a south to north arc of rough-hewn connected structures: an Angelus tower at the south end connected by an archway to an arch-roofed oratory with a stall and vestments leading north down a set of steps to his domed cell, thence to a kitchen with a fireplace. Behind the structure Hawes built a cistern, a sundial and planted a garden that supplied him—and many of the islanders—with fruit and vegetables. He would later add a guest cell off the kitchen to accommodate the increasing number of visitors that Hawes, the hermit, would paradoxically have to accommodate—local people nearly every day, priests and bishops from near and far, even His Royal Highness, the Duke of Windsor, then Governor of the Bahamas.

For the final seventeen years of his long life, Fra Jerome walked Cat Island's stony paths in sack cloth, barefooted, in the relentless heat of summer, whipped by wind and rain in the time of storms and hurricanes, climbing the stony path he carved out of the hill at day's end, up through dense thickets of poisonwood, lignum vitae and Cassava, past the Stations of the Cross, to his stone cloister. Here he studied and meditated, ate meagerly and slept on a straw mattress laid on a board. But as much as he desired isolation and erasure, his fame only grew. A 1950 profile of him in *Collier's Magazine* quoted Bishop Bonaventure Hansen who called Hawes, "our Christopher Wren."

"Tourists," he added, "will be coming to look at his buildings for a thousand years."

I parked in the gravel lot at the foot of the hill and approached the triangular archway inscribed "Mt. Alvernia" topped by a cross. Beyond, the path rose up through thick bush and forest past the Stations of the Cross, the last three depicting in relief Christ's three falls on the way to Calvary. Another carries the legend, "WEEP NOT FOR ME BUT FOR YOUR CHILDREN." In the precipitous climb up to The Hermitage, it occurred to me that this hill was more like Golgotha than Alvernia, a place for suffering rather than repose. Alvernia's sooty streaked limestone, visible beneath bush and vine, reminded me of crushed skulls. The sanctum at the top was fronted by an 18-foot Celtic crucifix, flanked on the left by a tomb with a stone disk rolled away. The legend inscribed on the entry gate says, "BLESSED ARE THE DEAD WHO DIED IN THE LORD."

The Hermitage is a *pastiche* of styles and characters—elements of medieval English and Irish monasteries, of Franciscan retreats in Umbria and Tuscany combined—all Hawes, all seeming to grow organically from the summit of the hill. Of the Hermitage, Hawes's biographer, Peter F. Anson rightly comments that "there is nothing quite like it in the world."

Conspicuous, proud and commanding, The Hermitage offered a 360-degree view of the island. Only inside did you realize its diminutive scale and simplicity. Altogether it conveyed the impression of a dauber's clay nest, enlarged only enough to suit a man who needed to remind himself how small and insignificant he was. Hawes wanted the Hermitage to be close and rough. Its comfortless gray and black stone, like its cramped spaces, suited his need to mortify himself, to expiate his sins, to scourge his flesh and purify his spirit. The only regret he expressed was leaving the interior wall unplastered, its cracks and crannies offering the perfect breeding places for the flies, mosquitoes and scorpions that tormented him.

Squeezing chamber to chamber through its narrow passageways, silent but for the whirring of wasps, I could almost see with the eyes of this man. Sitting in the wall niche before the small wooden desktop in the oratory at which Jerome read and prayed, from which I could see the sky through the broken pane of the arched, east-facing window behind the Celtic cross on the altar, I could sense the hard-earned, genuine piety that isolation must have provided Hawes.

But looking away from this interior, out the narrow window to my right, I sensed another side of the man. The perspective here, encompassing the entire southern stretch of the island to its emerald waters and beyond, conveyed supremacy and an altogether different kind of power, not immortal but mortal. It was a proud height from which to look down over the island, if not a vain one, once you turned away from the dimly lit, humbling interior of the chapel.

In fact, The Hermitage seemed to me to express keenly contradictory impulses in Hawes, the church architect, builder, expert horseman, sailor and hermit. Erected far from the mainstream of European culture, it was obscure. Yet in this remote location, atop the highest point in the Bahamas, it asserted its own primacy. It announced the scope and measure of one man's imagination, his strength and resource. This place to which he retreated from the world's notice wouldn't escape notice, nor was it meant to. How odd a combination of drives made up this man, I thought. What a paradox. One aspect of his character aspired to timeless and transcendent Truth, to dwell with the mind of God and the architecture of heaven, invisible dimensions that dwarfed mankind's meager imitations. But another aspect of his personality compelled him to build churches in far-flung places, from England to the States to Western Australia to the Bahamas, earthly creations inseparable from himself, even boastful. He wished to erase himself from existence, to leave no prideful footprint behind, and yet he erected earthly temples across much of the world that bore witness to the powerful presence on earth of Father John Cyril Hawes.

Still, for all its rough beauty and pride of place, the Hermitage only confirmed the finiteness of human achievement and the supremacy of Time itself, asserting in its design and now in its emptiness and decay the impossibility of transcendence. It might endure for a thousand years but it would do so as a derelict structure. There was something Ozymandian about it. Abandoned for decades—no one officially tends the property today—it said "Look on my works, ye mighty, and despair!"

Father Jerome surely must have been a complex, even a tormented man.

"No, I really don't think he was." This was Francis Armbrister, another legend of Cat Island, describing the *monsignor* whom she had met while he was building the Hermitage and sleeping in the cave. "He had blue eyes, a serene face. He seemed at peace, walking the paths and rubble roads in his simple hooded frock."

At 89, Frances Armbrister—"Mrs. A" to islanders—was matriarch of the resort at Fernandez Bay, the oldest and most popular resort on the island which she had built in the sixties—nine cottages clustered at the edge of a lovely bay on the western side of the island, just north of New Bight. Charlotte Caffrey, who'd admired the site of Greenwood, had called Frances a national treasure. "The Queen of Cat Island," she was called. A Midwesterner, Frances had lived permanently on Cat Island for thirty years in her own airy cottage in the middle of the resort.

While biscuit-brown guests dined on the beach in the wild light of bonfires and tiki poles, I had taken my dinner up to her cottage, a tidy and comfortable main room, bedroom and kitchen on the main floor, a loft above. Three young teens—her grandchildren—appeared glued to a video of "How To Be A Player." They didn't look up when I entered. Frances sat cane-in-hand in a chair with her right leg propped up on an ottoman. I could tell by her features—lovely deep-set eyes, aquiline bones, and long, lovely fingers—that she had once been a beautiful woman. She was still lovely, though weak. She'd recently undergone a third hip replacement after falling just before the then Bahamian Ambassador to Japan, the actor Sidney Portier, a native of Cat Island, had arrived for lunch at Fernandez Bay. The surgery had left her frail and easily tired, though her voice was young, precise and strong. A curly-tail lizard scampered back and forth across the stone floor like a house pet as we talked.

We looked through her photo albums from the 30's—stills of Frances posing like Gretta Garbo, and another of dark-haired Cyril, her husband, with cravat and pipe, looking over his shoulder. He had been as handsome as she had been beautiful. They looked to be the perfect couple.

Over the next hour, as she drank wine and I rum and Coke, she told me her life's story. Born Frances Fintel in Des Moines, Iowa, in 1908, she moved with her family to Los Angeles where she graduated high school and enrolled at the University of Southern California. The producer Dudley Murphy noticed her in a play at USC, screen-tested her and signed Frances to a contract at MGM, where she had small roles in several films, including "The Night is Young" (1935) starring Raymond Navarro and "The Great Ziegfield" (1936) starring William Powell and Myrna Loy. At the wrap party for "The Night is Young," she told me, the screen writer and actor Waldo Salt introduced her to

Cyril Armbrister, a successful, twice married film, theatre and radio producer.

"I wasn't the least bit interested in him," she said. "Not at first, not until someone told me that he owned half the Bahama islands. As soon as I heard that, I said to myself, 'he's mine.'"

Frances had always dreamed of carving out a life in the islands, a challenge well-suited to her appetite for adventure. At 16, she had become the youngest woman in the Midwest to earn a pilot's license. And though Cyril Armbrister's family didn't exactly own half the Bahama islands, they had long ago staked claim to much of Cat Island. South Carolina Loyalists, the Armbristers like so many other prominent Tory families had been granted a charter for extensive tracts of land in the Bahamas by the English Crown. Among the first ex-pat families to receive a Royal grant, the Armbristers brought everything they owned, including slaves, to Cat. They set about transforming the island into a plantation, playing Prospero to island Calibans. They erected a stately plantation house, now in ruins, around which the settlement of New Bight grew up. They cleared the land for crops and watched as cotton and sisal fields yielded healthy crops. But, as with plantations across the Bahamas, in a couple of seasons plantations leeched the thin soil of nutrients and the crops failed. Like other Bahamian planters, the Armbristers cleared more fields which failed in turn, requiring the clearing of ever more land. And so on, until the indigenous forests of Cat Island were gone and their plantations dead.

Rather than stick it out (mercifully: had they stayed they certainly would have wreaked even more havoc with the fragile ecology of the Bahamas) the Armbristers abandoned their enslaved people for prosperous Nassau, where ten generations of the family occupied a place among the Nassauvian aristocracy, supporting their elevated status in part from the rent of their holdings on Cat.

When Frances met Cyril Armbrister, her husband-to-be had visited Cat Island only once or twice in his life. Nassau-born and English-educated, he became a successful motion-picture producer, thriving in the glamorous circles of New York and Los Angeles. Unhappy in his second marriage Cyril Armbrister was soon pursuing this beautiful young actress under contract with MGM. He and Frances were married in Ensenada, Mexico, in November 1938. She was nineteen, he was forty. A month later, Frances Armbrister made her first trip to Cat Island. After this all-too-brief honeymoon, they set up house in Manhattan where Cyril produced radio shows, including "Charlie Chan," in which Frances performed.

She hated the city, he loved it. She loved Cat Island, he was indifferent to it. Six weeks after her son, Ted, was born, she returned to Cat infant in arms; Cyril remained in New York. At the Bight she was met by an impromptu delegation of neglected, nearly desperate islanders. There was no paved road, no physician, poor water and almost no income from the land. An old man wearing ragged jeans, a Prince Albert hat and a gold earring fell to his knees and wept at her feet. "They greeted me almost like a savior," Frances said. "They had almost nothing to support them. They were the poorest people I'd ever seen, and yet the kindest. They took me in their homes, fed me, so glad to see someone from the outside world among them. I loved them for that."

From the earliest years of their marriage, the Armbrister's were a divided couple. While Cyril delved more deeply into producing movies and radio programs, Frances was drawn to the islands. But the primitive nature of Cat made it impractical to raise children there, so after the birth in 1946 of their second child, Tony, the Armbristers moved back to California, settling in Pacific Palisades, where Cyril continued his producing career in Hollywood. Three years later, they moved back to New York. Frances couldn't stand the place and after a year, she and the children returned to California. For the remainder of their life together, Frances and Cyril maintained a long-distance marriage.

After her children graduated high school, she moved permanently to Cat Island. This was in 1964. Her children made frequent visits to Cat and eventually built houses in Fernandez Bay, forming the nexus of what would become Fernandez Bay Resort.

There were great challenges and disasters along the way to building a world-renowned resort. There were no roads, everything from building supplies to generators had to be imported, and there were fires. In 1973, a butane tank explosion destroyed the main house and left Frances with severe burns from which she almost died.

Her son Tony oversaw the development and operation of the resort while Frances became a legend, driving her Chevy recklessly along island roads, taking visitors on tours of the island. She regaled guests with stories of her life and the legends of the island. A locked sea chest, recovered from Port Howe, sits in the main building at

Fernandez Bay Resort. It's never been opened but Frances swore that it held a king's ransom in pirate booty. She took Obeah stories on faith, ringing her cottage with entrails, salt and turpentine to ward off curses, and telling first-hand stories about the power of African religious beliefs. Newspaper and magazine articles broadcast her fame beyond the island. And Fernandez Bay began to attract the rich and famous. Donovan, the Irish singer, songwriter and musician, became a frequent guest. He wrote a song about Frances called "Lady of the Isle."

While she and her sons developed the resort, Cyril spent most of his time in New York and California, making only periodic visits to his family on Cat. In the spring of 1996 he suffered a stroke in the very chair where I was sitting and died a short time later in Nassau.

More than any other white Bahamian I'd met, Frances Armbrister had assimilated herself to the black culture of the island. She shared their lives as fully, I believe, as is possible. Though it was clear that she was the master of this domain, she didn't seem to think of herself as superior to the islanders. For nearly a third of her long life she had done business among them, attended their churches, cooked with them, shared their collective struggle. She had, like Fra Jerome, devoted much of her life and energies to Cat Island. Like him, she had worked with her hands and imagination and resources to build a monument, this one a resort among the palms, a cluster of villas where tourists now wandered about in a kind of tropical trance. For them this retreat was a temple of sorts, casting a spell as palpable as any house of worship. Every guest I spoke to was ecstatic about Fernandez Bay. One couple asked me not to write about Fernandez at all, saying it was their secret—sticking me with that sharpest of travel writers' paradoxes: writing about a relatively pristine and uncrowded place such as Cat Island would only alert others to its existence. The more people who came to Cat Island the more the characteristics that make it special would be lost.

Just before I left I asked her how long she had loved her husband.

"Oh, one or two years," she said ruefully, smiled and touched my shoulder. "That's about all one can expect."

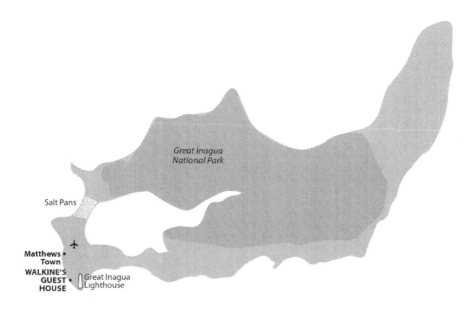

Great Inagua
National Park

Salt Pans

Matthews
Town

WALKINE'S
GUEST
HOUSE

Great Inagua
Lighthouse

GREAT INAGUA

N

Chapter 8
The Flamingos of Great Inagua

ALONE at a table in the bar of the Harbour Club in Nassau, I was lost in a reverie. The squall line that dumped buckets of rain on the island today had passed over the city to the west, trailing shards of purple clouds tinged with orange as the sun sank behind New Providence, lighting up the western faces of the enormous towers of the mighty Atlantis resort on Paradise Island. Out the window, fine boats cruised the harbor, washed clean by the rain, their hulls bright white. The bar was empty but for me, two American construction workers and a table of Nassauvians. On the radio Robbie Williams was singing "Millennium," with that riff with the dying fall from "You Only Live Twice." It wouldn't have surprised me if Sean Connery, wearing a blue suit with narrow lapels and a black tie, had walked into the Harbour Club and ordered a Vodka martini, shaken not stirred. I felt like I'd retreated to an earlier time, the Nassau of "Thunderball" when Gloria Patient, the shark lady of Exuma, had given Connery massages.

The Harbour Club was on East Bay Street, east of the bridges to Paradise Island, in an area of town not often visited by tourists. By no means shabby, it suffered for its location, not far from Fox Hill and high crime of the East End. This part of town was the haunt of shady characters from the Bahamian underworld. If not a spiffy Sean Connery then at least a haggard, anxious young man might come in, sit down, gulp two double Courvoisiers, open a briefcase containing millions in U.S. dollars, leave a c-spot or two on the table for the waitress—Charise from Baratarra, Little Exuma—and walk out without saying another word.

I had arrived at noon, checked in early and waited in the rain for the number 11 bus, which took me to the Bahamas National Trust on Village Road. My next-day's destination was Great Inagua, home to 60,000 West Indian Flamingos, second largest of the world's five species of flamingos, in a preserve managed by the Trust. The southernmost island in the Bahamas—just north of the Turks and Caicos Islands—Great Inagua is the second largest and the least populated in the archipelago. All week long I had sounded out the word in my head like a mantra, inn-aaa-guaa, inn-aaa-guaa. Tomorrow I would be there.

At the Trust, I had been greeted by a well dressed, aloof woman with a wicked cough who handed me a file containing fact sheets and feature stories on the Inagua National Park. The rain had stopped, so I took a table outside under a palm tree and, for the next two hours, rummaged through the archive. The story that emerged was fascinating. The Trust oversees the 287 square miles of park land that covers not quite half the island. The preserve is home to the largest concentration of the West Indian flamingo in the world. During the breeding season, the flamingos perform elaborate mass courtship rituals, the Flamingo Quadrille, involving thousands of birds simultaneously posturing and squalling, their necks writhing while males flash their wings and "a thousand voices set up a fearful hue and cry."

Things have not always been so good for Inagua's flamingos. Since Phoenician times flamingos have been hunted for their sweet flesh, especially the tongue, and their beautiful feathers. In the old days, Inaguans herded flamingos and clubbed hundreds of them to death at a time. The Inagua flock numbered fewer than 5,000 in 1952 when Robert Porter Allen, Research Director of the National Audubon Society, visited the island and began to spur conservation efforts. In 1959, an act of Parliament established the Bahamas National Trust as a non-profit, non-governmental agency dedicated to preserving national and natural resources. Four years later, the Trust took charge of the Inagua National Park and retained Samuel and Jimmy Nixon, skilled hunters Allen had first recruited, as its wardens. Samuel's son Henry is the third generation of Nixons to guard the preserve.

Back at the Harbour Club late that afternoon, photocopies in hand, I was pleased with myself for having gotten to and from the Trust by bus in heavy rain. I took a seat in the bar, ordered a drink, and began poring over the documents I had gathered. I overheard a woman at the locals' table next to me say that the enormous Atlantis resort on Paradise Island, just over the causeway from Bay Street, would be the salvation of Nassau and the Bahamas. A lot of Nassauvians felt this way. But I wasn't certain. Atlantis looks like an enormous happy invulnerable palace, but it's not.

Its fate is tied to a tourist economy and the vagaries of economic cycles. What's worse in the long run, there's a burgeoning stress on and consequent degradation of natural resources especially on New Providence. Every day, ever-expanding Nassau imports seven million gallons of drinking water from elephantine Andros Island, thirty miles away over the treacherous, very deep Tongue of the Ocean from New Providence. In September 2010, engine failure left the water tanker *Titas*, hauling 2.7 million gallons of drinking water from Andros, dead in the water. Immediately, authorities were forced to implement water rationing on the island. This isn't a rare occurrence. And the overstressed electrical grid regularly crashes, leaving Nassau powerless in the dark.

The huge Atlantis resort adds a significant risk of catastrophic irony that its name exuberantly exploits. The mythological Atlantis, after all, believed by many to lay off the shore of North Bimini, had crumbled into the sea. Not an impossible fate for the Atlantis resort should a catastrophic failure of the island's water supply occur.

The next morning I took another 30-dollar ride back to the airport, boarded the Dash-8 bound for Great Inagua and waited for forty-five minutes while workers repaired the landing gear on the plane. Inside the cabin it was sweltering hot and crowded. I seemed to be the only stranger on board. Everyone else, bound for Inagua or on to Mayaguana, were Bahamians, going about their inter-island business. There was a frocked priest, two elderly sisters wearing fine hats, a dozen or so men traveling alone, I presumed, to jobs. In the row beside me was a mother with her profoundly retarded child whose hair had been carefully woven with white ribbons. The little girl slept fitfully, crying and jerking her head every few seconds as her eyes searched frantically behind their lids.

The repairs completed, we sped down the puddled runway, lifted off, combed the top of a low cloud and banked toward Great Inagua 380 miles away. It was a straight shot southeast through a cloudless sky over the Exuma Cays, passing west of Long Island, Crooked Island and the Acklins. We touched down on Great Inagua in a blazing white heat and taxied to the terminal where chaos seemed to have broken out with the arrival of the plane.

Two U.S. Coast Guard helicopters parked on the tarmac were stark evidence of the ability of the United States to trespass on Bahamian national sovereignty in the effort to curb our access to drugs. The Coast Guard presence, combined with sophisticated surveillance cameras suspended from giant balloons tethered over Grand Bahama, Exuma and Inagua, which I mentioned earlier, ensure that the United States maintains a twenty-four hour watch over the entire nation, able to track the movement of every boat and aircraft in the Bahamas. Still, in 2010, the DEA reported that 5% of all illegal drugs reaching the US came through the Bahamas.

Henry Nixon, for sixteen years the warden of the Inagua National Park, met me outside the terminal. On the way into town we passed a convoy of trucks belonging to Morton Bahamas Ltd, one of the largest salt-producing operations in the world. A few miles north of Matthew Town, giant pumps at the Morton Bahamas plant suck seawater through narrow ports, flooding dozens of shallow pans that cover thousands of acres of this flat island. Over six months or so, these evaporation ponds dry into salt rinks. The salt is then harvested, piled into blaze-white hills, processed, loaded onto tankers and shipped away to Miami. Fitted with stainless steel hulls, the tankers return to Matthew Town filled with drinking water, Great Inagua's lifeblood.

In addition to providing the island's only source of potable water, Morton supplies the island's electricity, owns a general store, the liquor store and the main guesthouse. Everyone on Inagua, either directly or indirectly, lives off this one company. The thousand or so people who live in Mathew Town, the island's only settlement, are themselves vastly outnumbered by wild donkeys, seed cattle and feral hogs, in addition to flamingoes.

My first choice for a place to stay, the Morton Main House, was booked up with company executives when I called six months in advance of my trip. With no proper hotels or resorts and only three or four guesthouses, Matthew Town was unprepared to handle visitors. And despite the draw of the flamingos, only fifty or sixty people visit the Park annually, and Matthew Town couldn't accommodate that many at one time.

Henry dropped me a Walkines Guest House on Bay Street, a two-story cinderblock structure at the edge of town painted sky blue and set in a garden of Elephant ears, pepper bushes, guava and yellow elder. Shading the courtyard was a large tamarind tree in which raucous Bahama parrots fed. At 65 dollars a night Walkines was a pleasant surprise. I got a spacious air-conditioned room on the second floor with a large bath and satellite TV.

I unpacked and met Henry Nixon on the street an hour later for my first trip into the preserve.

Thirty minutes into a jarring ride along a maze of rubble-strewn dikes flanked by shallow salt pans, Henry pulled the Ford pick-up to a stop at a little rise and cut the engine. There was a merciful, joltless silence. Beyond us, hidden by a thick bank of red mangrove, was another hypersalene lake from which I heard one plaintive honk and knew I was about to see what I had come to Great Inagua for. First one, then three, then 20 and 30 more flamingos rose over the green, leafy fringe of mangrove. Pumping their red and black wings, they banked left over the truck and sailing across the pan to the right settled, slo-mo running on spindly legs just before touching down in the water.

Flamingoes, which just seconds before had been to me little more than yard ornaments, were suddenly and magnificently real. In flight they were simply incomparable: flaming winged arrows, an equipoise of leading neck and trailing legs slightly arched in the middle, their wing feathers jet black in the slanting afternoon sun, their beaks menacingly hooked, and their honks baleful and lonely.

"My God," I shouted from the back of the truck. "That must have been 100 birds!"

Just then a trailing juvenile, only faintly pink, soared over the truck and joined the flock.

"Nah," Henry replied, "that's just a couple-a-birds, mon. I seen times when the bottoms of the clouds turn pink when the sun shines like this, reflecting off the clouds, they be so many birds."

Periodic droughts have crippled Inagua throughout its history. In 1873 and again in 1883, drought combined with unreliable shipping from Nassau, brought famine and disease to the island, causing widespread suffering and death especially among the very young and old, not to mention drastically reducing the bird population. This year's withering drought meant that I was seeing a hundred flamingos at a spot where Henry Nixon was used to seeing 5,000. The show was out of town, the rookery having set up house in more hospitable quarters, southern Cuba or Yucatan perhaps, where it wasn't so dry. Still, 100 flamingos at a time were enough to astonish me. The deeper we got into the Park that afternoon, the more birds we encountered, the more desiccated the landscape became. Dry, stinking ponds everywhere and the bone-gray trunks of tamarind, lignum vitae and buttonwood were evidence of the desert-like conditions on Inagua. We passed tall, branching cacti that Inaguans call dildo cactus, for obvious reasons, another reminder of how dry and untamed Inagua is, how different from casino-ridden Nassau which draws tourists like shavings to a magnet.

The next day we entered the park through a different route and came upon flamingos almost immediately, several hundred wading on spindly legs in a pan to the right. The wind was stiff, blowing yellow foam balls across the dyke, but not strong enough to muffle the sound of the engine. At our approach the flock got up and flew out to the middle of the pan, well out of reach of my 70-300 mm lens. It didn't take long to realize that if Henry cut the engine before we got to a promising site—usually a salina protected by mangrove—and I hiked a quarter mile or so ahead, I could get quite close to the birds, at least near enough to get good photos of them. Everywhere there were animal tracks crossing the roads, and spent shotgun shells. Earlier we had passed several donkeys in the brush. I asked Henry about their effect on the nesting birds.

"No, the donkeys ain't no problem. They make very narrow tracks. Very careful walkers. They don't disturb the nests at all. It's the pigs that do the damage. They root into them nests and do a lot of damage. Damn nuisance. There'd be more birds here if it wasn't for hogs. They do more hurt than poachers, for sure."

I asked about poaching, which in the past had taken a heavy toll on the rookery. "There ain't that much poaching now. We arrested one guy this year that was shooting birds. The guy that was supposed to be watching had fell asleep. We just drove up on them. Got them with no problem at all."

On the final leg of the morning's drive, we passed the huge mountains of salt at Morton Bahamas on the coast. Visually it was spectacular. The pure white salt hills against the bone-colored crushed limestone road, and the deep green of the water under a porcelain blue sky.

Back in Matthew Town, I lunched on provisions I'd brought from home—canned tuna, cured ham, tortillas, crackers and Cheez Whiz—in the Kiwanis park on the main street. I ate with two men who complained that Morton Bahamas paid them starving wages. This would be easy to dismiss as isolated disgruntlement but for the fact that the exploitation of workers has been an element of Inaguan culture since the island was settled in the early nineteenth century. Too dry to sustain agriculture, Inagua produces only salt, and Inaguans have always lived by or off it.

Commercial salt production on Inagua began in the nineteenth century. In 1849 Timothy Darling enlisted five prominent Nassauvians to form the Inagua Salt Pond Company, the first such operation on the island. In 1865 the company laid rail tracks, the first in the Out Islands, and reformed as The Inagua Tramway and Salt Company. Aided by its location on the Windward Passage, the community grew not only by the salt industry but also by the presence of shipping agents who processed transient stevedores for shipping. Fifteen years later Matthew Town had a population of 1,100, larger than today. Behind Nassau, it was the most important settlement in the Bahamas for much of its history.

In the earliest days of the salt industry, Inaguans were victimized by a truck and credit system, a conspiracy of shipping agents and merchants that required workers to get food and supplies—often-inferior products charged at exorbitant rates—from the company. Encouraged to take advances against their future earnings, many workers owed their entire wages, everything but their souls, to the company store. This was a form of universal economic slavery so egregious that workers sometimes owed more to the company than they could hope to earn in a year. Not surprisingly, a huge gulf developed between owners who grew rich and workers who languished under the burden of debt and poverty.

Labor tensions increased in the twentieth century when the Erickson brothers from New England revitalized the dormant salt operations (strangled by protective U.S. tariffs) as the West Indian

Chemical Company, increasing production six fold from 1935 to 1937. At the time Inagua laborers were making two shillings per day, less than half of what Nassau workers were making. Violence erupted in August 1937 when two local workers, who seem to have been little more than thugs, shot and wounded a commissioner, Arthur Fields, and one of the Erickson brothers near the hospital in Matthew Town. In the course of what became a rampage, the Duvalier brothers killed a company employee, burned company buildings and the radio station. "The rest," Craton and Saunders write, "was as much farce as tragedy." With Fields, the Erickson brothers retreated to their yacht in the harbor and attempted to flee, but their vessel broke down and drifted across the Old Bahama Channel to Cuba where they were arrested for possessing firearms. When news of the troubles on Inagua reached Nassau, the government sent a mail boat loaded with armed policemen to the island. It too broke down and marooned the detachment on Rum Cay. Alerted that the police were on the way, the Duvaliers retreated to Haiti where they were arrested and extradited to Nassau. They were arraigned on murder charges, tried, convicted and hanged in November.

Minus the violence, work stoppages and strikes are more common today than ever.

Some nights later, I heard a passionate complaint against the exploitation of workers on Inagua. There was a party three miles out of Matthew Town for the retiring harbormaster. The whole town was invited, with free food and drinks for everyone. Morton Bahamas was footing the bill. I'd eaten mainly peas and rice for several days and the thought of conch salad and grilled chicken, potato salad and roasted corn was invitation enough for me to walk the three miles—there were no rental cars available on Inagua—to the Crystal Beach View hotel, a dilapidated "resort" near the airport. I started hoofing it about sundown but wasn't a hundred yards along the road when a truck slowed beside me and the driver shouted past his two mates, "Goin' to the party?"

I climbed into the back and we were off.

One of two white people in Matthew Town during this week, I stood out like a trout in a bathtub but never felt anxious or threatened, and only this one evening would I feel conspicuous. When I arrived at the party, Soca covers of American R&B tunes were blaring from the DJ set, and an early crowd of revelers was already rocking. The retiree, a dignified man in coat and tie, sat with his wife not two feet from the deafening music machine. After my third generous rum and tonic, I ambled outside for a cup of conch salad (the best I've ever had), peas and rice, salad and wild donkey, shot just this day when it strayed into Mathew Town. I was choking down the donkey—thick and burnt and very gamy—when a buffed young man, six-three or so, got in my face.

"I am a slave," he shouted, "we are all slaves of Morton. Slaves, I'm telling you, mon. This is what we are, and that is our story. I will tell it to you. I will come to your hotel tomorrow and tell you the whole story."

Caught off guard with a mouth full of donkey, I managed to say that that wouldn't work. If he wanted me to tell his story, he should write it down, sign his name to it and drop it by my room the next day when I would be away watching birds. He said he would do that, though I suspected correctly that he wouldn't, and he disappeared into the crowd. A few minutes later another young man saw me admiring an attractive woman and approached.

"You like her?" he asked.

"She's very pretty," I replied innocently enough.

"You want her, she's yours."

Feeling suddenly overwhelmed by the party, I said no thanks and aimed myself down the road. I was still in sight of the party when a pickup slowed and offered me a ride into town. The friendliness and hospitality of Inaguans made rental cars unnecessary. Any traveler who sets out to find Eden will, it's true, arrive at Disappointment, but Inaguans were exceptionally open and helpful to me as well as each other. I could hardly take a walk without someone stopping to offer me a ride.

The next day we made two trips into the park, one in the morning and another in the late afternoon, when it was cooler and the light better for photography. We fine-tuned our technique of approaching the flamingos on foot, using stealth to get the best shots, but paid a high price in mosquito and fly bites. Returning from the afternoon trip Henry dropped me off in town where I walked its gridded streets—Matthew Town was founded as a planned settlement—and ate fried shrimp and bread at a tiny eatery where I tried to talk to an older man, the only other person in the room. It was useless. He was glued to "The Young and the Restless" on the TV. Afterwards, I killed an hour at a picnic table in the park feted by two impromptu entertainers, Ryan Walker and Myra Farquharson, aged seven, then headed back to

Walkines. Near the guesthouse, I passed a group of men sitting on metal chairs and drinking rum in the shade of an almond tree. I joined them and fell into conversation with a light-skinned, freckled man in his fifties who was happy to see a visitor in Matthew Town.

"We need to do more to encourage tourists to come to Inagua," he said. "If I can do anything to make your visit better," he added hospitably, "just let me know." He offered me his card. It read: "Hon. Vernon J. Symonette, M. P. Minister of State for Family Island Affairs." In nearly ten years of traveling in the Bahamas, I had finally encountered a ranking member of the Bahamian government, and he was drinking rum under an almond tree in Matthew Town, Inagua, 400 miles from Nassau! A native of the settlement—one of his ancestors was involved in the 1937 uprising—Symonette was a fourth-term Member of Parliament responsible for directing the activities of local governments throughout the Family Islands, a charge that required him to visit each of them several times a year to meet with elected officials.

We fell immediately into a sometimes testy conversation, cupping our ears to hear over the cassette player booming Soca songs from the window of an abandoned building. Symonette was confident that the nation was in better shape than it had ever been, and that Hubert Ingraham's Free National Movement government would gain seats in the Assembly in the event that an election was called. "We are prosperous now, compared to what we were in the past." I agreed, but criticized the FNM administration for selling Gorda Cay to the Disney Corporation. He fired back that the U.S had sold Rockefeller Plaza to the Japanese. But that wasn't the same thing, I said, it being a private transaction between non-governmental entities. Could he imagine, I asked, the U.S. selling Rhode Island to the Japanese? "Well, it's the same thing," he said dismissively, and I changed the subject.

I admired Matthew Town and the Park but said I was disappointed to see so few facilities for visitors. He agreed, stressing "a national priority" to build modern infrastructures—roads, water and utility systems, as well as hotels—on the Family Islands. I added that without driving off foreign investment in the Bahamas the government should provide incentives and opportunities for Bahamians to build and own resorts. In my years of traveling in this nation, I had found only one Bahamian-owned resort in the country, a small operation off the beach in New Bight, Cat Island. He reeled off a short list of legislation, including the Hotels Encouragement Act that offered

Bahamians incentives to start up tourist operations. There was some evidence already, he said, that such moves were helping Bahamians gain a foothold in their own economy. Without saying so—I didn't want to alienate Mr. Symonette—I doubted it. Apart from teachers, preachers and politicians, virtually the entire nation seemed to me a powerless group of day laborers working for Americans, Canadians, and Europeans who often disdained them as lazy and shiftless.

"But you have to understand," he continued, "that we Bahamians have it hard. It is very difficult and expensive to run anything in this country. Imagine how different it would be in the States if each of them, Kansas, Massachusetts, New York, was separated by large bodies of water, if no truck or train or automobile could cross a state line without loading its cargo onto a ship or a plane. We're a nation of islands scattered across the sea, and it is not easy to bring all these along at the same level, at the same time. We face challenges that you don't."

I didn't want to bring up the labor issues on Inagua, but I couldn't resist asking Vernon Symonette what he thought of Morton Bahamas, Ltd. "Thank God for the salt company," he said, raising a cup of rum to his lips. "If it wasn't for Morton Bahamas, this would be a wasteland."

On the surface at least, he was right. Relative to other settlements in the southern Bahamas, Matthew Town was prosperous and picturesque. Cars and trucks were numerous and of recent vintage, houses trim and freshly painted, surrounded by blooming Poinciana, hibiscus and bougainvillea. There were new houses going up at the edge of town. At the Kiwanis park in the middle of town emerald green water swept up onto a fine white sand beach. On clear, dead-calm days the hump of southern Cuba, 45 miles across the Old Bahama Channel, was visible. A mile south of town, a working lighthouse built in 1868 rose chalk-white 120 feet into the sky.

But the workers told a different story.

Without a doubt, Morton Bahamas had been good for the flamingos of Inagua. The salt pans are prime feeding grounds for the rookery, supplying the diet of brine shrimp, mollusks and water snails that, in four years, turns the flamingo its deep, mature hue, closer to scarlet than pink. Without this enormous grid of evaporating ponds, there would surely be fewer flamingos on the island. In their turn, the flamingos do Morton a huge favor by ridding the basins of crustaceans, thereby eliminating one stage of the purification process, saving Morton considerable time and money. The usually conflicting interests of corporate profits and natural habitats coalesce here on Great Inagua in a rare and remarkable way. With poaching all but eliminated and the rookery flourishing as never before, this island is a spectacular yet largely undiscovered destination for bird lovers.

Over five days of exploring the preserve, I had seen flamingoes by the thousands, even though the rookery was much smaller than usual, enough to cloy the appetite for these magnificent creatures. And there were many other birds: cranes, herons and egrets too many to count; roseate spoonbills, ruddy turnstones, plovers, and sanderlings, American kestrels and burrowing owls in the dryer sectors and, nearer to the huge mountains of salt at the Morton Bahamas, Ltd. salt works on the coast, white-tailed tropicbirds and royal terns. Marauding hordes of Bahama parrots invaded Matthew Town every morning and night.

I slept fitfully on my final night on Inagua and awoke early, in no mood to spend my final morning on Inagua being tossed about in the back of a pickup. I had arranged with Henry Nixon to take me for a short trip out of town to an area not within the park but where there were plenty of flamingos. I called Henry and cancelled. I packed and checked out of Walkines, then walked to the Morton Main House for a proper breakfast of eggs and bacon, toast and grits with Vernon Symonette. Afterwards, I walked back to the Kiwanis park and killed time before my flight back to Nassau. As the heat rose on this Sunday morning everyone and everything, even the sick and starving dogs of Matthew Town, sought shade out of the midday sun. I sprawled on a picnic table under a palm tree, lulled in and out of sleep by the rasp of waves sliding up on the beach, fanned by the gentle breeze, disturbed periodically by the squawking racket of parrots feeding in a nearby almond tree. Sometimes when I closed my eyes I would see scarlet birds on the wing against a pale blue sky.

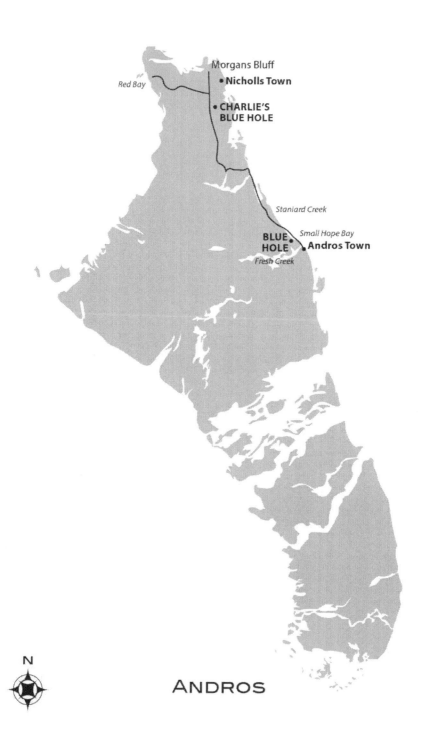

ANDROS

Chapter 9
Down and About on Andros

THE descent into Fresh Creek from Ft. Lauderdale was a roller coaster ride from the west over the vast abandoned reaches of Andros, the largest island in the Bahamas, and one of its most sparsely inhabited. On final approach to the airport—breezy, 85 degrees, a mix of sun and cloud—my view of the runway from the co-pilot's seat of the twin engine Cessna was commanding but frightening. Wind gusts tossed us about and the engines whined as we lined up on final approach. Touching down, we sped past a crashed plane, blaze white, suspended in a pine tree to the left of the field.

"He ran out of gas," the young pilot said offhandedly, as we taxied to the terminal.

I had arrived safely on Andros, "Bone-fishing capital of the World." But I wasn't here for the fishing. I've always held with Dr. Johnson who remarked that fishing was a sport conducted with a worm at one end of the line and a fool at the other. I was here for the diving. The Mecca of bonefishing, Andros is ringed by the world's third largest reef system, and the dive program at the cozy Small Hope Bay resort is the best equipped and most experienced operation on the island—actually three islands—of Andros.

I count Jacques Cousteau's development of the modern Aqualung in 1943—a compressed air canister attached to a regulator—among humanity's greatest inventions. Reefs are phenomenal natural theaters, which man is blessed to have discovered the means of entering. The thrill and beauty of diving is payoff for achieving an unnatural perspective on the natural world, one we weren't by nature meant to achieve. It's like looking at a snowflake through a microscope, or watching the earth rise from the moon.

Andros, whose reefs are not only vast but healthy, promised to be the most intense and challenging diving I had done to date. I was so excited I slept fitfully the first night, but I felt reasonably well the next morning as we checked out equipment from the dive shop at the end of a long dock and boarded the boat for the twenty-minute ride out to the dive site. The plan was for three dives this first day—ninety, fifty, and thirty feet. For the first thirty feet of the first dive my heart was racing and I was sucking air; after that I'd calmed down and barely noticed my steady descent to ninety feet. While I hovered above a mossy ledge, four of the divers with me disappeared into the black depths beneath, plunging to 185 feet. After a few minutes of hanging alone on the ledge, staring in amazement as an enormous loggerhead turtle worked the coral, I felt their bubbles feathering past me, and the four divers—two young Austrians expensively equipped, and a father/daughter team from Rhode Island—emerged like apparitions from the darkness.

At this depth, there was little color and utter blackness beneath me but magnificent shapes lurked all around, and I felt a comfortable density that came with tripling the pressure upon my body. We glided up the face of a ragged, sponge-draped ledge into warm, brightly-lit water. Coral heads, painted in varied hues of brown, yellow and red, erupted from patches of pure white sand. Parrotfish, triggerfish, mottled wrasses, trumpetfish, tangs and tiny majestic fairy basslets worked the structure. Underneath a stand of Elkhorn coral, I paused as a rainbow parrotfish, head tilted down, hammered the coral. Undulating bands of weirdly iridescent aqua and yellow against a background of reds, oranges, taupes, and tans created a scene of brilliant color such that no film or photography could hope to reproduce. I thought, had God not meant for man to dive, just as certainly as to fly, the rainbow parrotfish, like others in its family, would not be so breathtakingly beautiful. I don't mean to romanticize tropical fish. The parrotfish's blunt workman jaws—in the stillness and silence between breaths I can hear it feeding, crunch, crunch, crunch, on the reef—reminded me that there are scientific explanations for what I was watching. Avoidance of predation, reproductive drives, molecular logic. The rainbow parrotfish is, after all, a fish. But these explanations seemed, in this moment, narrow at best and frankly irrelevant to the lurid beauty I was experiencing. No strictly utilitarian drive—predation, protection, sexual attraction—could account for the creature I was looking at, its freaky lipsticked mouth of black and blue stripes, like something out of a makeup artist's febrile dream, giving way to a yellow-orange throat, then gray to electric green from mid-body back to its pectoral fin.

Back on the boat after the day's final dive, I was, as usual after diving, filled with an extreme euphoria. I had conquered the depths three times, rising smoothly and effortlessly up to the light, and felt now like I could probably walk on it. We dried out in the sun as the boat raced through the wind back to the dock at Small Hope Bay where drinks and dinner and a video of the day's dive awaited us. We talked over the day's experience—the fish, turtles, and coral—at the cabana before sitting down to a splendid feast of conch chowder, baked grouper, artichokes, potato salad and rolls.

We were an eclectic group united by the love of diving. In addition to the Austrians and the Rhode Islanders I had been paired with, there was a woman from Seattle on her eighth trip to Small Hope Bay, a couple from Paris, another from north Florida (very nice equipment also) and—most improbably—a woman from my own hometown neighborhood who the night before tapped my shoulder in the buffet line and said, "You look familiar." Sometimes, it really is a small world. Brenda and I belonged to the same swim and tennis club.

Dinner finished, we watched the video with the breeze getting up under a lovely rising moon, the rum flowing freely. Afterwards, I walked out to the cabana to mingle with a small group who hadn't been on the dives.

I spent most of the next three days underwater. While the more adventuresome divers descended to ever greater depths, Brenda from my neighborhood (her husband spent his days bone fishing) and I explored the coral heads and sandy flats at 60 feet. More brilliant coral formations, more beautiful fish. At this comfortable depth, with perfect weather, unlimited visibility, vibrant colors everywhere, I developed a Zen-like peace that is among the very deepest satisfactions I've known.

Between dives, I learned more about John, Brenda's husband. He had lived a charmed life. He'd met his wife in boarding school in Switzerland when they weren't teenagers. They'd fallen in love playing the leads in *Macbeth*. After their marriage, they'd returned to the States and John had taken a job with a pharmaceutical giant. He had been part of the team that formulated AZT, the AIDS drug. After that smashing success John had started his own company and, from the looks of his fly rod, tackle and gear—not to mention the costly guide he hired every day—had done very well.

Typically failure drives people to religion, but the opposite was true of John. In his late forties, now apparently retired, John had found Jesus. Having no theological training whatsoever he'd formed his own nondenominational church. He was a pastor now, a fisher of men as well as fish. There was an awkward moment one evening when, knocking back Mount Gay and tonic, he invited me to come to his church when I got back to Durham. He promised there would be plenty of guitar music, no traditional hymns or classical junk. This was unappealing to me. Though I'm not a regular church-goer, as the son of a Methodist minister, I was raised with traditional church music. I love hymns. I choke back tears when I hear "Just as I Am" or "I Come to the Garden Alone." It's my past haunting me.

The winter had been bleak and sad—my friend and office mate, the novelist, memoirist and poet Tim McLaurin was enduring his second bout with a deadly form of cancer, and my brother was drinking himself to death alone in Charleston, South Carolina. Within a year both would be in their graves. I've always been a pained doubter, feeling somehow incomplete and inadequate, left out of the confidence with which my parents lived their faith in The Word, like a man missing some crucial faculty like hearing or sight or taste or memory, which everyone else has. I envied John and Brenda their faith.

My last day on Andros I was ready for a road trip. Anyone wishing to explore the southern stretch of Andros by car faces some real challenges. South of Fresh Creek, at Behring Point, the island is cut by three bights, which means you have to take a ferry across two of these, the North and Middle which form Big Wood Cay, to reach Moxey Town, then take another boat across the third bight to pick up the highway at Driggs Hill for the drive through Congo Town and Kemps Bay to the end of the road at Mars Bay. Logistically, this was almost impossible. Since there was no car ferry across these bights, I figured that if I wanted to make it to Mars Bay, I'd have to hitch a ride to the dock at the end of the road, then catch a boat to the south side where I'd have to hire a car for the run to Mars Bay. Congo Town on South Andros haunted my imagination, but I just couldn't get there efficiently. Besides, I had good reason to rent a car here at Fresh Creek and drive north from Small Hope Bay to Nicholls Town at the blunt end of the island, sixty-five miles away.

In the early 1970s, a widowed aunt of mine from Pennsylvania, whom I'd met only once as a child, had pooled money with a friend and bought two villas in Nicholls Town. Why Mary chose this settlement I didn't know. But for the next twenty years these two women spent the winter months in Nicholls Town. Though I had never known her, Mary Hamilton and I had much in common. Like me, she was an English teacher and writer, and like me she loved the Bahamas. Before I left home I promised her daughter Beth that I would see if I could find her mother's villa in Nicholls Town.

I picked up my rental car—an early 90's compact Chevy—at Donald's Auto Body Repair and Welding Shop at Love Hill a few miles up the road. I turned the key and she purred reassuringly. Donald being a mechanic I trusted that the car was in good operating condition, unlike the Cat Island Merc, and other cars I'd hired in the Bahamas. Donald's only warning was that when the fuel gauge reached three-quarters empty, it was in fact nearly out of gas. The tank was almost full when I picked the car up, and so I figured I could make it to Nicholls Town and back before gassing up.

I headed west on the dirt track leading behind Donald's shop on a road that led to a large, unnamed blue hole miles back in the pine forest. Common on many Out Islands of the Bahamas, blue holes are inland lakes, some hundreds of feet deep, fed by the ocean through a system of underwater caverns and tunnels. Thirty feet or so down the water is fresh. Below thirty feet, the sea finds its level and the water becomes saline, oceanic. Experienced divers, especially cave divers, love these structures. Even for me, who would never dare to dive one, blue holes were fascinating. The blue holes of the Bahamas were featured in a recent issue of *National Geographic*.

It was 10:30 in the morning and already wickedly hot and still as I drove over a dirt track through the inland woods of the largest island in the nation, well out of the trade winds that bathe the eastern coast of

Andros. A mile or so along the bumpy road I began to worry about breaking down or blowing a tire. The engine was purring on and the needle on the temperature gauge hung steady midway between cold and hot. But the farther I drove, the rougher the rubble track became. Every revolution of the wheel was a yard or so that I'd have to walk back in the event of a breakdown or, more likely, a flat.

Three men in rags carrying machetes appeared. They didn't respond when I tipped my hand in passing. Farther along was a fork in the road, but no sign indicating the way to the blue hole. I paused for a moment and considered turning back, but the gauges were still good and I thought, what the hell, I'll keep on. The track to the right looked better traveled than the one to the left, so I took it. Another mile along, the way narrowed and branches scraped the sidewalls of the car as I crawled along.

By my estimate I was now three or three and a half miles into the woods with no blue hole in sight. The track was so narrow and the bush so thick that I couldn't turn around, so I could only go deeper inland. Then, up ahead, I saw the rear panel of a blue vehicle blocking the way. Pulling to a stop behind it, I noticed that the high-riding, old style van bore Nassau tags. My first thought was that I should have turned back at the fork. Who knew what the occupants of the faded white van were up to this deep in the woods—a drug deal perhaps—or what mischief they might have in mind for me, a lone stranger coming upon them. I cut the engine, noticing a path into the woods to the left, and in the quiet I could hear voices. I picked up my camcorder and set off along the path. I was anxious. A few yards into the woods I saw them—three men standing on a platform overlooking the blue hole. One shouldered a sophisticated video camera, the kind television stations use, and another was a tall, handsome, casually dressed man holding a microphone.

"Hullo," I said as I emerged from the trees. "Hullo," they replied and I joined them on the platform atop a ledge overlooking a circular lake a couple of hundred yards in diameter. They were from a TV station, filming a spot on the blue hole.

"Wow, this is quite a sight to behold, eh?" I said, enormously relieved. "This is something else."

Very lame, I thought, very lame. You should be able to come up with something better than this for a reporter.

"Yes," said the reporter in a friendly way. "And why are you here?"

"Well, I heard there was a blue hole somewhere out here, and I came to see it."

"And where, may I ask, are you from."

"The States. North Carolina."

"And you came all the way out here just to see this magnificent blue hole?"

"Well, this is just my first stop for the day. I'm on my way to Nicholls Town."

"And what is your name?"

"Marvin Hunt."

The reporter motioned to his cameraman to train his lens on me.

"Mr. Hunt, we're from Channel 13 in Nassau, here on Andros to do a feature on the island's natural wonders and resources, and how difficult it is to reach them. About how there's no signs along the way, and how difficult this rubble road is to travel. Do you mind talking on camera?"

"Not at all," I said cheerily.

And so began one of the strangest encounters of my Bahamian travels, being interviewed by a Nassau television crew in the middle of nowhere. On camera I gave them what I thought they wanted to hear, that the Bahama islands were richly blessed with natural wonders and resources, that Bahamians as well as visitors deserved better access to them, that the drive out here had been unnerving if not frightening, and that Bahamians ought to expect better from their government. Stepped down from the platform, I filmed the reporter's introduction to the segment he had just filmed.

"In five, four, three, two, one," he said under his breath, then loud and enthusiastic in his best TV persona: "According to a visitor visiting the blue holes here, Mr. Marvin—cut. What was the last name?"

"Hunt"

"Okay, in five, four, three, two, one . . . . according to a visitor visiting the blue holes here, Mr. Marvin Hunt from North Carolina, he says that it can be a frightening experience traveling some four miles through rocky roads with no signs. He said that proper promotion leading to this hole can be an ideal experience for all tourists."

As I was walking back to my rental car, they told me to make sure I tuned in to channel 13 at six o'clock on Tuesday when the segment would air. By then I would be long gone.

On the way back to the highway, I passed the three machete men, my car's engine still purring, and then arrived, home free, at Donald's auto shop. Donald was arc-welding something underneath a shed. I was chuckling at the strange meeting with the TV crew when I turned left onto the hard surface of the Queen's Highway for the drive to Nicholls Town.

I had a CD player, headphones and a stack of discs with me—the incomparable Youssou N'dour, a Sergio Mendes record, and a Smithsonian compilation of authentic Bahamian music that included six or eight rake-and-scrape tracks, an *a capella* version of "Sloop John B" (loved by Frances Armbrister and popularized by The Beach Boys), and three songs by the wonderful Natty Saunders of Bimini who, in his eighties when these recordings were made, was a virtuoso banjo player, and a writer of catchy and very clever songs.

In his best song, "Lynn," Natty asks a woman called Drana to find him a wife. Drana searches from Bimini to Freeport to find Natty a bride. She finds Lynn, his everlasting love. He and Lynn marry.

"I owe it all to Drana," he wails in "Lynn," "All over Freeport she been / She catch the plane, come back to Bimini and tell me / That she find a nice girl named Lynn."

The music and the open road made me cheerful. As much as I enjoy diving, I'm happiest in the Bahamas when I'm driving a reliable rental car through a landscape I've never seen, where every turn in the road reveals something new. Cruising up the Queen's Highway, listening to Sergio Mendes' version of Jorge Ben's "Pais Tropical," I felt blessed in my own deformed way.

I came upon the first wildfire a few miles south of Stanyard Creek. This wasn't a total surprise. For the past two days, returning from dives, we'd seen columns of smoke rising from the streak of green forest north of Small Hope Bay. But I hadn't expected to be stopped dead in my tracks on the Queen's Highway. Yet here was the reality of the situation: engine humming still, wheels not turning, me glancing anxiously in the rear view mirror. Ahead of the car a sinking blanket of smoke covered the road like a Maine fog. I got out and walked toward the heat. The fire, strangely, seemed confined to the roadsides. It was burning evenly down the pavement but not moving back into the woods, consuming the low brush and vines, scorching pine trunks but not reaching high into the trees. In a few moments, the pall of smoke thinned and I saw through to the other side that the way was clear and straight.

This entire region of the world, from Florida south to Great Inagua, where the lack of rain had driven the flamingos from their rookery, was in the grip of a prolonged drought. Here on Andros there was no fire fighting equipment, no one and nothing to challenge these flames, started by cigarettes or even bottles on the roadside that act like magnifying glasses in the tropical sun. Not even a flagman to warn traffic of what was ahead. So these fires were left to burn themselves out. Maybe the crew from Channel 13 would come along behind me and film the scene.

The situation was starkly ironic. Blessed with abundant fresh water, Andros ships millions of gallons of drinking water every day to thirsty New Providence, from a port at Morgan's Bluff near Nicholls Town. And yet Andros can't fight its own fires.

Stanyard Creek was a flower-strewn and scorched settlement of colorful houses, junked cars and palm trees laid out on a spit of land between the broad shallow creek to the west and a lovely beach to the east. The village seemed virtually deserted as I turned down its narrow streets. The stench of recent fires was pronounced. In the heart of Stanyard Creek, I passed a house surrounded by yellowed palms that had been burned up to their fronds. They were still smoking, but the house seemed untouched.

North of Stanyard Creek, I ran another gauntlet of flames near Blanket Sound where the highway turned sharply inland toward the west across a narrow bridge over another pale green creek. On the long, straight run to San Andros, the landscape changed subtly. The bush didn't reach the roadsides, and there were ferns underneath stands of pine trees. I soon passed a patch of forest that had burned as far into it as I could see. And not just scorched trunks either. These trees were burned all the way to their tops, the whole wood turned a sickly rust color.

Somewhere on this road I passed a development under construction: a couple of McMansions going up at the verge of a broad lagoon. I found out later that this was the brainchild of a wealthy American hoping to attract investors to North Andros.

The airport at San Andros was small but neat and clean, a reflection of the increasing prosperity the farther you traveled into North Andros. A few miles south of Nicholls Town, I turned right off the highway onto a rubble road to explore Uncle Charlie's Blue Hole. Only a half-mile long, the path ended at a clearing where five or six white men were milling about, all in straw hats. They wore gray, long-sleeve shirts, suspenders attached to long pants, and work shoes. They were young Mennonites, members of a community that operated a large and prosperous farm nearby that supplied produce for the entire northern half of the island. The vegetables I had for lunch and dinner at Small Hope, I later learned, were grown by Mennonites from Pennsylvania. I parked and walked through the bush to the blue hole only a few yards away. Several young black boys in long pants and shirts were making ready to jump into the hole. With every plunge the Mennonites howled with laughter. The last boy hesitated and they goaded him to dive rather than jump—"head premier," one said. Perhaps the boy was Haitian.

Just outside Nicholls Town the road widened and came to an end at a T intersection. There was a sign "Nicholls Town" with an arrow pointing to the right. It was Saturday and two schoolboys passed in front of my car. I offered them a ride, thinking they might have heard of or remembered Mary Hamilton, my aunt. At least they might know an old man named Merton who had been Mary's gardener. I asked about Merton.

"Yeah, he still live in Nicholls Town," one said. "But I think he's sick, in Nassau." I asked if they knew where he lived. "Down next to the Hotel." I asked and they agreed to show me Merton's house before I dropped them off. On the way into town we passed a fine building housing a police station and a health clinic, and another government building under construction—evidence that North Andros had a good friend in the Nassau government. Nearby there was a u-shaped structure that would pass for a strip mall, though it seemed abandoned.

Littered with bougainvillea, hibiscus, poinsiana, and almond trees, Nicholls Town was the prettiest settlement I'd seen on Andros. Laid out in a palm grove behind a bluff at the top of a nice beach that sloped down to The Tongue of the Ocean, it felt snug and safe and sane. There was a ruined brick hotel at the top of the bluff, its windows knocked out by a hurricane. Magnificent Norfolk Island Pines guarded it. The boys said someone was fixing it up, but I didn't see any evidence of that. Farther along I came to a lovely cemetery with plots surrounded by low, whitewashed concrete walls. Against a background of green water streaked with darker blues marking patches of reef, its graves looked out to the ocean, a view fit for eternity. Two side-by-side plots had triangular concrete headstones, waist-high, pointing toward heaven. Their hand-lettered legends were inscribed beneath the sign of the cross. One said: RIP/ SARAH/ SWEETING/ 1896-1997/ I LOVE YOU. The other memorialized Elsie Clarke, 1915-1997, with the same unconditional, eternal present tense. Down the slope behind the cemetery was Merton's small house painted in aquamarine, yellow and pink geometric shapes. The door was open but nobody was at home. The boys pointed out Mary's abandoned villa. It wasn't yet ruined but the yard had gone to seed. I took photos of them for Beth. The villa belonging to Coralea Jackson, my aunt's friend, across the street was neat and yellow and nested in an impressive garden of palms and flowering trees. She wasn't home.

I dropped the boys at someone's house and then stopped to get gas. The station's owner told me that Mary Hamilton no longer came to the island. I told him she was dead. He reacted indifferently but added that Coralea still came down for the winter. He thought Merton was ill.

I left Nicholls Town with nothing more than a glimpse at Mary Hamilton's villa and a snippet of superficial information about her life here. She was little more to me than an excuse for having come to this settlement. But really, that was enough. If I'd had more time, I might have met her ghost, but I didn't have time to spare. It was nearing late afternoon and I had another destination in mind: the settlement of Red Bays twenty miles away, the only village on the western shore of Andros.

The lateness of the day meant that I had to pass up Morgan's Bluff, named after Sir Henry Morgan (1635-1688), a Welsh captain who raided Spanish interests in the lower Caribbean and Central America. At least tacitly Morgan was not a pirate. Considered a privateer rather than a pirate, he doesn't appear with Blackbeard, Steede and others in Captain Charles Johnson's 1725 *History of the Notorious Robberies and Murders of the Pirates*. Yet, he seems to have been a pirate at heart, and a very successful one at that. Like most buccaneers of his time, Morgan took refuge in the sympathetic culture of Port Royal, Jamaica, the unquestioned capital of pirates. He grew fabulously wealthy raiding Spanish outposts in the Caribbean, was knighted and become acting governor of Jamaica at age 45, Vice-Admiral, Commandant of the Port Royal Regiment, Judge of the Admiralty Court and Justice of the Peace—handsome rewards for a career devoted to plundering the enemy in peacetime. Unlike most of his kind, Henry Morgan died in his bed, of dropsy.

I wanted to visit Red Bays not only because it was the only settlement on the western shore of Andros but also because it was founded in the nineteenth century by Seminole Indians from Florida driven off the mainland during the Seminole Wars, a series of protracted and criminal campaigns that robbed Florida's Indians of their land. American troops displaced and killed thousands in order to make room for settlers filing into Florida from the colonies. I hoped to see some light-skinned people like those of Sandy Point, Abaco.

Cut through to the settlement in 1969, the twenty-mile road to Red Bays was the first hard surfaced right off the Queen's Highway south past Uncle Charlie's blue hole. It was a dusty drive through some of the driest, most desolate country I've ever seen. Not a single car or building interrupted the wasteland of interior North Andros, just scrub and stumpy pines lining the long straight shots ending in sweeping turns on the road to Red Bays. Occasionally my car flushed ground doves from the cover of the roadside, but there was no other sign of life on the way to Red Bays. It was getting to be late afternoon, and my enthusiasm for the trip was waning. I'd listened to all my CDs, and the radio station from Nassau played an uninteresting mix of nondescript Soca tunes. I was slightly dazed from the drive and mindful of the wildfires and the sixty mile run back to Small Hope. The twenty miles to Red Bays seemed more like fifty.

At the edge of the settlement I passed kids on bikes, a ball field and scattered houses. Under a shed several light-skinned women were weaving baskets for which Red Bays is known. I didn't stop. I drove on thinking I'd come to something more recognizable as a settlement but came instead to the end of the road, a gravel parking lot and a stumpy dock. Some boys were swimming, jumping from a jonboat into the water. Their black bodies gleamed even this late in the day against a celadon blanket of shallow water that stretched to the horizon. Nearby, older boys were diving for the sponges they would store in circular impoundments constructed of young pine trunks. This was exciting to me, the only time I had seen this ancient Bahamian work tradition, virtually eliminated now with the introduction of synthetic material.

Once again I'd come to a place like Barattara on Great Exuma or Fox Town on Little Abaco, an end of the road in the middle of nowhere at the water's edge. It sounds chauvinistic, but these boys swimming and the women under the shed seemed forlorn, and I felt sorry for Red Bays being so remote and cut off from the world. Where I had come from they would probably never know. I was seeing them but they would never see me, tucked into my purring rental car behind tinted windows. I didn't want to talk to anybody, I don't know why, and so I stayed in Red Bays for only a few minutes. I had a gauntlet of wildfires to run on the way back to Small Hope Bay.

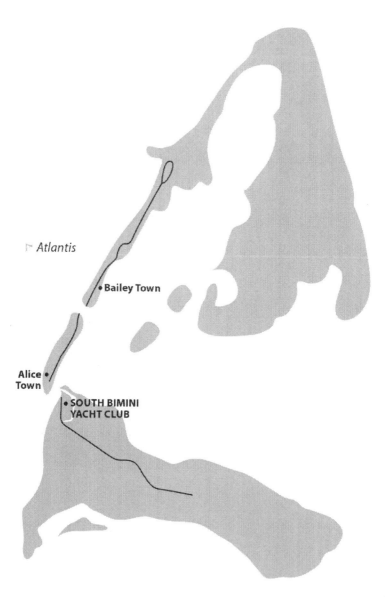

⌐ *Atlantis*

• **Bailey Town**

Alice •
Town

• **SOUTH BIMINI**
YACHT CLUB

BIMINI

N

Chapter 10
Orpheus and Atlantis on Bimini

Goldfinger: Your share of Operation Grand Slam will make you a very rich woman, my dear.

Pussy Galore: Why else would I be in it, Mr. Goldfinger?

Goldfinger: Retire to England, I suppose?

Pussy Galore: No, I've spotted a little island in the Bahamas. I'll hang up a sign: no trespassing. Go back to nature.

~Goldfinger

THE twin-engine Cessna climbed over the grid of streets and multilane flyovers of Ft. Lauderdale, rising over white roofs and palm trees, canals and swimming pools, eastward toward the uncluttered blue expanse of the Atlantic. I leaned back in the noisy back seat, a dry sink at my elbow and a flapping cabinet door overhead—relics of opulence, or at least comfort, when this plane was new and swank. Now, I could only hope that it was air-worthy.

In front of me were three pretty, very hung-over young women from Orlando taking their first trip in a small plane. Terrified, the two facing me in the rear held hands, gulped and looked earnestly at me, through the bumpy ascent out over the water. As we reached cruising altitude a mile out over the ocean, the trip smoothed out into a vast theater of puffy white clouds, deep blue sky and the weirdly green/white/blue floor of the water below us.

The prettiest of the Orlando women took off her shoes, propped her bare feet in the empty seat next to me and closed her eyes. She twisted open the little nozzle blowing air from the panel above her. Our pilot, a leggy platinum blonde from Norway named Krista, engaged the autopilot and stepped back from the cabin to join us, four lovely women and me in a plane that was flying itself. Half an hour across fifty miles of ocean separating Florida from Bimini, the closest Bahamian island to The United States, we were about to add a new chapter to the Mile High Club.

So sue me. That part about Krista coming back from the cockpit and making a wild dream come true didn't happen. But the three women with me in the plane were real. And Krista really was our pilot.

The exhausted Orlando women slept through the descent into South Bimini. Krista glided us down to an easy landing at the strip and we taxied up to the two-room International airport, climbed out into the thick heat of early afternoon, cleared customs, and waited for our bags. Inside the terminal, a peacock strutted, shuddered and fanned out his brilliant plumes.

Never again, I said to myself, would I be likely to fly through a fantasy out of Goldfinger, the only male in a manifest of lovely women.

Two islands divided by a narrow harbor, Bimini has a rich history. You could be forgiven for thinking that it received some special level of cosmic attention at its creation; it bears the imprint of the paranormal. In 1513, it's falsely reported, Ponce de Leon located The Fountain of Youth here—Bimini was actually the early name Spaniards gave to Florida. It's thought to be one point in the Bermuda Tringle where, according to popular belief, ships and aircraft are sucked into oblivion by mysterious vortices. Even now, New Age apostles gather to swim naked at night in a secret location east of the islands.

But it's best known for the Bimini Road, believed by the deluded and harebrained to be the ruins of the sunken City of Atlantis, described by Plato in the *Timaeus*. In 1934, the psychic Edgar Cayce, awakening from a trance, knowing little or nothing about Bimini, announced that Atlantis lay sunken just off its shores. In 1954, ten years after Cayce died, local fishermen reported to scientists a curious formation of sunken rocks just off the coast of North Bimini. Divers found 1500 feet of rubble now said to be the ruins of the fabled city, 15 feet under water.

Bimini might have remained a couple of tiny, obscure islands in the stream had not the United States Congress passed the Volstead Act of 1920. Prohibition brought unprecedented wealth to Bimini, almost instantly. Overnight, scores of rumrunners set up businesses here, converting houses and yachts and ships at anchor into liquor warehouses. Others sought their fortunes running rum from Bimini to Florida in fast boats. By some accounts—again, there is evidence to the contrary—one honest bootlegger gave American English a new expression for genuineness. Unlike other dealers, McCoy refused to dilute his rum, and customers quickly identified the purest Bimini hooch as "The Real McCoy."

With the repeal of Prohibition in 1933, Bimini's fortunes declined, though the islands continued to attract the famous and infamous alike. Ernest Hemingway spent the spring and summer of 1935 and 1936 on Bimini, drawn by its growing reputation as a superb game fish destination, especially the giant marlin. On Bimini he wrote *To Have and Have Not*—which is about smuggling—and got the idea for *The Old Man and the Sea*. He fictionalized his seasons on Bimini in the first section of *Islands in the Stream*, published posthumously in 1970. Other famous (and infamous) people have also been drawn to Bimini. In November 1963, the disgraced Rep. Adam Clayton Powell from New York exiled himself to a house on South Bimini. He quickly became an enormously popular and colorful friend of the local people—"Keep the faith, baby," he would say—as well as an expert angler. Powell remained on Bimini, a fugitive from American justice, until his death in 1972. And Martin Luther King, Jr. wrote his Nobel Prize acceptance speech during a retreat to Bimini.

By the time I cleared customs, Bobby Epstein of Scuba Bimini had arrived to drive us—me and the three Orlando women—to the South Bimini Yacht Club several miles down a crumbling highway from the airport. "Yacht Club" misrepresented the three-story cinderblock building fronting a canal. I didn't see anything that would pass for a yacht or a club. But I hadn't been misled. The photo of the club posted on the Bimini website didn't suggest anything grand. The nearest beach, lovely and deserted, was a quarter mile walk through a maritime forest. The canal in front of the hotel faintly stank, and a field of rusting machinery flanked it. The plate of peas and rice I ordered for lunch in the bar/restaurant—ample and nicely prepared—boded well. My room on the top floor was a bright omen, too. Recently refurbished, it was air-conditioned, had two comfortable queen-size beds, wall paintings and a fully functional bathroom and shower. If the food, the diving and the room at the Yacht Club were even acceptable, I'd be in for a happy stay.

The nearly brackish water from the sink and shower would soon be a thing of the past, with a state-of-the-art desalination plant going up near the Yacht Club. Built by the developer of the new Bimini Sands Resort south of here, the plant would effectively be a private utility, supplying water to Bimini Sands first, and then other destinations in South Bimini. Later an underwater line laid across the harbor will feed the densely populated north island, greatly enriching its owner for the foreseeable future.

Fresh water will be especially helpful to Alice Town and Bayley Town on North Bimini—venerable, historic, and crowded towns strung out along a narrow curvaceous main road called, as everywhere in the Bahamas, The Queen's Highway.

The next day Epstein took me on a tour of dive sites. In his 30 foot Apache with twin 300 horsepower engines, we fairly flew over several miles of green water south of Bimini to the wreck of the *Sapona*, a World War I-era ship of 2,795 tons that ran aground here in 1924 in 15 feet of water. Thirty feet of its hull, weathered to the color of roasted chilies, rose above the wreck like the ruins of a Greek temple. Its hull, with regular vertical openings between ribs like columns, was festooned with graffiti and pockmarked by shell holes from naval gunners that used her for target practice. A 1926 hurricane had broken off her stern. Today, sail and motor boats were anchored around her. Like bees on a hive, snorkelers worked the waters amidships while brave young men and women took turns jumping from the bow.

Built in Wilmington, NC, during the First World War, the *Sapona* was one of a fleet of 17 transport ships built of concrete and rebar, materials cheaper than iron and steel. But concrete and iron made for unacceptably heavy vessels, greatly limiting their load capacity, and like the rest of the concrete fleet, the *Sapona* was never pressed into service. Decommissioned after the War, she was purchased for $5,000 by the wealthy Floridian, Carl Fisher, who had her towed from Norfolk, VA to Miami where he planned to put the ship to use as a floating nightclub. His plan didn't work out, however—Prohibition got in the way—and Fisher eventually sold her to Bruce Bethell, a rum-runner from Nassau who planned to tow her to Bimini and convert the ship into a liquor warehouse. But *en route* to Alice Town she hit the submerged wreck of a Spanish galleon five miles short of the island, and ran aground.

Undaunted, Bethell announced that he would fit her out as a lavish offshore nightclub including a glass dance floor on her foredeck above an enormous aquarium where, according to Bimini historian Ashley B. Saunders, Bethell planned to entertain guests with the new sport of shark fighting. In an Alice Town bar, he offered a $100 reward for anyone who captured a 20-footer for his shark tank. Saunders quotes Bethell as boasting that shark fighting "will be to the Bahamas what bull-fighting is to Spain."

In July 1928 Bethell, who had lost an arm in World War I, set out for the *Sapona* in a dinghy, to chart the conversion of his ship into his dream nightclub. With him was a Biminite named John Mimms. It was a stormy day. While Bethell was making construction notes on her main deck, Saunders writes, Mimms tripped and fell from the deck 30 feet into the water. Bethell grabbed a plank and jumped in after Mimms, who was being swept away in the strong current. Unable to save Mimms or swim back to the ship, Bethell drifted toward Turtle Rocks several miles west of the *Sapona*. Nineteen hours later two Biminites, who mistook him for a turtle, rescued Bruce Bethell at Hawksbill Bar. Mimms had drowned, and a ruined Bethell took to drink. Saunders reports that he died a madman in a Nassau asylum.

The *Sapona* is the western tip of the so-called Bermuda Triangle, where five Navy Avenger bombers disappeared on a routine training flight from Ft. Lauderdale on December 5, 1945. Led by a reportedly hung-over Lt. Charles Taylor, the other pilots on Flight 19 were trainees. Shortly into their mission Taylor's compass malfunctioned and he elected to fly by dead reckoning, using landmarks to make his way back to his mainland base. The weather deteriorated. Apparently disoriented, Taylor neglected to turn his radio to an emergency frequency, which might have provided a way out of the crisis.

After reporting that he had the *Sapona* in sight, Taylor seems to have led his patrol northeast out to sea rather than west toward Florida, flying out of radio contact and eventually out of fuel, ditching somewhere in the ocean. The five Avengers and 14 crewmembers of

Flight 19 were never found. The first plane dispatched to search for the flight crashed on take off.

The Avengers, some claim, had been sucked into the notorious Bermuda Triangle, a mysterious vortex of which the *Sapona* is now a boundary point—a porthole through which ships and planes vanish.

On our way back across to South Bimini, Epstein throttled down the Apache near the remains of a plane, a DC-3 belly-up a hundred yards off shore. The wings and fuselage seemed relatively intact, a dark undulating shadow under our boat. The landing gears, protruding two feet above the water, were locked down, the right wheel still inflated and streaked white with guano. The nose pointed out from the shore. This orientation suggested that the pilot, attempting to land, hit the water at a shallow angle, spun around, and flipped the plane over on its back. Or they were heavy and dropped shortly after takeoff.

Either way, the pilot and co-pilot, with time only to freak out, died on impact. Their haul of drugs was lost to the investors.

This was a ghostly reminder of a time when drug dealers large and small, from huge cartels down to local mules working in the Family Islands, vigorously plied the trade under the benign neglect of the highest government officials. In this period, Lynden Pindling, the nation's first Prime Minister, almost certainly facilitated the drug dealing. Sad but not surprising—true, in fact, to the nation's remote and recent past. Marooned slaves settled much of Eleuthera in the 17th century. Pirates founded their republic on New Providence in the early 18th century. Rum-runners plied their trade in the islands during Prohibition.

The next morning we dove the *Sapona* and Turtle Rocks, a limestone outcropping a few miles west of the wreck. Under better conditions—clear sky with no wind or current, surge or chop—the *Sapona* would have made for an excellent shallow dive. Listed at 15 feet, my depth gauge never registered below 12. And the *Sapona* is penetrable, a true rarity in a dive that shallow. But our morning on the wreck was overcast, with a moderate current pushing from stern to bow, stirring up the floor, muting colors and limiting visibility. To make matters worse, for someone like me who's especially buoyant, shallow dives are irksome. With 15 pounds of lead on my weight belt and a full tank, I still have difficulty staying down in shallow water, especially as I use up air. The effects of diving are most pronounced the first 30 feet down, where you double the atmospheric pressure on your body at sea level. This means that in shallow water you have to clear your ears as you move only a couple of feet deeper.

Even so, the massive stern of the *Sapona*, broken off by the 1926 hurricane, was impressive, especially the huge screw. And there were thousands of fish working the wreck, smaller species such as grunts and wrasses, yellowtail and grey snappers, damselfish and sergeant majors. Inside, the hull thwarted the current and cleared the water. It was fun cruising the grid of collapsed bulkheads looking for interesting fish resting in the shadows.

The next tank, at nearby Two Turtles, was much more fun. Forty feet down I had no problem with buoyancy, and the massive coral head that marks the site, said to be one of the largest in the Bahamas, teemed with fish. The clouds had burned off and the sun brightly lit the underwater scene in all directions. At this depth you had space to relax, to glide over sandy swells between coral outcroppings, trailing unusual fish—two queen triggerfish, several large hogfish, and rainbow parrotfish, the most outlandishly colorful fish of the reef.

Then I made a serious error of judgment. Pumping my new high-thrust fins I led my dive buddy rather far afield of the boat and the other divers. When I realized what I had done, I paused and thought, where are we? Though we weren't exactly lost, neither of us had a compass, and the underwater landscape that had seemed so varied a few minutes before, now looked monotonous, markerless. I turned us back in what I thought was the direction of the boat, using the angle of the light as a guide, looking up and ahead occasionally for the black shadow of the boat. After fifteen minutes we hadn't come across any of the divers or the boat. I was becoming concerned, afraid we'd have to surface to find out where we were. I was below 700 pounds of air when we came upon a reef and began to rise up through thirty feet to twenty to fifteen, then ten feet when I popped to the surface at the very edge of Turtle Rocks. Teenagers were climbing on the scalloped limestone. The dive boat was an embarrassingly long swim behind us.

The dive group staying at the Yacht Club this week was from Jacksonville, Florida. Good, working people making their third trip to Bimini. An outsider, traveling alone, I sometimes felt strange among people who knew each other. But I liked these divers, especially Chuck and Vicky who worked for a company in Jacksonville that manufactured extruded foam products such as automobile seats.

Chuck was a tall, handsome man in his thirties whose neatly trimmed goatee framed a white, toothy smile. He no longer drank but he smoked cigarettes one after another. Still, he ran three-and-a half miles in the morning, before the day's dives. His consummate wish was to hike the Appalachian Trial end-to-end, from Georgia to Maine. Vicky was a smart, unpretentious woman, very American in her mid-thirties, at the time of a woman's life I find most attractive—subtly ample and experienced.

I gauged Vicky's mettle the next day when, coming up from a dive, we heaved ourselves out of the water onto the stern of the boat. Clad in glittering thongs, the three Orlando girls, drinking Kaliks, "The Beer of the Bahamas," were in the bow when we came onboard, giggling and playing sex games.

They'd quickly discovered that diving wasn't for them. "When I got my head under water," one said breathlessly, "I started to panic real bad." After that, the only time they got in the water was to pee.

"Oh, please," the bent-over blonde panted, feigning passion to her girl friend holding a tube of sun block, "rub it on my butt." This, before a group of rapt divers coming up from the beautiful world of tropical fish, coral and sea fans.

Sizing up the moment, the dive master asked me, *sotto voce*, "Say, man, you like the view better under water or up here on the boat." A Miami radio station blared funk-rap over the boat's speakers. Vicky asked the dive master to turn down the volume.

"There's something wrong," she said to her husband and me, of the Orlando girls, "when you care so much about your own ass."

The main reason I'd come to Bimini wasn't the diving or Hemingway or the mysterious forces associated with this island, but the hope of meeting Clement "Natty" Saunders. Behind Youssou N'dour, Natty Saunders was my favorite singer/songwriter at the time. In 1997, a friend had leant me a Smithsonian Folkways compilation of traditional Bahamian music titled "Islands of Song," which I had taken with me to Andros. The selections included "rake-and-scrape" instrumentals (saw, goatskin drum and accordion), fine and deeply felt gospel songs, including the wonderful song "Lay Down, My Sister," a lonesome old man singing "Let Me Call You Sweetheart," and "The Sloop John B."

My favorite cuts were three songs by Natty Saunders, of Bayley Town, North Bimini—"Girl, If I Write You," about a man writing a letter to his intended who doesn't know how to read; "Round and Round the Bar Room" about chasing pretty Bahamian women. And my favorite, "Lynn," about Drana who finds Natty his true-love on Grand Bahama. Driving the crowded and dangerous Interstate from my house to work and back I listened to these songs, especially Natty's. He played the banjo almost like a mandolin, wrist strumming rather than picking. But his playing was every bit as complex, varied and brilliant as any banjo player—picker or not—I'd ever heard. Living most of my life in North Carolina I'd listened to countless banjo players, good, bad and indifferent. Natty's technique was astonishing: wrist-driven, fast-time strumming, with complex chord changes and subtle modulations of volume. His songs were melodic and unpretentious but nicely structured, verse, bridge and chorus designs fleshed out with witty lyrics. To boot, his perfectly pitched voice rose above the music like a weathered bird, as fine, hard earned and exact as the finest blues singer.

Natty was in his mid-80s when the Smithsonian recorded these three tracks in Nassau in 1996. When I first emailed Bobby Epstein about coming to Bimini, I'd asked if he knew whether an old man by that name was still alive. Bobby wrote back that Natty was very much alive. He owned a bar called the *Precious de Paris* Club just up the Queen's Highway from Alice Town. He went under the alias, don't ask why, of Piccolo Pete.

I set out to find Natty on Saturday night.

Fortified with dinner and plenty of rum, we happy divers from Scuba Bimini loaded ourselves onto a water taxi and cruised half a mile through the darkness across the cut from South to North Bimini. We stepped out on the wharf at the government dock where clusters of reveling tourists were milling about under the street lights. A long night in Alice Town lay ahead.

At the wharf I hitched a ride on the back of a golf cart headed north toward Bayley Town. Crowded with two-story, haphazardly stacked buildings, cluttered with apartments over shops for the whole route, this street was curiously out of character, un-Bahamian.

The kind woman driving the cart—her two children sitting beside her—dropped me off in front of a hanging sign that said *Precious de Paris* Club.

"Natty live up there, up them steps," she said.

I gave her a fiver for the ride, climbed the stairs, and entered the top-floor room. An old man was asleep in a chair at a table lit by garish light, his chin on his chest. He was small, muscular and blue-black, with large ears, a chiseled nose and hair that ought to have been white but was slate gray. This had to be Natty Saunders.

This was an extraordinary moment in my life, a rare, almost impossible dream come true. My life had spun out the thread that linked infinitely iterable songs on a CD to a life in time, bringing me here at this hour when I met Natty Saunders. Happening on this still, thick night above a narrow winding street in Bayley Town, this alone justified the effort and expense of travel even if nothing else did.

People yearn for closure, but not me. I'm afraid of it. Closure is a coffin lid eased shut in a funeral parlor; it's Sam Pedican stuffed in a coffin in The Bluff, Eleuthera. And my younger brother now reduced to ashes in a marble urn. And Tim McLaurin's corpse stretched out in his homemade coffin and concrete crypt in a field outside Fayetteville, NC. There will be such a place for me, for all of us, someday. But not now. I was on the road, not knowing what would happen next, underwater or above it, the next minute, the next hour, the next day. Vital uncertainty, which John Keats called "Negative Capability," is the region of creativity. Had I remained at home, static, satisfied with the normal and predictable, I would never have met Natty Saunders.

"Mr. Saunders," I said, nudging him, "I've come to see you." He opened his eyes and looked up at me dreamily. I introduced myself, said that I had come from America, that I knew his songs and was a great fan.

"You're one of my favorite song writers. And you're a great player, too."

When he realized what I was saying he hitched himself up in the chair, rose and walked to the bar, taking my sudden and effusive praise in stride. An obscure artist, Natty nevertheless knew how to conduct himself in the light of admiration. He smiled but didn't look up from pouring my drink while I sang the chorus from "Lynn."

"Those are good songs on that Smithsonian record," Natty said, as we took seats at a small table across from each other. I was sweating profusely in the heat and excitement; Natty seemed comfortable. "But Smithsonian get the money for that record. Not me. I got many, many more songs better than those."

Then the dynamic shifted. I must have seemed like an apparition to Natty Saunders, come in a dream like a ministering angel. He looked around at his equipment—a tattered amp, mike stands, cords snaking across the floor—and wasted no time touching me for money.

"If I just had two thousand dollars I could make the best record of my songs. The best you ever heard. My amp is broke and the mikes, too. And you come here from the States, knowing my music. Just two thousand, I could do it. The best record you ever heard."

"You see," he said, "it is very difficult working here in Bimini. To get the money and support you need to record your songs, I mean. Nobody really appreciate what you trying to do. A man needs money to make his dreams come true."

I didn't doubt that. "I intend to write about you," I said. "Maybe that will help." Natty wasn't impressed. But I didn't have the money to make Natty Saunders' dream come true. When I said so plainly, he dropped the plea. This angel had no wings, it wasn't even an angel.

If Natty Saunders—now 90—were American rather than Bahamian he would be revered as a national treasure, a John Lee Hooker, Doc Watson or Pete Seeger, recording and living comfortably in the glow of national admiration. It was even more disappointing that while Bahamians had forgotten Natty, they still reveled in the success of "Who Let the Dogs Out?"—a stupid, immensely annoying, retooled Soca tune, covered by a popular Bahamian trio some years before.

When I asked if Natty would play awhile, he took his ornate banjo from its case on the floor, tuned up and broke into the up-tempo "All Around the Bar Room," which praises Bahamian women as "tigo"— "tiger," shaped, that means, like Coke bottles:

> *Bimini gals is tigo, tigo, tigo.*
> *Bimini gals is tigo, tigo, tigo.*
> *Round and round the bar room*
> *Round and round the bar room,*
> *Round and round the bar room.*
> *Go look for your Nassau tigo.*

Natty played for the next hour, talking between songs about how he got women, how he wrote, how he helped out Ernest Hemingway on Bimini in the 1930s. Not once did Natty miss a stroke or a beat or a note, either playing or talking. And he wasn't exaggerating when he claimed to have unrecorded songs better than the ones I knew from the Smithsonian Folkways CD. This display of consummate musicianship, songwriting and singing left me speechless.

In this impromptu concert, Natty dropped a couple of bombshells. The first—that he was the love child of Henry Ford—I dismissed out of hand, if for no other reason than that Natty was very black. His claim to have known Ernest Hemingway, on the other hand, was at least plausible, though nothing in the liner notes to the Smithsonian Folkways CD mentioned a connection with Hemingway. Neither had anyone I'd spoken to about Natty Saunders brought up Hemingway's name.

But Ernest Hemingway did in fact spend the springs and summers of 1935 and 1936 in Alice Town, living a mile down the road at The Compleat Angler. Drawn by the exploits of legendary big-game anglers Kip Farrington and Mike Lerner, Hemingway arrived in Bimini from Cuba aboard his boat *Pilar* in the spring of 1935. Marlin, the supreme saltwater game fish, was his quarry. A pelagic species so large and fast and powerful that it feeds on grown tuna, the blue marlin is a fleet oceanic nomad, rutting and hunting through thousands of miles of ocean every year. Its deep ocean wanderings are still only partly understood. The giant females of the species, dwarfing their males, can grow to weigh 1,000 pounds. Their eyes are the size and blackness of eightballs.

By the time Hemingway came to Bimini, he had already landed a hundred game fish in the waters off Cuba and the Florida Keys, using crude tackle, the sport being in its infancy. I don't know how many trophy catches he made during his four seasons on Bimini, but it must have been a prodigious number. Grainy photos of Papa standing with friends in front of enormous strung-up marlin in Alice Town hung from the walls of the Hemingway Museum at The Compleat Angler.

In Alice Town, Hemingway established an immediate bond with Lerner, the larger-than-life conservationist, philanthropist and angler, founder of the International Game Fish Association and later the Lerner Marine Laboratory on Bimini. The next year, 1936, Hemingway's wife Pauline and their children accompanied him to Bimini, living at the Blue Marlin Cottage up the rise from The Compleat Angler.

I didn't know it at the time but Natty Saunders is Louis in the first section of Hemingway's *Islands in the Stream*. The section includes a fictionalized account of one of Hemingway's most notorious fistfights.

Hemingway, wearing his trademark straw hat, was waiting on the dock when Joseph F. Knapp, publisher of *Collier's* and *McCall's* magazines, arrived in Alice Town aboard his yacht. Knapp appears to have been drunk. The two exchanged words, Knapp slurring Hemingway for his size and throwing the first punch. According to Natty, "Papa Hemingway said something ordinary. No harsh words. So Mr. Knapp call Mr. Hemingway a big fat slob. And Papa ball his fist and pow! Hit him and put him to sleep."

In *Islands in the Stream*, a wealthy, effeminately handsome, inarticulate man (a version of Knapp) arrives in Alice Town aboard his yacht. That night as the painter Thomas Hudson (a version of Hemingway) and his friends get rowdy aboard a nearby boat, Hudson's friend the writer Roger Davis (another, more honest version of Hemingway) gets very drunk, starts cursing loudly and fires a flare-gun up the hill at the Commissioner's house.

The local boys hanging out on the dock wish him good aim at killing the white Commissioner. "Burn him. Burn him," they shout. "God give you the strength to burn him."

The pretty man in creased whites, who earlier in the day had beaten his wife and insulted the locals, then passed out in his cabin, steps up on the deck of his boat. Halting and hung over, he complains that the shots and foul talk are bothering his wife. Hudson's drinking friends slice the man in white to pieces with their razor wits, freely playing upon Knapp's stunted verbal skills. It's a merciless lampoon of the publisher of two widely distributed magazines.

Roger Davis fires a flare over the man's head; outraged, he lamely retorts by calling Davis "a big fat slob." Davis explodes on him, beating his face to a pulp in a protracted scene of such intense and murderous violence that it leaves the reader wondering whether the man in white is still alive.

When Alice Town wakes the next morning, the beaten man's boat is missing from the dock. He's never again mentioned.

Shortly after the fight, Natty made a popular song of it called "Big Fat Slob." I found the lyrics framed on the wall of the Hemingway Museum at The Compleat Angler:

> *Mr. Knapp called Mr. Hemingway*
> *A big fat slob*
> *And gave him a knob.*
> *Big fat slob in Bimini*

This night we have fun.

Oh, the big fat slob in Bimini
This night we got fun.

Mr. Knapp look at him and try to mock
And from the blow
Mr. Knapp couldn't talk.
At first Mr. Knapp thought
He had his bills in stalk
And when Mr. Hemingway walk
The deck rocked.
Mr. Knapp couldn't laugh
Mr. Ernest Hemingway grin
Put him to sleep
With a knob on his chin.

After writing and fishing, boxing was the major indulgence for Hemingway on Bimini. He built a ring at the wharf in Alice Town where on Sundays he pummeled local challengers. Hemingway was a "good bar-room or survival fighter," according to his brother Leicester, who also committed suicide. Another Hemingway specialist put it to me more bluntly. "Hemingway was a sucker puncher. He'd beat up people who were smaller or drunker than he was."

Hemingway won most of these Sunday boxing matches. And he left a fighting legacy on Bimini. The island developed an impressive boxing tradition, producing more champions of the ring than any other island in the nation, a distinction it enjoys even today.

Remembering Bimini in *Islands in the Stream* Hemingway focuses his anxieties upon his children. After the fistfight on the wharf, Thomas Hudson narrates a scene in which his kids go "goggle-fishing" somewhere called Signal Rock—this could be Turtle Rocks, where I'd gotten lost on a dive earlier in the week. In a truly terrifying episode, Thomas Hudson's children are attacked by a huge hammerhead. Seeing the shark approach Hudson fires three shots but misses each time. Its dorsal fin slicing the water, the shark is setting up for the kill when the first mate and cook, Earl, fires from behind Hudson, hitting it.

The hammerhead rolls on its back and desperately pumps its tail, exposing its white underbelly. Earl puts two more shots into the frantic, dying beast while the children climb aboard the boat. Then it sinks into the deep water where not even Earl can dive to cut a trophy from it. The scene is in some ways reminiscent of the ending of "The Short Happy Life of Francis Macomber," published in 1936, one of Hemingway's best short stories.

But another episode in *Islands in the Stream* even more clearly provides a frame for one of Hemingway's later stories, the one that won him a Nobel Prize. On another outing Thomas Hudson's son, David, hooks a giant swordfish and struggles for four hours to land it. Finally, his hands bloodied from the line and reel, his feet bloodied from gripping the rail, just as they are landing it, the magnificent fish breaks the line and disappears into the depths of the Gulf Stream.

As a precursor to *The Old Man and the Sea*, the fish becomes an emblem of nature's highest challenge, and the failure to land it the sign of heroic—or pathetic—failure. David must bear it earnestly and with resignation, that night telling his father that he loved the fish most at the moment when he lost it.

"Well," David says, "in the worst parts, when I was the tiredest, I couldn't tell which was him and which was me. I loved him so much when I saw him coming up that I couldn't stand it."

At the end of the summer the boys return to their mother in the States. Soon they're in school in Paris. Within only a few weeks after leaving, Hudson gets a telegram reporting that all three—Tom, David, and Andrew—have been killed in a car that plunged off a bridge. The Bimini section of *Islands in the Stream* ends with Hudson leaving the island to attend their funeral. It's as mawkish, gratuitous and pathetic an ending as it is abrupt.

When Hemingway arrived on Bimini in 1935, he was reeling through an extraordinary life—a middle-class Michigan youth followed by a stint in journalism, then a baptism by fire in World War I, followed by the Paris of Stein, Fitzgerald and Picasso, then the bullfighters of Spain, hunting in Africa and fishing in Cuba. During his four seasons in Alice Town Hemingway continued to live large. He fished often and drank hard, fought and wrote *To Have and Have Not*.

This 1937 novel concerns a once-upright fishing guide, Harry Morgan—the name copped from the pirate/privateer—who's forced by treachery and unrelenting bad luck into a life of smuggling. The gods singularly curse Morgan. The harder Morgan struggles, the harder he falls. *To Have and Have Not* is sentimental, violent and technically flawed. At times, reading it is like sitting down next to a drunk at a bar in a strange town and listening as he spins a boozy, disjointed, overly intense story. Morgan smuggles people and hooch, anything he can be paid for or can rationalize, between Havana and The Keys, once slaughtering a boatload of Chinese men he's been paid to smuggle out. Later he's horribly wounded running a load of illegal booze to Key West. This comes five years after the repeal of Prohibition, which makes Morgan's actions seem not only gratuitous but pointless. At the end of the book, Morgan is double-crossed and fatally wounded by a gang of thugs. He dies as the Coast Guard fishes him out of the water, pronouncing mawkishly that "One man alone ain't got no chance."

In *To Have and Have Not*, Hemingway, according to *The Oxford Book of American Literature*, "for the first time showed an interest in a possible solution to social problems through collective action." Seeing himself more privateer than pirate, Harry Morgan is presented as a proletarian hero of the sea. No doubt, he stands for the disposed men of the 1930s, living through Depression-era dire straits, when circumstances forced countless average men to make desperate decisions that sometimes killed them. The problem is, of course, that Hemingway's Morgan is little more than a thug, hardly a folk hero.

To address that problem, the 1944 film version of the novel, starring Humphrey Bogart and Lauren Bacall in their first screen pairing, featuring Hoagie Carmichael and Walter Brennan, directed by Howard Hawks with a screenplay by none other than William Faulkner, radically changes the book. Hawks once said he made "To Have and Have Not" to prove that he could make a good movie from Hemingway's worst book. As a way of countering the wanton and gratuitous nature of Morgan's character (Harry becomes Steve), the movie transfers the action from Cuba and Key West of the thirties to Vichy Martinique of World War II, an island swarming with German operatives and plenty of displaced men and women either violent or inured of violence. Having Bogart resist the Nazis elevates him above what Morgan is in the novel. Even so, the movie never really works for me. Its only enduring scene comes when Bacall, walking out of his room turns to Bogart, her future husband, and says: "You know how to whistle, don't you, Steve? You just put your lips together and blow."

It's a genuinely erotic moment perfectly done, one that guaranteed Bacall film immortality. But it has nothing to do with Hemingway's novel. In fact, there's no ingenue, no version of Bacall, in *To Have and Have Not*. There's only Harry's long-suffering wife—a strong, attractive woman in her forties, enduring the repeated beating, wounding and, finally, the death of her husband.

Even while he chased big fish and thrashed local boys at the Government Dock in Alice Town, Hemingway's time in Bimini was coming to a close. He had discovered a cause larger than fishing, fighting and drinking, in Europe where the brewing civil war in Spain portended the global cataclysm of the Second World War. After Bimini, he went to Spain where he wrote passionate newspaper stories from the front supporting the freedom fighters, and gathered the material for his longest novel, *For Whom the Bell Tolls* in 1940, which depicts the catastrophic results of outlawing freedom. Despite repeated invitations from Lerner and others to come back to Bimini, Hemingway returned for only two days in 1937 and never came back again.

The decade and a half after For *Whom the Bell Tolls* was a long sunset for Hemingway, who wasn't even forty when he left Bimini. He was fading from critical attention, writing ever more bitter and pathetic stories that were either ignored or scorned. Yet a final miracle awaited Hemingway. In 1952, *The Old Man and the Sea*, his parable of heroic failure, made Hemingway again the focus of popular and critical acclaim. Two years later, in 1954, Ernest Miller Hemingway was awarded the Nobel Prize for literature.

A fading genius, the inevitable health problems brought on by heavy drinking, hard living and age offered Hemingway only one solution. In 1961 in Ketcham, Idaho, Papa shot himself in the mouth.

As I was leaving the *Precious de Paris* Club, I asked Natty for his autograph. From a room adjacent to the bar he fetched an undated poster with a photograph of himself in a suit and tie posing as a candidate for mayor of North Bimini. I asked him to sign it to "My Best Fan" and he did. I left a 20-dollar bill on the table, and Natty Saunders walked with me down the steps to the street. He flagged down a passing golf cart, we said goodbye and I climbed into the back behind the driver and her small children.

Whirring down the street toward Alice Town, it was as if I were riding through an especially lurid Bosch painting come to life. Not only were the more-or-less perpetually drunk tourists rioting, but

Biminites too, enjoying the long Bahamian Labor Day holiday weekend, were carousing wildly. It was past 11, the shank of the evening. Bleary-eyed men and women in wild array, locals and tourists shoulder to shoulder, choked the narrow Queen's Highway, staggering and laughing and threatening from alleys and front yards. Stunned by exhaustion, a toddler in a white shirt sat unattended in a yard just off the street. Farther along, a drunken, cursing, shirtless man threatened us with a bottle.

By the time I got out in Alice Town, the bemused disbelief I felt riding in the cart from Bayley Town had soured. Mostly young and toasty white people from the yachts, very drunk, littered the courtyard at The Compleat Angler. I passed a college-aged kid vomiting in the flowers. I needed to cash a traveler's check to pay the ferryman for the ride back across to South Bimini, but the bar was packed with people waving bills at the harried bartenders. Elbowing my way through this throng of people, and shouting over the noise of a cover band mangling Jimmy Buffet tunes, didn't seem worth the effort.

I loathed these people. Most couldn't report one solid fact about the Nobel Prize winning writer who spent four seasons here, though the Hemingway museum was adjacent to the bar. They'd certainly never heard of Natty Saunders. Indifference and stupefaction would consign Papa and Natty alike to oblivion.

And soon a catastrophe would erase The Compleat Angler from the record. It, and the adjacent Hemingway Museum, were destroyed by fire in January of 2006.

For these tourists this bar, this town, these islands had no past. They just wanted to get seriously drunk. But why seriously drunk? What was eating at them? They were the antithesis of Harry Morgan. Times were good. The Great Recession, which lurked unseen in the future, probably wouldn't affect them. For now, they were living off their parents' wealth. Fair children of fortune, they came ashore from yachts costing hundreds of thousands, even millions of dollars. Their buffed, crisply tanned bodies were clad in the priciest of casual attire. And they drank so prodigiously that they puked in the garden. Perhaps I was being cynical, but I hoped they'd suffer. I wanted to see failed relationships, torpedoed careers, ill health—Hemingway's life without its accomplishments—in the futures of these hard bodies desperately sickening themselves tonight.

I walked south from The Compleat Angler in the lurid yellow light cast by streetlamps to The End of the World, a one-room saloon that was the favorite haunt of Adam Clayton Powell, the disgraced U.S. representative from New York who took up residence here, a fugitive from American justice, in 1963. He bought a beach house on South Bimini and settled in, defying the Bahamian authorities to extradite him. He immediately put himself forward as a "friend of the people," preaching in churches and exhorting people in the street to live a righteous life. Powell rallied Biminites against injustice. He was fond of shouting, according to Saunders the Bimini historian, "keep the Faith, baby, and spread it gently." He held press conferences and delivered speeches on the importance of economic independence for black people. But mostly, it seems, Adam Clayton Powell fished and drank and played dominoes. He was known as the "Wahoo King," having landed 15 of this superb game species on his best day. Walking into The End of the World he would announce that "The Wahoo King is here, and he's ready to play with the domino," then order a round of drinks for everyone, and a scotch and milk for himself.

Other than being Powell's favorite watering hole, The End of the World saloon is known for the fact that all kinds of undergarments— thongs, bikinis, balloon britches and F-cup bras, boxers and briefs scribbled with inanitics—cover its walls and ceiling. I got to the bar with no trouble, and the lady tending it cashed my 50-dollar travelers check when I ordered a rum and tonic. Meanwhile, the crowd had turned its attention to a vacant-eyed redhead who came out of the bathroom, panties in hand. A round of hoots and cheers greeted her.

I would have bet heavily that no one in the crowd this night at The End of the World could identify Adam Clayton Powell in an impromptu, one-for the-money, all-or-nothing "Who Wants to Be a Millionaire."

I took my change, downed my drink and walked back to the dock where the water taxi waited. We cruised in the pitch black across to South Bimini to the landing where I paid the ferryman. I walked up the empty street half a mile to the yacht club. Lights off, the restaurant closed, the place seemed vacant. I climbed the stairs, entered my cool dark room, stripped naked and laid down in bed. Natty's songs pounded in my head and I became disoriented. Somewhere behind me, my wife appeared and I called her name; wild revelers and dark waters swirled up to my consciousness. I had the sense that I was losing something, that time was rushing through me, eating me up. Somewhere in the future my severed head floated down a river.

The next morning I was wretchedly hung-over, sweating, aching and dizzy. Well, okay, I thought, I've been here before. There was a message in this painful morning. Back in the 1980s, I had quit cocaine while high on the drug, teeth chattering, sometime in the wee hours of the morning. The drug all but talked to me that dawn, telling me never again to find myself in a moment like this, or I'll kill you. Now, as then, the pain of doing an unhealthy drug was a message from the drug itself, telling me not to do it. The devil telling me to leave him alone; evil acting as conscience, and so showing itself not entirely evil.

Queasy and dry-mouthed, I faced eggs and bacon in the restaurant with a delegation of equally hung-over men from the Jacksonville dive group. In one corner, the wide screen monitor carried a satellite feed of a woman with enormous breasts and a man with a huge schlong fucking in the surf. When the first of the dive party's sleepy-eyed wives walked in and noticed what was on the screen, I expected someone to change channels. But no. Forking slices of cantaloupe, the women seemed perky and uninterested. The men were disappointed, grew solemn and began settling their bills. One, a tow-headed man with a red face, ordered a Bloody Mary.

Soon everyone, including the three Orlando women, had left for the airport, and I was the lone guest at the South Bimini Yacht Club. I went to bed and nursed my hangover in the cool darkness of my room. Late in the morning Bobby knocked on my door and asked if I wanted to dive the Atlantis Road after lunch.

That this might be the ruins of any manmade structure, much less the fabulous city of Atlantis described by Plato, is of course twaddle. The formation is actually a line of beach rock, so common in these islands. Formed during mini-ice ages when lower sea levels exposed much more of the limestone shelf that forms the Bahama islands, rock newly exposed to light and air cracked into sometimes surprisingly regular shapes. As the sea level rose again, these rectangular slabs were submerged again. The best formation I'd seen was in Graham's Harbour, San Salvador, some years earlier where the beach rock looked remarkably like a sunken road.

We motored out of Bimini harbor, crossed the bar and cruised north along the west coast of the north island. It was a beautiful day, bright sun and calm water. With just the two of us being tended by three dive assistants-in-training, there was nothing for me to prepare or look after. A tank had been fitted to my buoyancy control vest and moved to the stern even before we reached the Atlantis Road, perhaps a quarter mile offshore in 15 feet of water.

Since it was such a popular dive site, known throughout the world, I expected very little from the Atlantis dive. But it was actually quite fun. The water instantly refreshed me. There was no current or surge to work against, and it was crystal clear to the bottom. Hundreds of gray and yellow-tailed snappers were schooling around the structure. In such a shallow dive, only air supply (an hour's worth) limited our dive.

And the Road itself was much more interesting than I had expected. Instead of being a line of simple beach rock, it really did look like the ruins of an ancient city, or at least the walls of a city. While I was prepared for symmetrical stones a couple of feet wide, what I found surprised me: scores of thick slabs 10 feet or more across, each weighing tons, lying end to end exactly as if an ancient wall had been downed by a cataclysm. It was a virtually straight line twenty feet wide in places stretching for 656 yards west where it made a 90-degree turn and continued north for another 328 feet, making a long flat L. It looked like no natural formation I'd ever seen or could imagine.

Still, if this were really a man-made structure, you'd think that would yield definitive evidence of habitation—pottery fragments or building tools, plinths, columns and capitols. But nothing of significance has surfaced, even though in 1975 David Zink, a former English teacher at The United States Air Force Academy who spent 70 days mapping the Road, claimed to have recovered a tongue-and-groove building block and a marble animal head at the site, which he delivered to the Bimini commissioner. I have no idea whether this is true or, if true, where these artifacts presently are. I was sure, however, that it was another excellent shallow dive in a region of abundant opportunities for beginning divers.

I was ready to end this trip, but not quite. Earlier in the week, lounging half asleep at the dock on North Bimini, I had been yanked out of my reverie by the roar of propellers whipping the air. I stared in amazement as a magnificent seaplane, blaze white with purple engine cowlings—a true flying boat—rushed through the harbor. Its elegant profile crossed left to right, clean and bright against the matte of green water and casuarina trees on the far shore. It was simply the bravest, most beautiful airplane I'd ever seen. I quick-stepped it down the street past The Hole in the Wall to a two-room terminal where the plane, having paused to lower its landing gears, throttled up a ramp out of the water. Spraying us with a fresh, cool mist, the beautiful bird roared across the street into a vacant lot and, turning on a dime, came to a stop.

The pilot killed its engines. The doors opened and passengers began to climb out. I was overcome by déjà vu. I'd been here before. I looked back up the street toward the dock and realized what was happening. This was the long, continuous final shot in "Silence of the Lambs" where Anthony Hopkins as Hannibal Lecter watches a man step out of a seaplane and tells his cop nemesis, Jodi Foster as Clarisse, on the other end of the phone call, "an old friend has just arrived for dinner." I had watched the scene over and over before coming to Bimini, trying to get a feel for the island.

The plane was one of the small fleet of Grumman Mallards operated by Chalk's Ocean Airways. Founded in 1919 by Arthur Burns "Pappy" Chalk, a native of Peducah, Kentucky, Chalks advertised itself as the world's oldest scheduled air service. In the early years of aviation, Chalk barnstormed the South, then served in the Air Corps during World War I and afterwards settled in Miami where he founded his air service to the Bahamas. Chalk's timing was impeccable. With the passage of the Volstead Act the following year, Bimini became almost overnight a bootlegger's free state, reminiscent of the Bahamas's pirate history. Pappy's fortunes took off. Over the next 13 years, he ferried hundreds of bootleggers and rumrunners—as well as the federal agents that pursued them—between Miami and Bimini.

After the repeal of Prohibition in 1933, Chalk's continued to thrive, flying Errol Flynn, Judy Garland, Howard Hughes, Al Capone—and Hemingway—to and from Bimini. Pappy Chalk died in 1977 at age 88 from injuries sustained in a fall from a ladder while trimming a mango tree in his yard, but that didn't mean his seaplanes would be retired. Chalk's continued to operate under a series of different owners—Resorts International and a division of Pan Am—flying daily out of Miami with a stopover in Ft. Lauderdale, then to Bimini and on to Paradise Island across the harbor from Nassau and back.

I wanted to take the final leg of Chalk's route, from Bimini to Paradise Island, very badly. I checked the arrival and departure board at the terminal. Since the plane from Bimini touched down in Nassau Harbor, exchanged passengers on Paradise Island, and then flew straight back to Bimini, I could make the round trip in a matter of a few hours. But at $160 this was a steep price for a man traveling on a tight budget.

Over the next few days I debated whether this excursion was worth the cost, and finally decided, to hell with the budget. This might be my only chance to fly in a seaplane. The morning after diving on Atlantis I set out to fly to another Atlantis—the opulent resort on Paradise Island where top floor suites cost thousands of dollars per night. Just before noon, I crossed over to the north island, walked to the Chalk's terminal and smacked down my Am Ex card on the desk. I explained to the ticket agent that I wanted to fly to Paradise Island and back to Bimini.

"But, why?" she asked.

"Just want to see what it's like to fly in a seaplane."

"But people don't just fly to Nassau and come straight back."

"But that's what I want to do."

She checked and there were seats available on the Bimini to Paradise Island leg, but she wasn't sure about the return trip. She called the office at Paradise Island and asked if there were seats available.

She nodded into the phone. "So, you know, this man just wants to get there and come straight back on the plane." She nodded again into the phone and looked at me, smiling. She was warming to me.

She hung up and wrote out a ticket. "Have a good flight, Mr. Hunt." For about the tenth time in my travels in the Bahamas, at airports all over the nation, I was thinking to myself that Bahamian women must be the most attractive, engaging and helpful airline agents and flight attendants in the world.

I walked into the lounge to wait for the plane, which was expected at any time. Sweating and thirsty, I got a cup of water from the dispenser and picked up *Island Scene Magazine*, the official publication of the Bahamian Ministry of Tourism, from the table. I sat back down and thumbed through the slick, full-color pages to the centerfold of large curvaceous roseate flamingos, a beautiful two-page spread with only the title of the story cluttering the brilliant photograph: "Counting Flamingos on Great Inagua."

It was my own story, published the year before in *The New York Times* and reprinted without my knowledge. I had worked long and hard on that story, but though it had my name on it, it no longer belonged to me. I wasn't even sure I'd been paid for the *Island Scene* reprint of "Counting Flamingos," though back in the winter I had received a check from the *Times*, which my editor at the paper couldn't explain. Now in every hotel in the entire nation of the Bahamas my article was the centerpiece of a slick magazine. And I wouldn't make a cent for it. This ought to be illegal, I thought.

Almost immediately the whirring of turboprops blasted the air, and the seaplane skidded through the water behind the terminal.

I walked outside, *Island Scene Magazine* in hand, just as it was climbing the ramp out of the water. Within minutes I was belted into a choice window seat behind the co-pilot. Beside me was a dead-seating Chalk's flyer along for the ride, and behind us tourists and local people on their way to Nassau. The spare pilot was a wealth of information. Built in 1947, he told me, this 17-seat Grumman G-73 Mallard had recently been modernized. Pratt and Whitney PT6 turboprops replaced the original rotary piston motors, an avionics package had been added—"no better than what you'd get in a used Lexus," he said—and the interior of the craft refurbished. Still, the plane had no autopilot, it wasn't pressurized, had no lavatory or flight attendant.

At 53, she was older than the combined ages of its pilot, 23, and his female copilot, 26. Hell, the plane was older than me.

The crew finished their preflight check, revved the engines and we shimmied across the street, down the ramp and sank easily up to the windows in the harbor. Pulling a lever between their seats, the copilot raised the landing gear, which closed with a thump, and the pilot pointed her nose north into the harbor. In an instant, she proved why she was so different from other boats. The pilot—a cocky young man with sculpted features, dusty blond hair and with a large mole on his cheek—pushed forward the overhead throttle with his right hand while the copilot—a trim, attractive woman wearing sleek sunglasses— covered his right hand with her left, adding her strength to his to hold the throttle full open. We roared through the water. The pilot played the yoke wildly as we rode the waves past Alice Town and Bayley Town toward the north end of the island. After the longest takeoff I've ever experienced, we lifted off. A thin mist of water from the emergency exit door beside me moistened my calf as we rose over the fringe of the island.

The flight from Bimini to Paradise Island was a lovely 50-minute cruise above luridly beautiful water, through puffy clouds and finally rain squalls as we descended toward Nassau from the northwest. Touching down, we sliced into the harbor with the sound of a hail storm on a tin roof. Then it was smooth, no bouncing or lurching at all as we sailed past a cruise ship, slowed to a stop and sank to the windows. Down went the landing gear with another thump, and we throttled up the ramp to the Chalk's terminal on Paradise Island at the foot of the enormous Atlantis resort.

I walked through the Chalk's terminal to the street and took photographs of the twin towers of Atlantis rising from the island like an enormous sand castle, and walked back inside just as my return flight was boarding. When I checked in at the counter, the woman said, "You're not listed on the passenger list. You can't take this flight"

"Well, I know they called from Bimini to make sure there was seat on the return flight," I replied

"Didn't nobody talk to me," she said. "Bedsides, nobody fly from Bimini to here and then turn around and fly back to Bimini. You can't do that."

"Oh, yes I can. I got a ticket to ride," I said, humming the tune.

The flight back was dramatic as we rose from the water and banked west in the direction of Bimini, then smooth and pleasant as we cruised back to Alice Town, touching down smoothly again in Bimini Harbor.

I had no sense of being in special danger during the flight to Nassau and back in the Grumman Mallard, but I really was. Two years later, on December 19, 2005—a month before The Compleat Angler burned—a Bimini-bound Chalk's Ocean Air Mallard crashed on takeoff from Miami, killing all 18 passengers and the pilot and copilot. The fatalities—mostly Biminites returning from a Christmas shopping trip to Miami—included three children under two years old. Sergio Danguillecourt, a member of the board of directors of Bacardi Ltd and great-great grandson of the company's founder Don Facundo Bacardi Masso, along with his wife Jacqueline, also died. The pilot and copilot were Paul DeSanctis and Michelle Marks—undoubtedly the same young man and woman who had piloted us to Nassau and back from Bimini. The National Transportation Safety Board found that metal fatigue had caused the right wing to sheer off, bringing the plane down into the cut.

The NTSB noted many maintenance problems on the aircraft. "The signs of structural problems were there but not addressed," safety board chairman Mark Rosenker reported. The entire Chalks operation was shut down. It was the end of an era, for an airline and an island, too.

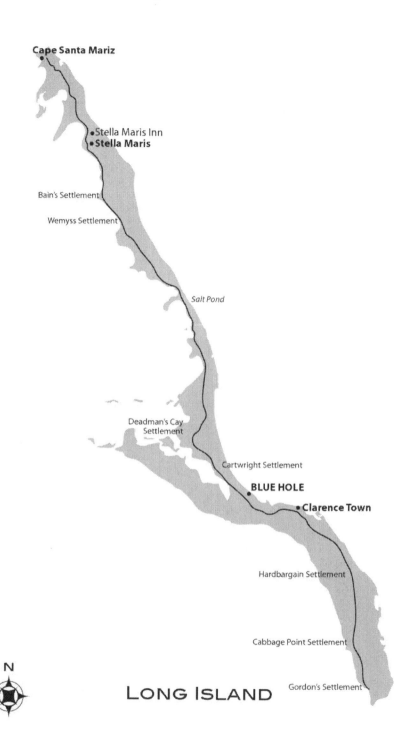

Cape Santa Mariz

•Stella Maris Inn
•**Stella Maris**

Bain's Settlement

Wemyss Settlement

Salt Pond

Deadman's Cay
Settlement

Cartwright Settlement

BLUE HOLE

•**Clarence Town**

Hardbargain Settlement

Cabbage Point Settlement

N

Gordon's Settlement

LONG ISLAND

Chapter 11
Seeking Sancutary on Long Island

L URCHING down on approach to a place called Deadman's Cay would be unsettling anytime, under any circumstance. In this instance, it wasn't the equipment—a Bahamasair twin-engine De Haviland Dash 8—that troubled me. In thirty years of service as the national airline not one soul has been lost on a Bahamasair flight, and the Dash 8 is the mainstay of the fleet. No, it was the name, Deadman's Cay, that gave me the sweats. My timing could be wrong. After all, I had flown that Grumman Mallard that later crashed in the cut next to the Port of Miami, killing all on board. Dead for a name was all I could think—the wrong name at the wrong place at the wrong time—as we wheeled down into Deadman's Cay.

But once again I cheated death. We had a smooth touch down at Deadman's Cay and a safe takeoff for the hop up to the airport at Stella Maris in the northern sector of the island.

It was early June, and the Long Islanders were prepping for the annual regatta, a three-day sailing party that attracts virtually every Long Islander, and scores of yachters from other islands too. Long Island probably doubles its population of 3,000 during the regatta, on the Labor Day and Whit Monday holidays.

But Long Island place names were a greater attraction to me than the regatta. Who could resist settlements called Burnt Ground, Hard Bargain, Salt Pond and Deadman's Cay? Then there was the florid

Stella Maris in the north, one of only a few proper resorts on Long Island, where I was booked.

I would spend a week at the nearly forty-year old Stella Maris, a 1,500-acre compound of rooms and cottages, swimming pools and cabanas, nestled in a grove of coconut palms on a hilltop sloping down to the teal-colored Atlantic on the east side, and far off to the emerald green waters of the Great Bahama Bank on the west side. Both were visible from the summit above the clubhouse.

Early June is the rainy season in the Bahamas, not always the best time to visit. But the chance of rain is offset by off-season rates and, especially in the Family Islands, by the rioting local flora—coconut, bougainvillea, sapodilla, mango, hibiscus, Poinciana. Even the "century tree," a noble name for the humble sisal so important in the 18th-century plantation history of these islands, was blooming at Stella Maris.

Named by its German founders and still family owned, Stella Maris was well appointed and quietly elegant, among the best private resorts I've seen in the Bahamas. No televisions, no locks on the doors, it was a place you could relax, eat well and soak up the sun. When you'd had enough of doing nothing, you could dive or snorkel, bike around the settlement, rent a scooter or hire a car and drive the 80-miles of Long Island end to end.

I was nearly alone at Stella Maris early in the week, taking my dinners with an engaging couple who had retired to the Florida Keys from Buffalo. I lounged about for two days, waiting for enough newcomers to make up a dive party. The third day a mini-convention of Piper pilots and their companions checked in to Stella Maris.

The next morning six divers and two dive masters cruised out of the Stella Maris harbor on the lee side of the island and turned north past Hog Cay into darker, deeper water. A strong, steady wind from the south—perfect conditions for the regatta—was bad news for divers. We anchored out of the wind, and dived on a series of coral mounds.

That was fine by me. I enjoy this kind of diving more than any other. In good visibility, such as we had, you glide around, through and above brilliant sunlit underwater architecture, enormous limestone towers covered with brain coral, bright sponges, purple sea fans and fire coral: massive underwater apartment buildings rising from a white sand floor at street level.

The spectacular tenants were about their daily work: deep blue and yellow fairy basslets, wrasses, sergeant majors, yellowtail damselfish, yellowtail snappers, blue tangs, bar jacks and a tiger grouper. On every descent, two or three barracudas materialized and hovered ten feet over my shoulder. Barracudas have an annoying but harmless tendency to follow divers, attracted by silver tanks.

In addition to the usual suspects, there were uncommon encounters. I saw my fifth rainbow parrotfish in ten years diving, my first ever yellowtail parrotfish, and several hogfish. At the end of the last dive, three large ocean triggerfish cruised by thirty feet above me as I scanned upwards and around for the silhouette of the boat.

Later that day, I was scribbling in my notebook outside the clubhouse when one of the divers sat down beside me.

"You know there was another writer here last week," he said.

"No," I replied. "Who was that?"

"Somebody famous. James Michener, I think."

I imagined a spectral Michener gliding through the rustling, wind-whipped fronds of the coconut grove at Stella Maris, like a ghost out of a Du Maurier novel.

My next thought was more unsettling. Some well-connected travel writer had gotten to Stella Maris before me. Already back home, I feared, he or she was preparing to file a story. I had been scooped before. Years ago, driving the length of East Coast U.S. 1 from Ft. Kent, Maine, to Key West, Florida, I interviewed a priest in Ft. Kent who asked: "Are you with those *National Geographic* people who came through last week covering the road?" Now as then, I had the crippling feeling of the oxygen being sucked out of me.

The next morning I headed out in my rental car south along the Queen's Highway aiming to drive until I ran out of road at Gordon's, the last, southernmost settlement on the island, seventy miles away. Peter Kuska of Stella Maris had annotated a map of the island with special stops and excursions along the way. My main objective was to visit Father John Hawes's churches at Deadman's Cay and Clarence Town.

At Simms, a hardscrabble village fifteen miles down the road, I stopped at Her Majesty's Prison, two dark concrete rooms with a small high barred window on the back wall, a relic of the colonial past closed only in 1990. Its heavy door was flung open and I was free to walk inside. Rich graffiti adorned the walls: "Farquharson, you bitch, watch your back."

I didn't know of Hawes's Church of St. Andrew at Wemyes at the time, so I missed it. Hawes designed and built this simple but charming structure—his only entirely new church on Long Island, I believe—in 1909 and 10. John J. Taylor, author of *Between Devotion and Design: The Architecture of John Cyril Hawes* (University of West Australia Press, 2000) admires the trademark Hawes features: "a bell–cot located over the chancel arch, a Romanesque altar, a vaulted sanctuary ceiling, and a simplified circular 'rose' window over the west entry doors." Hawes described it as "the Gothic type of an English village church." The altar set of six brass candlesticks once graced the altar of the Church of the Holy Redeemer in Clerkenwell, London. I regret passing St. Andrews by. It's a great hazard of travel writing that, most of the time, you get only one shot at a destination and you're bound to miss things you should have seen or done.

Salt Pond was next. For the past two days, late in the afternoon, I had driven the 20 miles south from Stella Maris to Salt Pond, the site of the Regatta. Both times, the settlement had been crowded with revelers, most of whom were hammered drunk, passed out under trees, or staggering around booths that sold conch fritters and crab patties, curried goat and mutton. The single-masted Bahama boats were riding at anchor in the expanse of pale green water of the spectacular bay. Neither time had I seen a boat under sail.

Today was no different. Boats swung at anchor in a steady breeze and, though it wasn't yet noon, spectators were already deep in their cups, some menacingly drunk. I braced myself for the long drive south with a gin and coconut water, and pulled out of Salt Pond, wanting no more of the Long Island Regatta. I listened to the radio from Nassau, site of the major Labor Day celebrations—speeches, bands and parades—interspersed with songs apropos of the occasion—"Drunk Again" and "Gin and Coconut Water."

"Everybody want to go to heaven / But nobody want to die."

Driving the hilly terrain south through Guano Cay, The Bight and Grays toward Deadman's Cay offered terrific vistas of the lee waters of the island. The list of Bahamian islands I hadn't visited—Grand Bahama, Crooked and Acklins, the Berrys—was shorter than the list of islands I had. Hands down Long Island, with its high ridge running down the middle of the island and scores of lovely coves on the lee side, is to me the most beautiful island in the Bahamas.

At The Bight, I found Hawes's Church of St. Mary the Virgin, rebuilt in 1910. Today, this once fine church sits ruined in a field of weeds. Writing in 1910, Hawes claimed that St. Mary's was the oldest standing church in the Bahamas. He added the stone domed apse and rebuilt the campanile which in 1910 looked, he wrote, "as if they might have smiled a thousand years ago across the plains of Lombardy."

At Deadman's Cay, I stopped by the lovely Church of St. John the Evangelist, which Hawes rebuilt and made additions to (like most churches on the island, the original structure, erected in 1883, had been destroyed by the hurricane) in 1909 and 10. From the debris of the wrecked church he built a shack in the church yard where a long desk he used as a drawing board doubled as his bed.

The natives were horrified that he would sleep among the dead. The shack, a villager noted, was next to the grave of one Abdenego Macandry who was "a terrible wicked ole man." Hawes replied that there was "plenty of room still for the dead people and me as well." Off opposite sides of the nave, he built two side altars with statues— the northern chapel of St. Francis and the larger southern chapel of the Blessed Virgin.

For the 30' x 15' Virgin chapel, Hawes built his first 'rock roof' to the amazement of his helpers. They couldn't believe that such a structure could stand. To prove them wrong, when he took down the last support, he climbed a ladder and "danced on the crown of the arch." Inside, a rood screen and a two-sided apse with stain glass windows depicting the Burning Bush and the Tree of Life grace the chancel. Above it, he erected a baldachin made up of four Doric columns that carry semi-circular arches that meet in a pyramid. He added a sacristy off the Chapel of St. Francis on the north side.

Most of this interior description is by report. St. John the Evangelist was locked when I saw it and I was limited to peering in the windows. I could have climbed in through one of these, I suppose, but that would have been a desecration, and very difficult to explain should someone happen along.

Near Cartwright I ate a rather too heavy lunch of curried goat, potato salad and rice at the Hillside Tavern and Bar. Soca music blaring from massive speakers out back made it impossible to concentrate on anything except eating, but I couldn't help noticing the unusual racial characteristics of people coming and going: some had dark skin and kinky hair but Caucasian features.

Miscegenation is a legacy of Long Island's colonial past. Two centuries after the indigenous Arawak Indians of the Bahamas were destroyed, and a half-century after pirates raided shipping from the shelter of its coves, Long Island, like many other Bahamian islands, was settled by American Loyalists. With the failure of the plantations and the abolition of slavery in the 1830s, many planters moved to other more fertile locations in the Caribbean and south Florida. But others stayed behind on Long Island, surviving an unthinkably difficult life of subsistence farming, working shoulder to shoulder with men and women they once legally owned and thought of as property. People being people, the two races discovered the beauty of each other.

The national telephone directory opens a window on the colonial history of Long Island. In the area of Stella Maris, built on the ruins of the Adderley Plantation, the 2003 directory listed 56 Adderleys. The area around the settlement of Cartwrights, of which the Hillside Tavern and Bar was the epicenter, takes its name from another major plantation. The phone book had 97 Cartwright numbers on Long Island, all living between Deadman's Cay and Clarence Town. The rowdy young men knocking back beers at the table next to me—one was a dark–skinned man in his twenties, blue eyes, and curly hair bleached blonde—were almost certainly descendents of the Cartwright planters. If I threw a bone from my lunch plate, I'd probably hit somebody named Cartwright. But these were big men and strong and well on their way to being drunk, so I wasn't about to test my theory.

The directory listed 15 Constantakises in the settlement of Pettys. I have no idea how or why Greeks came to settle in this tiny village.

At the rubble road south of Petty's I followed Peter's direction left off the Queen's Highway toward the Atlantic. The sign said "No Trespassing," but the chain was down. Peter had assured me that there were treasures down that road, and that guests from Stella Maris were okay. A half mile east, over a rough, rain-rutted ridge, the track ended at two perfectly curved beaches separated by a hill spar. Both were pristine, perfect coves refreshed by waves breaking over the lip of a rock barrier at the mouth—larger, more inviting versions of Neumann's Pool off Whale Point Road in North Eleuthera. I walked the rim of both; mine were the only footprints in the fine white sand.

A third cove, not far from the other two, was perhaps a half mile across, at the head of which was a pocked limestone cliff rising 50 feet above water so deep it was blue-black. Three feet from the edge, the water was only inches deep. 30 feet out, the bottom fell to a depth of 660 feet. This is the world's deepest known blue hole, one of the most extraordinary geological structures anywhere on earth.

Long ago I had stopped traveling with other people, partly for logistical reasons but also because traveling alone I didn't have to deal with someone else's expectations. But there is a sorrow to traveling alone. Standing on these remote beaches, not another soul in sight, I wanted someone to turn to and say, in true amazement, "Can you believe this?"

On the way to Clarence Town, I stopped at Max's Conch Hut, a cabana by the side of the road, and had a cup of conch salad. A mango I had picked up by the roadside a ways back and two stiff rums put me in a thoughtful mood. During my stay, Long Island had been majestically beautiful and bountiful, its waters teeming with fish and stunning coral gardens, its roads crowded with fruit trees, every cleared plot heavy with vegetables and vines. The place seemed Marvellian, a primordial garden, not so far from the Fall, where "Ripe apples drop about my head, / The luscious clusters of the vine / Upon my mouth do crush their wine; / The nectarine and curious peach / Into my hands themselves do reach; / Stumbling on melons, as I pass."

After resting in the cool shade of the conch hut, I continued south with mounting anticipation of seeing Hawes's Anglican Church of St. Paul and the Catholic Church of Sts. Peter and Paul at Clarence Town. Hawes' twin churches dominate Clarence Town, the first things you see approaching the settlement and the last you see leaving it. From a distance they are commanding, St. Paul's facing north, Sts. Peter and Paul facing south, both with twin towers rising above pitched roofs. I parked the car next to St. Paul's Anglican and walked around the gated exterior of the sanctuary, its entrance guarded by two angels. Its matching towers were penetrated with round arches and topped by wooden crosses that rose in three stages above the sanctuary. Pointed columns buttressed the thick white-washed walls of the building, behind which was a graveyard. The wind was high, and it was mercifully cool up here, despite the withering mid-afternoon sun. I photographed the exterior and then tried the door. It was unlocked. The interior was cool and lovingly appointed. Opening up from the narthex with a pedestal and font, the vaulted nave rose over a stone floor, the center aisle flanked by rows of pews and the pulpit to the right of the chancel, the dark wood contrasting with the white walls of the sanctuary. The Stations of the Cross, Hawes's signature motif, were depicted on plaques between windows. In the chancel, the altar and communion table, draped in gold-fringed satin, were flanked by candles and flowers.

The difficulties of its construction, and the turbulent spiritual struggles of its creator during this time, belie the serenity of St. Paul's. Hawes and his volunteers began erecting the walls in mid-1910, which were composed of a core of stones over which wooden forms were fitted and filled with wet lime, a kind of mortar known as tabby. The stone and mortar walls were necessary because hardwood on Long Island, as everywhere in the Bahamas since the arrival of planters, was scarce.

But tabby was plentiful. Huge mounds of conch shells, burned in open-air kilns, rendered lime. The lime was mixed with sea water, which Hawes and his helpers hauled in buckets up the hill, climbed ladders, and poured into the forms. Once the walls reached the desired height, Hawes set to work erecting the pointed arch vault of the chancel. When he completed the vault, he waited for the materials to dry sufficiently and took down the centering form.

He did so too soon; the tabby was still green. Disaster struck on Michaelmas Day, September 29, 1910 when, in his words, "a tremendous three-hours rain storm came—the arch had not properly set. Some hours after the rain had stopped—about midnight—the whole roof collapsed and fell in." The collapsing roof caused the walls to buckle. Later, he offered more details. "I was reading up in the attic of the Rectory—a perfectly still night—you could still smell the rain. Then suddenly a loud rumbling and mighty crash—cries of people running out of their houses up the street—'The church is fallen—the church is fallen!'"

Hawes didn't dwell on the catastrophe that had stricken St. Paul's. The next day he began clearing the debris and started rebuilding his church. His parishioners were to pitch in. To exhort them, he filled a basket with lime from the ruin, walked down the hill to the canal, filled the basket with water, lifted it to his shoulder, and climbed back up the hill. An eyewitness described what happened: "the wet lime . . . drained down his back to his waist and settled around his belt. He made several trips like this before he realized that his back was peeling and burning. The wet, white lime had seared into his skin and the skin of his back was peeled off in large blotches."

Hawes was forced to lie in bed on his stomach as his injuries healed. But the work went on once he recovered. He thickened the walls from a foot to four feet at the bottom tapering to three feet at the top. Hawes added a baroque stone altar and sacristy screen, as the building neared completion.

But for all the physical struggles and setbacks Hawes endured in building St. Paul's, he was undergoing an even greater spiritual crisis. On Long Island the pull toward monasticism and the Catholic faith had intensified. He could no longer resist its call. While building continued, Hawes held services in the rectory. On Sunday, January 29, 1911, Hawes failed to appear before his congregants and a catechist performed the service. Afterwards, a woman asked the catechist if Father Hawes was holding church at Deadman's Cay. "No, Marm," he replied. "I was taken by surprise . . . when Father Hawes came to my house this morning and he gimme the key of the church and [some] money, and he tell me goodbye. He ain't tell me why he gone and he ketch the mailboat leaving for Nassau."

Hawes didn't say how long he would be away. It turned out to be thirty years. Convinced that Catholicism alone could satisfy his need for isolation, stricture, ceremony and service, the thirty-six-year-old Hawes left Long Island for America where he was baptized as a Catholic at Graymoor, a former Anglican retreat in upstate New York under the auspices of the Society of the Atonement, a Catholic organization devoted to "Church unity and reunion with the Holy See." At Graymoor, Hawes designed the Chapel of St. Francis before returning to England to tell his parents of his conversion. Still unsettled, wanting "some breathing space," he set out on an extended odyssey, sailing back to America in a perilous voyage through storms and icebergs aboard the *Lake Champlain*, then took a train to Calgary where he found work as a muleskinner for the Canadian Pacific Railway and later as a farmhand near Regina. He was working his way back east across Canada when he heard his mother was gravely ill and returned to England in December 1911. In 1911 alone, the peripatetic Hawes traveled from the Bahamas to New York, crossed the Atlantic to England and back again, then forth and back across the breadth of Canada by train.

Early in 1912, he made his first visit to Rome and returned via Switzerland to England where he designed an addition to a local Catholic Church and made additional changes to his design of St. Paul's in Clarence Town, which was still under construction. Finally, near the end of 1912, Hawes returned to Rome and entered Beda College to study for the priesthood. Within a year, he sought admission to the Third Order of St. Francis and was invested as a tertiary in the Basilica of San Francesco at Assisi, fulfilling a spiritual desire that had been growing irresistibly within him since his youth.

At Beda, Hawes dreamed of returning to the Bahamas as a *monsignor*, but this was a dream to be deferred for a long time. Ordained as a priest in the Lateran Basilica on February 27, 1915, Hawes was posted to Western Australia where he spent nearly thirty years as a bush priest, church architect and builder. This was his most prolific period as an architect, and Western Australia is the site of perhaps his greatest creations. The prolific Hawes designed and/or built cathedrals, churches and chapels, convents, rectories, and hermitages in Geraldton, Mullewa and various desert outposts—twenty-four in all. The Cathedral of St. Francis Xavier in Geraldton remains his supreme achievement as a church architect and builder. In Western Australia, he also became an excellent horseman, winning the Yalgoo Maiden Race cup in 1926.

In Australia Hawes soon found himself a celebrity. He was loved by the people, feted by priests and bishops (though not without cattiness on the part of some of his seemingly envious colleagues). Now, three decades into his Australian mission, his aversion to notoriety and his peripatetic nature got the better of him and, on May 14, 1939, after the outbreak of war in Europe, he left Australia aboard the Italian liner *Romolo*, sailing west with stops in Ceylon, the Holy Land and Rome before arriving in England. From home, he turned his attention to the Bahamas again, and decided that Cat Island would make the perfect place to retire from the world and live as a hermit, arriving at Port Howe, Cat Island, aboard the *Roma* in February 1940.

From St. Paul's, I drove to Sts. Peter and Paul's on the next hill. Designed by Hawes while he was living as a hermit on Cat Island and built by the Benedictine Friar, Cornelius Osendorf, Sts. Peter and Paul was dedicated in February 1946. From the outside, it's a more imposing structure than St. Paul's, with its south facing prospect and tiered stairway flanked by stately palms leading up to its doors, above which is a recessed, circular grilled window. The exterior was blaze white in the mid-afternoon sun. The interior was cool, light and spacious, the walls adorned with the Stations of the Cross depicted on plaques between the windows.

Hanging behind the barrel-vaulted altar is a rood triptych, enamel over wood carved with a pocket knife, of great power and beauty. Mary and Joseph, vividly painted in regal colors, flank the crucified Christ whose side-wound seeps blood. Mary sheds tears but Joseph is stoic, in Hawes's words, "not the long haired spineless effeminate youth (as alas usually portrayed) but . . . a strong thoughtful face." Christ wears "a simple small blue loin cloth." His hair is "a dark 'burnt sienna' brown," Hawes wrote, "the neck, ribs, knees undercut in low relief and the fingers and toes painstakingly carved in fuller detail." If this work (like so many other Hawes's paintings) seems Gauguinesque, that impression isn't mistaken. Inspiration for Sts. Peter and Paul's triptych came, Hawes said, from the primitivism of Gauguin's "The Yellow Christ," painted in 1889.

I climbed the hot and narrow winding stairway of the eastern tower and from the top gazed out over Clarence Town. It was a brilliant prospect, offering a view of the entire southern section of the settlement down to the water. I climbed back down, knelt before the altar and said some words for my brother who had died a year ago this day in Charleston, and walked out into the blinding sun.

South along the Queen's Highway I passed through Dunmore and stopped at Hawes's Assumption Chapel, built in 1943, but I was churched-out and had another twenty miles to go to the south tip of the island and then the long drive back to Stella Maris. So I carried on through Hard Bargain, Roses, and Cabbage Point, where the road was flat and straight, lined by stone walls marking 18th-century property boundaries. There were scattered houses and at several places sunken fields flanked the road. These were small, defunct versions of the vast flamingo-feeding pans on Great Inagua.

There were more goats than people on the final stretch of the Queen's Highway, and the goats didn't concede my half of the road. I was stopped twice by meandering nannies with kids. Then a sign appeared—Gordons—marking the southernmost settlement on Long Island, though I didn't see any evidence of a village, just the end of the paved surface and a causeway to the right over a mangrove flat to another pristine beach with water the color of blended lime and cream. I drove over and parked under a casuarina tree.

Once again in the Bahamas—as at Barattara on Great Exuma, Crown Haven on Little Abaco and Red Bays on Andros—I had come to the end of the road at a place so remote that it wasn't well enough known to be called forgotten. With not another soul around me, I gazed out at the pale green water of the Great Bahama Bank that stretched to the horizon. Behind me was the rental car I'd taken to so many rough places on Long Island, the rubble causeway and the end of the road.

But the end of the road was only the end until I turned the car around and started back to Stella Maris. At that moment, the end became the beginning. It's all a matter of perspective. And timing. Checking out the next day, I came across this entry in the guest book, written the date I arrived: "Thanks for four wonderful days, John Grisham."

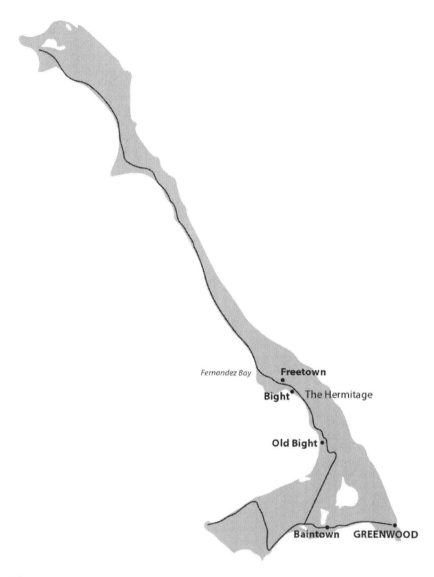

Fernandez Bay   **Freetown**

Bight   The Hermitage

Old Bight

Baintown   **GREENWOOD**

N

Cat Island

Chapter 12
Back to Cat: Stone Temples

A LONG the perfect mile-long arc of Fernandez Bay, a desiccated sea grape leaf cartwheeled silently past me down to the water. It was a beautiful thing, a sudden pleasure typical of the experience at Fernandez Bay on my second trip to Obeah-haunted Cat Island. Cozy cottages set among palms, hibiscus and bougainvillea, wind singing in the palms, sea grape leaves tumbling down in to the water. This was perfect.

I was taking it easy, soaking up the sun and recharging my batteries with simple pleasures. Up at 7:15, brew a pot of coffee, chuckle with P. G. Wodehouse for half an hour, then walk the beach under a brightening tropical sky to where the bay ended at a pocked limestone ridge covered with bonsai, wind-stunted palmettos and yellow hibiscus blossoms. Hang my towel on a ghostly spar of driftwood, take an easy swim along the base of the ridge to the mouth of the bay, threatened only by a nesting tern that dive-bombed me every morning. Afterwards, a slow walk back to the resort and a shower in the garden bath I shared with two truculent hermit crabs, and a curly-tailed lizard with voyeuristic tendencies. Breakfast at the lodge—fresh mango, cantaloupe, papaya, watermelon, cereal, toast and eggs with sausages—and then late morning excursions.

Much had changed in the years since my last trip to Fernandez Bay. Fran Armbrister was dead. She had fallen ill the day after

Christmas, 2001, and been airlifted to Holy Cross Hospital in Ft. Lauderdale, where physicians had given her up for dead. But she defied their prognostications and recovered sufficiently to return to her beloved Fernandez Bay where joyful islanders thronged to visit her. She died in her cottage on March 19, 2002, surrounded by her family and friends, and the lovely gardens and waters of the resort she had built and loved so much. Five ministers spoke at her memorial service. Her son Ted concluded his eulogy with the words of her favorite song, "The Sloop John B," which may have first been composed on Cat Island, rendered in the idiom of the island:

> *Call for the captain ashore—I wanna go home,*
> *I wanna go home, I wanna go home. I feel so break-up,*
> *I wanna go home.*

The old lodge had been replaced by a new, much grander main building erected closer to the center of the compound. Tony and his wife, Pam, still ran Fernandez Bay, which seemed lovelier than I remembered it. Sea Grape House, the two-bedroom, two-bath duplex where I was staying, was a mere thirty yards from the beach. The weather was wonderful. I had come back to Cat to take a closer look at Hawes's churches, but otherwise I planned to do as little as I could get by with—little other than gaze out at the electric green water from a beach chair. I was nearly alone at Fernandez Bay during the first part of the week but on Wednesday visitors began arriving, some by private plane. Mike and Sharon and their children flew in from Huntsville, Alabama, in a Piper Lance.

Mike loved to fly. I hadn't known him two hours when he invited me for an aerial tour of the island. After breakfast the next morning, clutching a placemat inscribed with a map of the island, I was strapped in the co-pilot seat roaring down the runway at New Bight and up into the wild blue yonder.

The island, covered with thick scrubby vegetation, was heating up and spawning thermals. The Lance pitched and yawed, bounced and swayed, making it difficult to follow the map. We flew north along the western, lee coast past Arthur's Town—Sidney Poitier's hometown— around the northern cape and back south down the eastern coast, flying 500 feet above miles of spectacular beaches to which there were only sporadic dirt tracks.

God, what a beautiful run it was—pure white sloping beaches fronting emerald green water beneath our wings. If the west side was placid, the eastern coast of Cat was dynamic. Twenty yards out from the beach, wild gardens of coral heads appeared as dark shadows beneath the water, hundreds of them stretching out to a reef line marked by white flashes of surf in winds fetching from Africa, the very winds that drove Columbus to this island sometime during his first voyage to the New World.

North of Columbus Point, Greenwood Resort and Dive Center came into view. Waldemar Illing had tutored me through my first dives here; I planned to revisit Greenwood the next day. From Columbus Point we banked steeply west and followed the scalloped southern bays of the island staying off shore where the air was smoother, passing the settlements of Port Howe, Zonicles, Bain Town, Devil's Point and Hawks Nest where we turned back over land. The plane's shadow crossed the lonely road north to McQueens, and only a running commentary with Mike through our headsets kept my churning stomach from rejecting breakfast, then mercifully we were back out over the Exuma Sound due north to New Bight in smoother air. We turned inland again and made three kidney bruising passes over Mt. Alvernia so I could click off some shaky photographs of The Hermitage. We approached the air strip from the north and Mike guided the Lance to a smooth landing at New Bight. I was relieved to be back on the ground but very happy to have made the flight. I offered to pay for the fuel we had used but Mike, who was the soul of kindness and generosity, wouldn't hear of it.

I paid the cab fare back to Fernandez Bay Village. Since my last visit, the government had passed a law prohibiting the once common practice of resorts shuttling their clients to and from the airport—this, so that local cab drivers would be guaranteed a cut of tourist money. The new policy had little effect upon visitors to Fernandez Bay, which is only a couple of miles from the airport, but added significant costs to people booked at more remote resorts like Greenwood and Hawks Nest.

After lunch, I took to the water. Fernandez Bay didn't have a dive service but the little cays in the mouth of the bay were excellent for snorkeling. The usual, unusual suspects worked the rocks: frantic tangs, fairy basslets, wrasses, snappers, a stoplight parrotfish. Once I came upon a family of Nassau Groupers—two enormous adults and a juvenile—hovering under a ledge. On the way back to the beach I paused above more stunning sights: a juvenile French Angelfish—silky black with bright yellow bars, vivid and near perfect as an artist's rendering, running vertically from dorsal to ventral. Farther along, a starfish a foot broad, arrayed in rust red and white lines, rested on the dusty bottom. Then the tail wing of an airplane reposing conspicuously on the white sand.

The flight with Mike had been exhilarating and my snorkel trips to the rocks in the mouth of Fernandez Bay lots of fun and always different; the rum flowed in the late afternoon, and my dinners were consistently excellent. I was having a superb time of it, but my days on Cat were running out and I had still to visit and revisit Fra Jerome's churches.

The next day, I started out early, drove south to the base of Alvernia, parked and climbed the steep path past the thirteen Stations of the Cross. I was alone at The Hermitage this morning. In the narrow confine of the oratory I sat as I had on my earlier trip to Cat, at the prayer desk by the window and gazed out over the southern reach of the island. The spirit of Father Jerome, this remarkable Franciscan architect, builder and monk, expert horseman and sailor, whose journeys I had tracked on Long Island and here on Cat, was again palpable. A noisy group of schoolchildren on a field trip appeared presently and broke the spell, so I left Alvernia to them and climbed down the hill.

At Freetown, I stopped at Father Jerome's splendid Catholic Church of the Holy Redeemer, ruined by a hurricane that struck on Sunday, October 5, 1941, and, like the Church of St. Paul in Clarence Town, Long Island, Hawes had rebuilt from the walls up. Though it lacks the grand setting of his two great Long Island churches, Holy Redeemer, consecrated in 1948, is arguably the summit of his achievement in the Bahamas. Outside, the plastered buttresses, blinding white in the sun, were angular and severe, the irregular walls they supported were built of exposed rough limestone blocks. Jerome was especially pleased with this "antique" effect. He especially admired the stonework, "weathered and stained with the rains." The structure was adorned with gargoyles and topped with a belfry bearing the legend "*Christo Liberatori.*"

Holy Redeemer is an oddly-shaped, asymmetrical structure. Jerome admitted as much, calling it a "queer-looking building." I found it powerful and deeply moving. The main entrance, on the side rather than the front of the church, opens into a vaulted nave of transverse arches with purlins, the center aisle divided into rows of pews leading to a lovely chancel and apse, the altar dominated by a large rood painting of the bleeding Christ flanked by Mary and John the Baptist, "fashioned after models of the Greek rite, the figures not being carved in the round but cut out of flat boards one inch by twelve inches," in Hawes's words. Its vivid primitivism reminded me, as the rood in Sts. Peter and Paul in Clarence Town had, of Gauguin. Beneath and behind the rood cross is an altar and tabernacle in front of a seven-light west window. The northwest corner of the apse leads to a small sacristy. Fourteen glassless, grilled windows, each of a unique design, punctuate the walls which are adorned with the Stations of the Cross. Niche altars are recessed into the north wall. Across from the main entrance is a baptistery whose centerpiece is an exquisite font topped by a praying angel.

The sanctuary contains—or once contained—a mural. I don't remember seeing it, but can't imagine overlooking such a wonderful painting. Perhaps it has faded, perhaps it no longer exists, but Hawes lovingly described it in his letters. Its centerpiece is—was?—a "high-pooped (fore and aft) schooner, flying the papal flag," complete with detailed and accurate rigging, ropes and cork floats. The background is a busy but calm sea composed of what seem almost Bosch-like details—popes, a snake, a raven, fishes and birds, a zodiac, "the gray wolf of Gubbio with snarling teeth and red tongue," a rat "praying for a bit of bread." Hawes described this fantastic painting as "primitive and crude, but outright and vivid, planned as a didactic catechism instruction."

From the cool sanctuary of Holy Redeemer, I stepped out into the murderous heat of the midday sun, got in the car and drove eight miles south to Old Bight, passing the ruins of the Armbrister plantation along the way, and stopped at another of Hawes's churches, the hauntingly beautiful and nearly derelict Church of St. Francis of Assisi, consecrated in 1945. Hawes undertook this project—with donations of £193 provided by the Tertiaries of Western Australia and £50 of his own money (among the last he had)—in response to the villagers of Old Bight who asked for their own place of worship such as Freetowners had.

With the exception of its thatched roof, which was constructed by local artisans, Hawes built this structure virtually by himself. He couldn't possibly walk the eight miles from the Hermitage to Old Bight, work all day, and then walk back home, so prior to undertaking the construction of St. Francis he built a tiny *portiuncula*, or priest's lodge, on site where he ate and slept. He erected the church's façade and walls, three gables, cot spire and fleche first, working from makeshift scaffolds and in constant danger of falling.

Above the north-facing entrance is a blackened gray limestone façade depicting St Francis in his cowl with his arms uplifted feeding birds that bears the legend *D. O. M. Et in Honorem Sancti Francisi Hoc Templum Sacrum* ("*Deo, Optimo, Maximo*—To God, Most Good, Most Great and in honor of St. Francis this church is dedicated.")

You enter through wooden doors into a pewless, hot and empty space dominated by a crucifix above a stone altar guarded by twin angels fixed to the southern wall. The crucifix is a dark-skinned and violently scarred Christ. "Why should we always present [Christ] . . . as 'White man'—?!" Hawes asked in his diary, "Or worse, pink! So I have made this crucifix figure dark skinned," he continued, adding, "not of a negro type, but of an Indian (Lucayan or Carib) type—long glossy jet-black hair and beard, and I have painted it very realistically—with all the black and blue—and gory-weals of the terrible scourging."

Dedicated to his beloved saint, to whose order he belonged, and whose example of poverty and simplicity he emulated, this once-lovely church was truly a labor of love and devotion. It was sad to see it abandoned and ruining in the bush of Old Bight. With no priest living on Cat and services no longer held in St. Francis, the only celebrations here are the occasional weddings arranged by Tony and Pam at Fernandez Bay. This important church is ruining in the bush of Old Bight.

Even so, St. Francis is faring better than other Hawes churches farther south. Another eight miles along the Queen's Highway I circled the roundabout at the southern extreme of the island, and took the eastern route through Bain Town, Zonicles, Port Howe and Bailey Town, settlements I had flown over earlier, toward Columbus Point. Hawes's Chapel of St. John the Baptist in Bain Town is completely ruined, a mere shell of a building sprouting weeds and bushes through vacant windows. I continued east all the way to Greenwood Resort to drop in, unannounced, on the Illings. It was roiling hot and cloudless but spectacularly beautiful and breezy when the ocean came into view at Greenwood.

Greenwood was more beautiful even than I remembered, with palm trees and flowers framing the view from the dining area down to the ocean. And completely empty. I walked down to the water and back up to the pool, called in the kitchen window but no one answered, then ambled back down to the beach. I remembered details of my last visit here—the heat, the food, the rattle-trap rental car, Hazel Brown the Obeah doctor, my first dives—while relaxing for half an hour in the shade of a palm. Then I heard a vehicle rumble up to Greenwood. It was Waldemar, sweating profusely, back from helping a neighbor restore an old house at Columbus Point. I was happy that he remembered me. It being the off season, the absence of clients at Greenwood wasn't troubling. In fact, Waldemar was busy with a project that would, if he could pull it off, greatly increase his profile, and boost the profitability of his Cat Island investment. Twenty five miles up the coast, he had discovered a nineteenth-century Spanish warship sunken in thirty feet of the Atlantic. It was an ideal dive site, ready-made. But a fifty-mile round boat ride to and from the wreck was practically impossible, so he had petitioned Bahamian authorities to permit him to cut a track east from the Queen's Highway across the interior to the coast where he would build a dock, boathouse and dive shop. So far, he had met with nothing but obfuscation from the government.

It was great to see Waldemar again, but he was busy and I had other stops to make. I left Greenwood for the ruins of the Deveaux plantation at Port Howe, where Father Jerome had made landfall aboard the *Roma* on February 4, 1940, after a perilous voyage from New Providence. At the time, a Deveaux descendant—as far as I know the last of the family—still occupied the house that was a virtual ruin even then. In this crumbling plantation house, Hawes celebrated his first mass on Cat Island before a congregation of three—Mrs. Deveaux, a mother and her infant child. Here's how he described the plantation in his diary:

> The house is bare and empty. Mrs. Deveaux sleeps downstairs—says there are 'Too many sperits' [sic] upstairs—it's haunted. I choose a large empty room (well haunted!) about 18 feet square upstairs—and they put up a table and chair in it. I sleep on the bare boards on the floor—but next day they bring a

grass stuffed mattress. It is an old 18th century house . . . walls two feet thick with window seats, sash windows, and shutters— first floor above empty ('haunted'!) and big attics on top—3 stories, balcony and verandas—but alas! all falling into disrepair and running to ruin. They use the nice old shaped ornamental balusters for daily fire-wood in the kitchen!

An architect on decaying architecture; a spiritualist on spirits.

An ancestor of this old woman had engineered one of the great coups in Bahamian history. The patriarch of the family, Andrew Deveaux Sr., was a rich planter and stock farmer in Beaufort, South Carolina, and a fervent Loyalist who abandoned his estate and lands after the American Revolution and accepted the grant of extensive lands in southern Cat Island. His like-minded son, Andrew Deveaux, Jr., joined the British forces in 1779. After the siege of Charleston, Lord Cornwallis commissioned Deveaux, Jr., to muster a regiment called the Royal Foresters, for which he was given the rank of colonel. With his band of Loyalist irregulars, Deveaux became an intrepid guerilla commander and warrior, capturing two rebel generals. When the British evacuated South Carolina in 1782, Deveaux and his men went south to St. Augustine, the capital of East Florida, but did not stay long.

Finding St. Augustine inhospitable, Deveaux and seventy followers sailed from Florida to Abaco in six vessels, the largest of which were the twenty-six gun *Perseverance* and the sixteen-gun *Whitby Warrior*. He declared uninhabited Abaco for England and sailed on to Harbour Island where he recruited and/or impressed "almost the entire male population and most of the local ships" for his great mission: to liberate New Providence—and thus the entire Bahamas—from Spanish rule. If the early historical accounts are true, Deveaux's stunning defeat of the Spanish is nothing short of biblical.

Arriving under the cover of darkness east of the main Spanish forces occupying Ft. Montagu on April 10, 1783, Deveaux, it's said, launched his force ashore in skiffs, some of his troops dressed as whooping Indians, some not men at all but fascines (bundles of sticks, the origin of our word "fascism") disguised as men. Once ashore, the invaders got back in their boats and, flattening themselves below the gunwales, returned to the mother ships. Deveaux repeated this ruse again and again while the Spanish, who far outnumbered the invaders, watched from the fort. Convinced that an enormous force was upon them, on April 18, Don Antonio Claraco y Sanz, the governor, ordered Montagu's cannons struck and surrendered to the English without firing a shot. Deveaux had retaken New Providence, and thus all the Bahamian islands, virtually without bloodshed.

Michael Craton and Gail Saunders dismiss this story as fanciful, noting the "Bahamian Liberator" himself embellished the incident "with exaggerated color," and adding that Claraco already knew that the return of the Bahamas to England had been agreed upon in the terms that would be ratified as the Treaty of Paris on September 3, 1783. They suggest that Claraco simply knew the Spanish loss of the Bahamas was a forgone conclusion and gave up.

Whatever the truth is—I expect it lies somewhere between the early romanticized accounts and the skepticism of modern historians—there is no reason to doubt the circumspect claim of Craton and Saunders that "Claraco was tricked and outmaneuvered by the guerilla methods of Deveaux and his second-in-command, Archibald Taylor." It was indisputably a great victory for Deveaux and Taylor, whose men—white, colored and black—were rewarded with large tracts of land in north Eleuthera and houses in Dunmore Town on Harbour Island.

Andrew Deveaux, Jr. was rewarded with thousands of acres on Cat Island, where his father was to relocate, but instead of settling on Cat he spend most of his time in England and the United States. It was his father, Andrew Deveaux, Sr., who built the manor at Port Howe, having transferred his slaves and livestock to Cat Island. He spent the rest of his life here, dying at the age of seventy-nine on December 23, 1814. He outlived all four of his sons.

It was low tide when I got to the ruined Deveaux estate at Port Howe, the marsh and rotting seaweed stank, it was buggy, snaky and murderously hot. Behind the ruin is a boggy marsh and a wide flat shoreline. I couldn't imagine living in such a hostile place. I walked through the first floor but even that seemed dangerous. At any step you might crash through a rotten board and break a leg.

In Bailey Town, just up the road from the skeletal ruins of the Deveaux plantation house, is perhaps the least known of Fra Jerome's standing churches, Our Lady of Sion. Fernandez Bay had arranged for someone to unlock the building for me, so I tooted the horn at the top of a dirt track leading to a small rectangular stone sanctuary in a clearing of tamarind and sugar apple. By the time I got out of the car, an old lady in a red dress and a straw hat was making her way down the drive with the key.

Completed in 1942, Our Lady, like some other Hawes churches on Cat Island, has not fared well. The interior walls were covered with cheap paneling. Yet it was not in ruins. I had the impression that its few congregants had lovingly tended Our Lady of Sion, like the corpse of a dear sister.

As I walked toward the rear of the church, the lady in red pulled back a curtain revealing a shallow sacristy containing a wooden rood propped up against the wall. Five feet tall, pristine, painted in still bright and vivid colors, it once hung above the altar in Our Lady of Sion. Oversized nails pierce Christ's feet and hands. In his right hand he holds a round communion wafer, a representation of his own body. Blood pours from his side-wound into a cup. The Body and Blood of the Eucharist. Sad-eyed, his head tilted, he wears a royal crown above which the legend reads "Jesus of Nazareth, King of the Jews." Mary and Joseph are missing. It's stylistically primitive and even more Gauguinesque than the other Hawes roods I'd seen.

For a moment I felt like I was trespassing, a meddler in this sacred place. This crucifix—the icon of a great private man, long forgotten— was made for his congregants, not for an interloper. And, propped in the sacristy, it was hidden even from congregants. Not for mortal eyes to behold, I suppose. But this uncomfortable feeling passed. Here in this hot chapel with this special guide—Father Jerome had christened the lady in red—transfixed by a rood tucked away for years in a tiny church on an obscure island, I felt an exquisite physical thrill. I had lifted another veil on the spirit world of Cat Island.

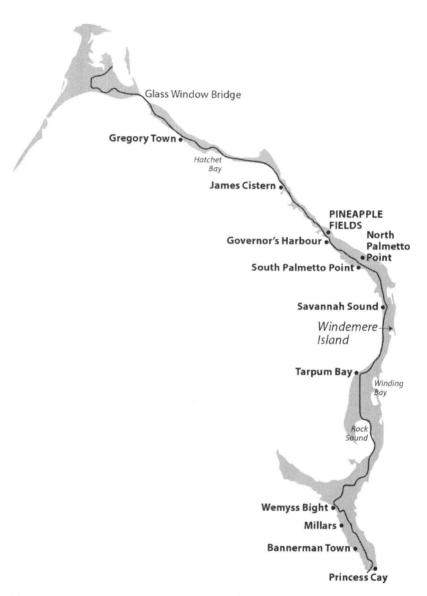

Glass Window Bridge

Gregory Town •

Hatchet Bay

James Cistern •

PINEAPPLE FIELDS

Governor's Harbour •

North Palmetto Point

South Palmetto Point •

Savannah Sound •

Windemere Island →

Tarpum Bay •

Winding Bay

Rock Sound

Wemyss Bight •

Millars •

Bannerman Town •

Princess Cay •

N

ELEUTHERA

Chapter 13
Eleuthera Redux, Harbour Island To Bannerman Town

I HAD managed to save some money over the school year, and so I decided to splurge. I had never really roughed it in the Bahamas. By no means luxurious, Cambridge Villas in Gregory Town, Eleuthera, the research station on San Salvador and Walkine's in Mathew Town, Great Inagua, were comfortable, and other places— Small Hope Bay, Fernandez Bay, Stella Maris were quite nice. Still, I hadn't stayed anywhere really luxurious, though there are plenty of grand hotels and resorts in the Bahamas.

I booked three nights at Pink Sands on Harbour Island. Chris Blackwell, founder of Island Records, bought the property in the early nineties and transformed it into a quiet paradise. An instant mecca for A-list rock musicians and actors. If you're lucky, you might see Jagger or Bono or De Niro at Pink Sands, or a bevy of runway models sunbathing on the three miles of truly pink sand fronting Pink Sands. If not the famous, then the simply rich—tanned middle-aged men and trophy wives wearing white cotton dresses, and their bonny children.

The water taxi slipped up to the government dock at Dunmore Town, one of the oldest post-Columbian settlements in the Bahamas and its colonial capital. It was just before 11 on Sunday morning—in time for me to make it up the hill to Wesley Methodist Church at the corner of Dunmore and Chapel streets, past pastel-colored, flower-festooned, hurricane-shuttered clapboard houses of this crowded little town founded perhaps as early as the 1650s. I slipped into the church and took a seat in the back pew.

This church hour, in a song-filled sanctuary out of the oppressive heat and blinding sun, would be my last immersion, for a while, in the world of ordinary Bahamians that had become so familiar to me over the years. The only Bahamians I was likely to encounter at Pink Sands would be serving me food and drink, or tidying my room.

Pink Sands was another quarter mile up Chapel Street, but a world away from Wesley Methodist. Three magnificent banyan trees prefaced a koi pool, an open-air lobby, dining area and lounge decorated in a mix of Balinese, Moroccan, and Indian influences. Designed by Barbara Hulanicki, the place had a nostalgic Raj-era feel about it, as if you might find white-linened Kipling reading in one of these over-stuffed chairs, beneath a whirling ceiling fan. Beyond the lounge and dining area the 25 cottages of Pink Sands were scattered over the crest of a hill on 20 acres of manicured grounds—coconut, sapodilla, almond, mango, casuarinas, hibiscus and bougainvillea swept down to the beach.

I checked in and waited for a golf cart and driver to take me to the garden cottage that would be mine for the next three days. Dixie Trail was a one-bedroom, four-square pyramid-roof structure designed after the derelict "leaf houses" I described earlier, especially San Salvador. It was a thing of beauty, its private patio facing down a winding path cut through a thicket of sea grape to the beach. Inside, it was aromatic and cool. The centerpiece was a magnificent bed of hand-wrought Balinese teak. The window shutters were Jamaican cedar, the floors fine marble. There was cable TV and a CD player and a collection of discs. The bathroom featured pink travertine tiles and a rain-shower.

I walked down to the beach and scanned the scene. It was a spectacular sight, the waves broken by a reef line a hundred yards offshore, the water inside pale green and calm, the sand indeed pink. Back at my pad, I put on Marley's "Exodus" and chilled on the patio, rum and tonic in hand. Then another. Then I went inside and fell asleep in a cool cloud of pillows.

At five, I showered and dressed for dinner—my usual tattered T-shirts and tattoos wouldn't do—and walked back to the lounge. The friendly bartender plied me with more rum and tonic and afterwards I had a fine dinner of spiny lobster and freshly prepared vegetables, aware all the while that there would be a steep reckoning for these luxuries at the end of my stay. The only other people dining were a family of four—a handsome man in his early forties, his beautiful wife and their two lovely little girls. I would later learn that she was a clothing designer from Los Angeles and he her business manager.

The next morning I had eggs and bacon at the Blue Bar just up from the beach. During his first stay here years ago, a bare-chested Robert De Niro famously made a scene at the Blue Bar. Asked to put on a shirt, the notoriously temperamental De Niro protested and a contretemps followed. The manager was called in; De Niro was told that there would be no exceptions. He must put on a shirt or leave. In the end, De Niro relented and became contrite, so I was told, and has since been a regular visitor to Pink Sands.

I ambled a quarter mile down the beach and settled under a cabana. It was a glorious day. There were no more than fifteen or twenty people in the water and on the beach. Near me, at the water's edge, three children played in the sand. Bored with his sand castle, a young one ran toward a beautiful woman under the next cabana. "Mommy," he begged. "Can I have another juice?" Only then did I notice she was topless. Euro-chic meets American home values.

The reef line was intriguing. I walked back to Dixie Trail, got my snorkel gear and returned to the cabana, snorkeled up and waddled backward into the undulating green water, warm as a bath, turned over, cleared my mask, and cruised out toward the reef. As I neared the structure, it was clear that something was very wrong. The reef was a featureless line of sand-blanketed coral topped with fleshy algae blooms swaying in the light surge. Not a fish in sight. I was perusing a dead reef.

Why this tragedy? Dying reefs are a frightening global phenomenon, of course, and the answers are complex. But here at Pink Sands the reasons seemed clearer. Storm-driven wave action had sucked sand from the beach back out over the coral, coating its complex and delicate lungs with a fine-grain phlegm. The hideous algae bloom was another problem and question. Maybe climate change was to blame, warming the water a degree or so, enough to feed a bloom that finished off the strangling reef. This was the case Conrad Neumann had pointed out to me years earlier at the Club Med beach on Eleuthera. But there was a more immediate possibility. Only three miles long and half a mile wide, Harbour Island is crowded year round. In peak season, thousands of people swarm the beaches and fill the shops and streets of Dunmore Town. Human waste, pumped deep into the limestone bedrock of Harbour Island from every house and hotel, leeches out over years.

It was a sad snorkel, for sure, but irrelevant to beach-combers. From the shore a dead reef and a living reef look the same. If it didn't dull the pleasures of Pink Sands, the dead reef did stay with me.

That night I had drinks and another toothsome dinner with friendly well-heeled strangers who were remarkably unaffected, including a young man and his new wife. He was the son of the owner of a NFL team and had been present the night that The Compleat Angler in Alice Town, Bimini, had burned in 2006. He showed me photos he had taken of the raging fire. Both were friendly and open, but she seemed dissatisfied, even unhappy. I was reminded of Fitzgerald's remark that the rich really are different from you and me, and Hemingway's droll reply, "Yeah, they have more money."

My final day at Pink Sands, I booked an off-shore dive, to see how widespread the damage to the reef system was. There were only three paying customers—me, the new owner of the Pineapple Club north of Gregory Town, and his daughter—on the boat. We cruised southwest from Harbour Island for twenty minutes in the direction of Eleuthera. The ride out was rough, the sea heaving beneath periods of bright sun interrupted by scudding clouds. We anchored half a mile off-shore, directly opposite Glass Window Bridge. The dive site, known as The Plateau, was a 10-acre system of coral canyons beginning at 35 feet and descending to 90. *National Geographic* had featured this area for its diversity of hard and soft coral.

Beneath the surge it was a magnificent descent into Wonderland—gliding down canyon walls darkened by clouds and then exploding into bright colors as the sun broke through, producing a kaleidoscopic effect. Fifty varieties of hard coral are found here, and they were all robust and beautiful, untroubled. What a contrast to the reef at Pink Sands! We cruised through a vertical seascape, rising weightlessly along underwater walls as richly varied and colorful as the desert at sunrise.

The canyons supported stunning swarms of fish—black durgons, yellowhead wrasses, parrotfish and angelfish, slippery dicks, blennies and tangs. We came upon a stack of sleeping yellowtail snappers. In the deepest shadowy region of muted colors, at 90 feet, the carapace of an enormous loggerhead turtle appeared. We had been promised a reef shark.

"We didn't see him," Andy the dive master later said, "but he saw us."

Back on the rocking dive boat I was rapt, gazing west to the cliffs of North Eleuthera where only twenty feet of rock under Glass Window parts the Atlantic and the Caribbean, separating the heaving blue ocean from bleached green shallows beyond the Bight. Half a mile out at sea I nursed a Kalik aboard the dive boat. Here the water was only 35 feet deep at places. Another mile or so out, the bottom drops to a thousand feet. This precipitous shallowing of the ocean floor approaching Eleuthera, abetted by the concave line of cliffs, propels huge volumes of water toward Glass Window Bridge, driving up monstrous, killing waves such as those that took Sam Pedican to a watery grave.

That night I had my last dinner at Pink Sands, and talked with the members of a rake-and-scrape band that entertained us. I asked if they had ever heard of Natty Saunders. "Yeah, man, we know Natty. He still alive and kickin'."

The next morning I checked out, took a cab to the dock ($4), then a water taxi across the harbor to Eleuthera ($5) and another cab to the North Eleuthera airport ($5) where I picked up a rental car. In the past few years, Eleuthera had become something of a darling of travel media, with a consequent influx of visitors. Major newspapers and magazines touted new developments and major changes to the island. My plan was to drive the 110-mile long island end to end to see what changes Eleuthera had undergone.

I drove north through the Bluff to the grave of Sam Pedican and then south through Lower and Upper Bogue. Just north of Glass Window Bridge I turned back north along Whale Point Road, parked and climbed the steep slope of pocked limestone. I was hoping I might find Marvin Gardens, or the shelf of rhizomorphs I had stumbled upon on my first trip to this area. But I didn't. Nearing the summit, I got down on my stomach and, inching toward the edge, peered over the cliff top. Seventy or eighty feet below, the Atlantic thundered into the base of the wall. Thrilled and terrified—slip up here and you would fall to your certain death—I looked out across the water to the place where, the day before, I had scanned the cliff face of North

Eleuthera from the dive boat. It was very strange that then I was there and now I was here.

I stopped at Glass Window and walked across the bridge. Since my last visit the span had been replaced—elevated ten feet and moved maybe ten feet west of its old position—to put it out of the reach of rages. It hadn't worked: rusted rebar was exposed in the concrete approach to the span. By 2008, the bridge had been reduced to a single lane. The government has hatched an ambitious project to replace the bridge with a causeway that will be strong enough to withstand the most powerful waves. I'll believe it when I see it.

Creeped out, I got back in the car and gunned it across the bridge, one eye on the road and the other on the Atlantic, blue-black under a cloudless sky. I drove south on the Queen's Highway, past the turnoff to Lenny Kravitz's house—the rocker's mother's family are Bahamian—toward Gregory Town. On the way I stopped by the Cove resort sprawled on a hillside on the western, leeward side of the island. Years before, I'd had drinks here; I had dived with the owner and his daughter the day before. Completely renovated, The Cove was handsome and inviting, though nearly deserted this day in early June. The high season—October through May—had been very busy, the desk manager told me, owing in part to publicity generated by stories featuring the Cove in the American and European press. I didn't see my dive buddies.

Cambridge Villas hadn't fared as well as other Eleutheran hotels. It isn't on the water; it's on the edge of town; it's not even villas, but rather the same pair of concrete buildings and a restaurant flanking a swimming pool. Though open for business, the place was deserted today. Resorts like the Cove, of which there are nearly a dozen on Eleuthera now, attract press attention but not, sad to say, locally owned hotels like Cambridge Villas, which could boast only good food and an average pool. Harcourt Cambridge, sitting alone in the restaurant, offered—as he had the last time I dropped in on him years before—to sell me the place at a bargain price.

Before leaving Gregory Town I stopped by the local surf shop. Since the sixties the stretch of beach from Gregory Town to Hatchet Bay has attracted hard-core surfers, as I'd found out years before. Steve, the owner, who had surfed this area since the sixties, moved to Gregory Town in the eighties and opened his shop. I asked about the pace of change on Eleuthera.

"Well, there's been change, for sure," he said, "but this island's not nearly as developed as it was in the sixties, before independence."

"Back then, this island was really going strong. A major playground for rich Brits, who poured money into developing it. You know those empty silos near Hatchet Bay?" he asked.

You can't miss these towering derelict grain bins, ghostly sentries on a rolling stretch of the Queen's Highway south of here.

"Those silos fed cattle that supplied beef for the entire island and beyond. That whole area was ranches. Once independence came, the British packed up and left. It was like the father driving along with the kids in the back seat hollering, 'when are we going to get there?' Dad gets fed up, slams on brakes, gets out and says to the kids, 'okay, you drive.' He comes back two years later and the car is exactly where he left it, rusted out, the tires all flat. That's basically what happened when the Bahamas became independent."

Ex-pat chauvinism, for sure, but there's certainly more than a grain of truth in it.

I drove on south passing the silos through Hatchet Bay and James Cistern toward Governor's Harbour, the first and largest settlement on the island, a lovely scattering of pastel colonial-style homes on a hill sloping down to a cluster of shops, a grocery store and bank, and a park flanking the beautiful harbor.

I had booked three nights at the spanking new Pineapple Fields on the Atlantic side, just up and over the ridge from Governor's Harbour. In the first phase of a planned 32 units on 80 acres, Pineapple Fields is a new kind of resort—the hotel condo. The target market is baby-boomers looking for an investment opportunity in paradise—with on-site management to handle renting the condos when they're not there.

The developers first built Tippys, a fine-dining bistro on the beach, and then began developing the condos across the road. An upscale deli and coffee shop, offering scones and lattes, meats, imported cookies and jams followed, and the developers have plans for an outfitter and dive shop. My new one-bedroom, ground level unit seemed to have been fitted into the landscape without cutting a single limb of a twisted Gum Elemi tree that hugged it. The deck looked out over lush native vegetation across the street to Tippy's and the beach beyond. The large living area (satellite TV) was nicely furnished and the kitchen (no garbage disposal) featured superior-grade cabinetry and appliances. The bath was spacious; the bedroom large and comfortable with a view of the ocean.

Given the environmentally sensitive approach to development, the quality of material and workmanship at Pineapple Fields, the venture seemed enlightened, likely to appeal to eco-travelers. The only dark lining to this silver cloud is the fact that Pineapple Fields, on the Atlantic side, is a sitting duck for hurricanes. One big storm could obliterate the condos, restaurant and deli—and everything else in its path.

It's easy to forget this peril while walking the gorgeous pink sand beach at Pineapple Fields. For a hundred yards I strolled beside a magnificent sting ray, four feet across, gently undulating its wings effortlessly down the beach less than a foot from the water's edge. Crickey.

Offshore was a dark reef line, similar to what I had seen at Pink Sands. Was this one also dead? I would find out tomorrow.

Back at Tippy's, a motley group of locals and ex-pats was gathering for drinks and dinner, while a large nurse shark worked the shallows just in front of the restaurant. Nobody took notice of the shark. The bartender told me that this was a regular stop for the animal. Food at Tippy's was consistently superb. The French chef treated the usual island fare—conch, grouper and lobster—with a continental flair of savory sauces and artfully carved vegetables. I liked the Old World handling of New World cuisine. Scrumptious desserts.

Mid-morning the next day I snorkeled the reef north and south of Tippy's. It was dead as Elvis, dead as the one at Pink Sands, or nearly so, and dead in the same manner—choked with sand and fleshy algae. I didn't have a camera with me but, cruising along, I came across a sight so shocking and vivid you'd expect to see it in *National Geographic*: a huge brain coral maybe five feet across, a brilliantly Byzantine maze, one of the wonders of the ocean, momentarily lit up by parting clouds as I looked down from above. The top section was pristine. The bottom two-thirds were covered in sand and algae. I was circling a silently drowning giant. How many people who come to Pineapple Fields, who drink and eat at Tippy's knew, or cared, what was happening just off shore?

That night, I fell into conversation with Ed, an affable, silver-haired man, brash but good-natured, in his mid-sixties, wearing shorts, a Tommy Bahama island-print shirt and flip-flops. He offered his opinion on women.

"If you're gonna get involved with a woman, make sure she's the mean type. Kind of hard, you know, a bitch." He whispered the word. "They can't get inside you. Won't have time. Short and sweet. They can be a pain in the ass alright, but it just won't last that long. They'll be gone before they can get much from you."

"It's the soft ones you've got to stay away from. The loving kind. They hang around too long, get too far inside you. You end up marrying them and before you know it the trouble starts. They get so far inside, and then they turn on you. You'll pay hell to end it, believe me. The ones that seem to be the most trouble at first do the least damage. The ones you'd think wouldn't hurt a fly, they end up taking you to the bank."

I liked Ed and bought him a drink. Just as the drink arrived, his dinner party walked in—three women, two men, and two children. His extended family, maybe. The women sat down across from the men. The oldest must have been Ed's wife or lover—she wasn't wearing a wedding band. She looked to be in her late fifties, brown, sun-damaged, with long, slender fingers and perfectly maintained hair. Diamonds dripped from her earlobes. I wondered if she was one of those "soft ones" that Ed described, who had gotten deep inside him and was now backing out with bags full of his money. Later I heard that he was worth millions.

"Hey," Ed said to the table, throwing his arm around my shoulder. "Let me introduce you to Martin. He's staying across the street. New in town. Say hello."

"Hello, Martin," they said in unison. I sensed I was about to be asked about myself. I've met my fair share of rich people in the Bahamas, and as a middling writer and minor Shakespearean, I'm always uncomfortable in such encounters. If I told the truth, they'd probably be disappointed.

"So, do you have a last name, Martin?" the oldest woman asked, as she unfolded her napkin.

"*Coeur de Fer*" popped out of my mouth.

"What's that?" she asked.

"Collier," I said.

"And what do you do, Martin Collier?"

"I'm in publishing."

"When I was a girl, my family subscribed to *Collier's Magazine*. Any connection?"

"You betcha. That's us," I said.

I needed to get out of this situation, and fast, before this lie could take root and grow out of control.

"So I'll leave you to your dinner. Enjoy your evening."

"So long, Martin." Ed said. "Maybe we'll see you tomorrow."

"Maybe you will."

I would make sure they didn't.

I walked out of Tippy's into a starless, black night. The clouds were so thick I had trouble finding the path up to my condo. The weather channel showed a large front rolling up from the south. The call was for rain, at times heavy, tomorrow.

The next morning the world had been transformed. The greens and blues of the ocean, the pastel buildings, the lush foliage around Pineapple Fields had all been erased, leveled to a writhing slate grey. White waves, rolling heavily up on the beach in front of Tippy's, went subterranean. Clouds lowered and whirled, and bands of rain swept the street and rooftops. Squalls twisted the treetops and set palm fronds writhing.

I drank coffee under the awning on the porch out of the wind and rain and then packed my cameras for the drive down to Bannerman Town at the southern end of the island, 60 or so miles away. The foul weather would make the trip something of a challenge, at the very least deadening the visual thrills of driving in the Family Islands. But this was my last full day on Eleuthera, and I was determined to drive until I ran out of road. I stopped by the deli, bought a sandwich and a bottle of juice that I tucked into a small collapsible cooler, then drove north, turning east down the hill into Governor's Harbour. I filled the car with gas, withdrew money from a nearby ATM and hit the road.

I crossed over onto Cupid's Cay and drove past Ronnie's Hi-D-Way, where Conrad Neumann and I had had drinks many years before. From Cupid's Cay, I made my way through a narrow back street and then across the causeway and turned south for a mile or so out of town where the street widened into a road and soon merged with the main highway. It was raining hard now and the wind was whipping up drenched leaves and fronds and flowers, scattering debris across the road. The highway to Palmetto Point was hilly and winding, the road punctuated with garages, shops and convenience stores. The leaden vista gave them an especially poor and shabby look, nothing dressed up or hinting at tourist appeal.

More steep hills and sharp curves on the drive toward Savannah Sound, where a side road leads east to Windermere Island, the location of a resort made famous in the 80s when Princess Diana was photographed there in a revealing bathing suit. South of Savannah Sound the highway hugged the long, elegant curve of Tarpum Bay, but the usual colorful menagerie of greens and blues had been repainted a flat, featureless grey, the waves washing up to the highway at places. From Tarpum Bay, the road turned inland for a straight shot down to Rock Sound, a major destination for yachters in the region and the hub of life in southern Eleuthera. Several airlines now serving the airport at Rock Sound with daily flights funnel tourists into this attractive settlement nestled along a lovely harbor.

I came into town from the north through a narrowing and surprisingly crowded street to where the road took a sharp left and the harbor came into view. The rain had stopped and the sky was lightening as I ate my sandwich in the car at the dock. On another day this would have offered a stunning view east across the Sound. Here it was still dark and turbulent. Behind me, a group of boys and girls—American scouts—wearing rain slickers trooped behind me along the roundabout at town center.

I would have liked to walk the streets of Rock Sound to get a feel for the place, but it was approaching mid afternoon and I still had long stretches of road to cover. I drove out of Rock Sound into the hinterland of South Eleuthera. This was a very different stretch of road—thick and lush, with bowers of trees forming at places nearly a canopy over the asphalt, with stretches of what appeared to be cultivated land beyond the tree line. Along other stretches, clustered houses too small for a name hugged the highway. And then more empty spaces with hills and scrub brush and white sand fringing the road. This was one of the loneliest places I had ever driven through, absolutely empty. Not a house or a sign or a side road or another car for miles. I kept up my speed but was cautious topping hills for fear of running over something and flattening a tire. My cell phone was useless out here.

At Tarpum Head the road came out of the bush and turned sharply to the left and the water appeared. The sun had finally broken through and I had a spectacular view of the long arcing bay and the waves frothing and running up the sand nearly to my wheels. It was less desolate here. There were cars, and boats working the bay. Then the road turned inland due south again and all signs of human habitation disappeared, though kestrels and mocking birds surveilled the road from wires and poles—at least the few people living this far south on Eleuthera had electricity—lining it.

The route turned west and then sharply to the south again through still more desolate country toward Waterford and Wemyss Bight. Just past the turnoff to Waterford, bulldozers were parked at the cut that takes you over to Cotton Bay. When it opens the new Cotton Bay Club, rebuilt on the site of the original private resort founded by Pan Am executive Juan Trippe in the 1960s, might transform this empty stretch below Rock Sound into a paradise for well-heeled tourists wielding (golf) clubs. But today nothing but heavy machinery and mounds of chalky rock marked the place.

From Wemyss Bight the road traversed the middle of the southernmost stretch of the island, up and down hills, with bush-covered slopes rising out the driver's side and distant views of the water out the passenger window, past the turns to John Millars and Millars on the drive to Bannerman Town, the last settlement on the island. I turned off at Bannerman Town and drove up the ridge into the village—a half-dozen houses painted in bright colors surrounded by flowers and lawn ornaments, neat gardens and cars. Nobody was stirring. I stopped and photographed one particularly attractive house—white, framed in royal blue—but didn't linger for fear that I would raise suspicions if spotted. I drove back to the road and turned right for the final half-mile of pavement.

Just before the road ended, I came to a sign—black lettering on a large white background—that said: Princess Cay. This was a peculiar find, on this remote stretch of southernmost Eleuthera, with tiny Bannerman Town the nearest settlement, and many miles from anything larger—Rock Sound. I drove up the rise and across the causeway and came to a fence and a gate that was unlocked. Sure enough, the truck parked just behind the gate had "Princess Cruise Lines" painted on the door. I didn't see anyone, so I got out and walked into the compound, passing stalls and pavilions and tables, down to the beach. This ready-made, swept-clean playground was utterly deserted. It would be thronged with tourists when enormous ships anchored offshore and disgorged passengers onto tenders, to this beach.

I crossed back over the causeway and drove to where the pavement ended in a little bowl of bush land. A dirt track continued over a hill toward the water and a lighthouse. The day was getting late, the weather steadily clearing, I was tired and faced a long drive back. Yet again, the end of one journey marked the beginning of another. I had reached another Bahamian conclusion, with a long run home ahead of me.

Abaco

Grand Bahama

Bimini

Eleuthera

New Providence

Cat Island

San Salvador

Andros

Exuma

Long Island

Crooked/Acklins Island

Mayaguana

Great Inagua

Bahamas

N

Epilogue

TWO WEEKS later, I woke in the cabin of an enormous cruise liner making its way silently in the early morning along the southern coast of Eleuthera. My wife and I drank coffee and watched as the ship rounded the stumpy end of the island and entered the calm waters of the southern lee. We ate breakfast as the ship wheeled around and dropped anchor, coming to a stop within sight of Princess Cay. I could hardly believe that in an hour or so, I'd be boarding a tender headed for a remote slice of Eleuthera I had reached from land only a dream ago.

But soon we were there, claiming our beach chairs as the crew ferried frozen burgers, hotdogs, fancily carved fruit, drink and souvenirs ashore, while more tenders unloaded their passengers. Presently the stretch of beach that only a fortnight ago had been abandoned was crowded with people old and young, fit and fat, in various states of undress feasting and drinking and snorkeling, all under the watchful eyes of lifeguards. I wasn't particularly happy with the experience—I preferred the place empty—though the weather was perfect and, as I would soon find out, the snorkeling was excellent. The underwater world was new to my wife and children, and it was really great fun introducing them to the wonders they could experience with mask and fin.

I had brought my dive gear along for the cruise—I had dives booked at Ocho Rios, Grand Cayman and Cozumel—but for the family I had to rent gear from a stand operated by local women.

"I was just here two weeks ago," I said to one of the Bahamians working at the stand. "Can you believe that?"

"You must be a rich man, taking two cruises in two weeks." She was a large woman, with fatty upper arms and a toothy smile.

"No, that's not the way it was. I came to Bannerman Town by road. Down from Governor's Harbour."

"You drove all the way down here from way up there?" she said in disbelief. "I ain't never been to Governor's Harbour but twice in all my life. We don't get no tourists in this area—except them that come off the ships.

"Why you come all the way down here?"

"Just wanted to see the place. Drive till the road ran out. You ladies live in Bannerman Town?"

"Yes, we doos."

"I drove through your settlement. Pretty houses. Took some pictures."

Surprised, one of the ladies said, "Was that you taking pictures from a car? My cousin tell me he see out his window somebody taking pictures. Thought you was from the government or something. Snoopin' round." They laughed.

"Well, I guess you could say I was snooping. But not for the government. Just admiring your houses. I especially liked the white one with the blue trim."

The ladies erupted in laughter. I had finally dispelled any suspicion they had that I was making this story up. "That be my sister's house, for sure. My cousin say he saw you get out your car and take pictures. White man taking pictures." I laughed too. I felt more comfortable talking to these Bahamian women than to any of the cruise passengers. But a line was forming behind me, customers needing attention.

I paid for the gear and was turning to leave when the woman in charge handed me a very nice laminated "Guide to Fish of the Bahamas and Caribbean."

"No charge for dat. You one of us. Come on back to Bannerman Town when you can. We cook up some peas and rice."

That was nearly seven years ago, and I haven't been back to the Bahamas since. Just before the trip to Eleuthera I had signed a contract to write a book about Shakespeare's *Hamlet*, which is not the sort of thing you can knock out in six or eight weeks. I knew—and regretted—that I would have to give up my travels for seemingly endless days toiling in libraries, poring over recondite documents, squinting at rare and musty books, and wading through nearly impenetrable essays on the most famous play and character in history. It was a sacrifice I would have to make. But much of my memory and imagination dwelt in the Family Islands of the Bahamas, among the people I'd come to love, while I was working on *Looking for Hamlet*. I know that now as I write this, life largely unchanged goes on among the children of the sun in Bannerman Town and Crown Haven, in New Bight and Clarence Town, in Cherokee Sound and Stella Maris, in Barattara and Cockburn Town and Matthew Town, and elsewhere in the islands. There are some islands—Mayaguana and Grand Bahama—I've visited that haven't for one reason or another made it into this book. Others—the Berrys, Crooked and Aklins—I haven't set foot on. No doubt, more of the people I've met in these islands are dead. But for me, they will never die, and when I go back—as I surely will—I'll find myself one day, happy and exhausted, pausing again at the dusty end of another Bahamian road.

"The Mail Boat to Crooked Island" sounds good to me.

October, 2012